Rhetorical Traditions and the Teaching of Writing

C.H. Knoblauch
SUNY at Albany

Lil Brannon
New York University

BOYNTON/COOK PUBLISHERS
HEINEMANN
PORTSMOUTH, NH

BOYNTON/COOK PUBLISHERS, INC.
A Subsidiary of
HEINEMANN EDUCATIONAL BOOKS, INC.
361 Hanover Street   Portsmouth, NH   03801-3959
Offices and agents throughout the world

Library of Congress Cataloging in Publication Data

Knoblauch, C. H.
  Rhetorical traditions and the teaching of writing.

  1. English language — Rhetoric — Study and teaching.
2. Rhetoric.   I. Brannon, Lil.   II. Title.
PE1404.K58 1983   808'.007   83-15712
ISBN 0-86709-105-3

Printed in the United States of America

91 92 93 94 95 5 4 3

Acknowledgments

Something every writer knows about and dreads is the smooth-tongued treachery of dumb ideas. Lurking on all sides, numberless, they oil their way into a writer's confidence, appealing to vanity, profiting from inattention, sneaking into acceptance when one's guard is down. At the same time, every writer knows the aloof integrity of smart ideas, difficult to locate, resistant to easy acquaintance, content to remain in more discerning minds if one is not wise enough to seek them out. We hope we have resisted a few dumb ideas and also happened luckily upon a few smart ones. If so, we have not done it by ourselves. For both blessings, we want to take a moment to thank some readers who have shown their friendship by sharing their insight and saving us from our foolishness where they could.

Particularly, we thank Ann Berthoff, whose clear-(not to say hard-)headed appraisal of our ideas enabled us to recognize some worth keeping and a good many to throw away. We have worked to profit from her knowledge. We can only aspire to her philosophical discipline.

Thanks also to John Mayher, who spotted several unusually dumb ideas and held them patiently in the light until we could see them for ourselves.

Thanks to John Clifford, Paula Johnson, Gordon Pradl, Nancy Lester, Pat Belanoff, Dan Hittleman, and David Hoover, each of whom read discerningly and helped us to revise.

Thanks to Jimmy Britton and Nancy Martin, certainly for their responses to our arguments, but more for their commitment to dignifying the teaching of writing as an intellectual enterprise. We have hoped here to make our contribution in the spirit of theirs.

Thanks to the many colleagues and graduate students who have listened to us, disagreed with us, provoked us to more, and we hope better, thinking.

Thanks to the students in our writing classes, whose intelligence and ability first demonstrated to us the inadequacy of our own traditional teaching. They have been the educators, as usual.

And thanks to Bob Boynton, who has held us to his standards when our own would have made life easier. We've given him the words; he has given us a voice.

Alas, dumb ideas are cunning and ubiquitous, and some have doubtless remained in our good graces. The reason, however, is not lack of diligence among our friends but lack of perceptiveness in ourselves. No one can save anyone all the time. But perhaps our new readers will prove themselves friendly as well by putting our arguments to the test of their own thought and experience. Though books appear to be monologues, their best use is in conversation. We hope to have joined an important conversation.

Contents

Foreword

JAMES BRITTON

Certainly, I take it as a compliment that the authors should want me to write an introduction to their book. So, "Yes," I say, allowing myself to be flattered in this way; and I read the book, and I am amazed by it, but now I have to recover from my amazement and find something to say. I have to "make connections," as the authors would explain. I brood over the problem of where the possible connections lie, passing threads of thought through my mind in much the way that fishermen, the world over, from Galilee to Tidewater, pass the strands of a net through their hands looking, not for connections, but for disconnections, the holes to be repaired.

And I come to a conclusion: this will *not* be an introduction. There is no way I could insert myself transitionally between the authors and their readers to improve on what they themselves have written. My attempt to create a bridge must end up as a hurdle, inevitably.

What else, then? A recommendation to potential readers — a way of canvassing the floating vote? Immodest thought! — no, I am not a television personality, "nor was meant to be." A grace before meat, perhaps — gratefully anticipating "what we are about to receive"?

Not quite that, I decide, though that was near to it: a *celebration*, a way of marking with appropriate utterance the birth, the launching of a very unusual work — a book without compromises, a book that lacks neither heart nor stomach.

"A celebration," and, writing the word, I realize that I must go carefully in this mode if I am not to incur censure from the authors: It is typical, they tell us, of the old rhetoric — "that old-time religion" — to take a "ceremonial view of discourse."[1] What I choose to celebrate must reflect my own exploratory musings in and around the authors' text, the "movement of mind" that has taken shape in this my text rather than rehearsing any litany of praise, any ritual of approval.

An important theme recurs in many contexts in this book. If I were to give it a title I would label it "the integrity of the individual utterance." A writer comes face to face (as I do now) with a complex set of demands — the constraints of conventional word meaning and of the syntax of the written language; the limitations potentially set by a reader's expectations and preparedness on the one hand, and, on the other, limitations in the resources he is himself able to bring to the task. The comment the authors make upon this situation is to point out that what the writer writes is the outcome of his *particular* purpose or purposes with *particular* readers. To exercise his competence as a writer is to be guided by perceived cues in the situation rather than by general principles, rhetorical, logical, or linguistic. "*Operational* purposes rather than idealized aims are what really motivate writers to make choices while composing. . . . They are not broad decisions to 'be transactional' or to 'be scientific' but are rather concrete reactions to single occasions for discourse, representing the desire to affect readers in certain ways."[2]

The notion of the integrity of the individual utterance forms a major plank in the arguments against an outworn rhetoric — against a rhetoric based on a ceremonial view of discourse, against a prescriptive conception of genres, and in support of the claim that the problems a writer engages are largely "discourse-specific."[3] On the positive side this leads to the refreshing and novel suggestion that what goes on in writing classes may be justified as a genre of its own — a "freer pursuit of meanings" appropriate to that two-sided learning situation where learning to write and learning through writing go hand in hand.

On the negative side, however, the idea can be taken too far and lead to the error I have elsewhere[4] called "a global view of writing": "writing is writing is writing." Kellogg Hunt, for example, based his developmental stages in structural maturity of writing (his mean length of minimal terminable units) on *any* thousand words of continuous student writing, only to find subsequently that Faulkner's fiction achieved on this scale Grade 12 level, whereas Hemingway's was at Grade 4 level.[5] And when in our London research we applied the T-unit measure to writing differentiated according to the nature of the task, it was clear that T-unit length was a resource that able writers varied in accordance with the nature of the task.[6]

The authors have stated that they "see problems" in the use of taxonomies of function for writing, but it seems clear that much of the difficulty disappears when it is recognized, following Jakobson's lead,[7] that many or all functions may operate together in any piece of writing, but that they will tend to be hierarchically ordered and it will be the dominant function that most influences the organization, the form of the writing. And that influence will be exercised as it were indirectly, being a part of the context of expectations shared by writer and reader, a socially derived, socially modifiable pattern of predictions. To defend the integrity of the individual utterance is to view these mutual contextual expectations as a resource for the individual writer rather than as a restriction.

A principal source of amazement for me in reading this book has been the courage displayed in the authors' statements of faith. I cannot forbear to quote — here are two examples:

> "Unlike the ancient intellectual world, which it has permanently displaced, this new world features a perpetual search for knowledge, where learning is an endless adventure in making sense of experience, an exploratory effort in which all human beings are both teachers and students, making and sharing meanings through the natural capacities for symbolic representation that define their humanity. It is a world founded on this perpetual search, not on the authoritarian premises and unassailable dogmas of antiquity, not on the passive veneration of conventional wisdom or the declarations of privileged ministers of the truth."[8]

That on the intellectual changes that grew from the philosophical crisis of the seventeenth century; and this, nearer to our teacherly hearts, about the capabilities of the ordinary student, the ordinary child:

> "An important implication of modern rhetoric is that what is true of composing on the sublimest cultural heights has relevance down in the valleys as well. *All* human beings share in the creative ingenuity which is supremely articulated by Shakespeare, Kant, or Einstein."[9]

This confidence, clearly born of experience, is maintained throughout the book, to culminate, in the final chapter, in a proposition regarding "the myth of measurable improvement": after a careful consideration of grading and assessment procedures, the authors conclude:

> "The judgment of instructional worth should be a function of the perceived relationship between teaching and its desired end, which means *focusing on the known long-term benefits of classroom activities whatever the difficulties of assessing their short-term results.*" (my italics) [10]

Taken out of context, these declarations of faith may look like easy and unrealistic optimism: in fact, the whole book is a double justification of what is claimed. It is, in the first place, a closely reasoned philosophical statement — written not for philosophers but for teachers; and in the second place, it is an exemplification of the way practice may be affected by such theoretical underpinning. It is in no sense a teaching manual, to be thumbed over before taking a writing class; but in showing how practice flows from intellectual belief, it manifestly reflects highly sensitive and highly successful teaching.

As I have said, this is a book that makes no compromises: it may inspire you or infuriate you, but it won't leave you cold.

JAMES BRITTON

References

1. See p. 4.
2. See p. 28.
3. See p. 40.
4. Britton, Burgess, Martin, McLeod & Rosen, *The Development of Writing Abilities, 11-18,* Macmillan Education, 1975, p. 1. And having made this known elsewhere, it would have been a breach of friendship *not* to have referred here to this difference of view.
5. Kellogg W. Hunt, *Grammatical Structures Written at Three Grade Levels,* N.C.T.E. Research Report No. 3, 1965.
6. H. Rosen, "An investigation of the effects of differentiated writing assignments on the performance in English composition of a selected group of 15/16 year old pupils," Unpublished Ph.D. thesis, University of London, 1969.
7. Roman Jakobson, "Linguistics & Poetics" in T.A. Sebeok (ed) *Style in Language,* New York, Wiley, 1960, p. 353; Roman Jakobson, *Selected Writings,* Vol. 2, Word and Language, Mouton, The Hague, 1971, pp. 556-8; Britton *et al., op. cit.,* Chapter 5.
8. See pp. 51-52.
9. See p. 73.
10. See p. 166.

Rhetorical Traditions and the Teaching of Writing

Chapter 1

Philosophy in the Writing Class:

Teaching with a Purpose

Our book is for teachers of writing, for anyone who plans to become a teacher of writing, and for anyone concerned about the ends and means of writing instruction. Naturally, therefore, we will have much to say about the questions that matter most to teachers: what to do in the classroom and how to do it. But we want to insist at the start that our main interest is not in "method" in a narrow sense, the isolated techniques and strategies, assignment ideas, class activities, and tricks of the trade that teachers share with each other during coffee breaks in order to find something entertaining for the next day's lesson. We're not opposed to enlightened "recipe swapping," but we're not very interested in it either. Though we will certainly end up with some coherent images of the writing classroom, we want to make a beginning somewhere else—with what comes before method and makes it pertinent, directed, and organized. Our priority throughout what follows will be the attitudes and values, the beliefs and suppositions that give rise to method, that cause teachers to prefer doing things one way rather than another. In short, we will be talking about the philosophical context of instruction. We want to encourage writing teachers to become philosophers in their classrooms.

Page one and already a problem. Teachers have their hands full just doing their jobs day by day without taking on the added burden of theoretical hardware. New teachers especially find Monday morning an urgent, looming reality, and they need practical information to cope with it. Who has time or inclination to become a philosopher? We acknowledge this urgency and sympathize with the demand for practical information. The trouble is, we can't extend the same sympathy to certain assumptions underlying a restrictively practical viewpoint: the assumption, for example, that teachers can be purposeful and effective while remaining unconscious of the intellectual motivations supporting their work; or the assumption that all classroom activities reflect identical arguments about how people write and learn to write, so that choosing among them is a matter of personal taste in the context of equally legitimate alternatives; or the assumption that any one teaching practice can be joined with any other without affecting the

1

coherence or quality of instruction. As we see it, methods derive from philosophical perspectives whether teachers wish to become philosophical about them or not—perspectives on language, on meaning, on communication, on learning, and on the ways of assisting learning, among others. Moreover, they frequently derive from differing perspectives which are opposed rather than complementary, for instance, mechanistic versus organic views of language. Most important, some perspectives are demonstrably preferable to others because they offer more accurate, more comprehensive, and more productive understanding of the nature of discourse and the development of verbal competence. We believe it's important for teachers to become conscious of the philosophical dimensions of their work because nothing short of that consciousness will make instruction sensible and deliberate, the result of knowledge, not folklore, and of design, not just custom or accident.

What does it mean to be "philosophical" about the teaching of writing? In general, it means being aware of what one is doing and why. It includes having an exploratory and reflective attitude toward ideas, issues, and questions pertinent to how people write and how they develop as writers. It means observing writers' actual practices as the test of plausible generalizations about what composing involves and how it occurs. It means speculating about the significance of what is observed in order to enhance or revise earlier conclusions. It means applying personal conclusions to the larger conversation about writing and teaching that is going on today in professional journals and conferences[1]—and that has been going on for centuries. It means teaching from sound conceptual premises that are understood, consciously sustained, and continually modified in light of new knowledge about composing and accumulated experiences in the classroom. It means conceptual as well as methodological flexibility, a willingness to discard comfortable old beliefs and practices or to adopt unfamiliar new ones when there are good reasons—rooted in careful observation and rigorous speculation—for doing so. The idea that writing instruction is such a sophisticated, intellectually respectable enterprise has only recently come to enjoy broad support. Therefore, the habit of mind we wish to encourage among writing teachers is not necessarily one to which they are accustomed, though it's common enough in academic disciplines whose evolution has been less accidental, less subordinate to other subjects, and less narrowly pragmatic in popular conception. But the pertinence, directedness, and coherence of teachers' methods, to say nothing of the eventual success of their efforts, depend on their intellectual maturation in a field which is itself maturing and therefore expecting more of its practitioners.

We're not implying that writing teachers have intentionally aspired to ignorance of their subject. The problem historically has not been laziness but rather a disjunction between the traditional academic preparation teachers have received and the demands of the work they are called upon to do. Since most writing instructors have been trained in English departments, and therefore have become students of literature, they know the perspectives and concepts of a field which is related to composition in some respects, but which is by no means equivalent to it. They have learned to analyze literary texts as the happiest outcomes of the writing process, but they have not learned to inquire into the process itself. They can evaluate completed writing according to various standards of critical taste, but they have not thought much about how texts come to take the shapes they have, or about the operations that make up "composing,"[2] or about how unpracticed writers develop the expertise that literature specialists find demonstrated in the texts they study. Lacking preparation in concepts relevant to an understanding of the composing process, writing teachers have tended for years to rely on a mixture of literary ideas ill-suited to the ends of writing courses (for instance, the concept of "fine style") and folklore about writing (such as the necessity of thesis statements) sanctified by tradition but unsupported by the actual practice of writers. Meanwhile, until recently, teachers could find little motivation to improve their knowledge of composing because of the prior commit-ment to literary study and the perception, which English departments have not strained themselves to discourage, that writing instruction is a tainted academic endeavor, a public service grudgingly extended to the underprivileged, a blue collar job requiring minimal expertise but a good deal of patience and a tolerance for large workloads. Only in the past twenty years or so has composition work begun to aspire to the intellectual respectability cheerfully afforded the study of literature.

What has most impeded the development of theoretical sophistication is the fact that the philosophical perspectives and concepts historically most rele-vant to composition instruction belong to an esoteric discipline called "rhetoric," which long ago disappeared from the standard academic curriculum, even at the graduate level. Teachers are simply unacquainted with the once vital subject from which their views of the nature of writing and many of their classroom practices are chiefly derived. Writers such as Aristotle, Cicero, and Quintilian rarely attract the publicity of Chaucer, Shakespeare, and Milton in English departments. This might be less surprising were English departments not responsible for the teaching of writing (though important ancestral relationships between rhetoric and litera-ture make it surprising enough in any case). But since they have accepted that responsibility, however grudgingly, the omission is noteworthy, for these writers have profoundly influenced traditional composition theory and instruction. Meanwhile, more recent contributors to rhetorical thought, including Vico, Adam Smith, Coleridge, Nietzche, Whitehead, and Kenneth Burke, are similarly neglected, despite their contributions to a series of dramatic revisions of classical assumptions and ideas. The history of rhetoric is an enigma to English teachers, its texts unread and its evolution misunderstood. The closest most teachers get to a glimpse of rhetoric is their composition textbooks, which have been written mainly by other writing teachers who are equally uncertain about the rhetorical tradition and who have based their books on personal teaching experiences with occasional, haphazard reference to other textbooks as unfamiliar with the con-cepts of rhetoric as their own. The consequent sterile repetitiveness and historical naiveté of these books create the impression that rhetoric is a monolith, that nothing has changed between Cicero and Kenneth Burke, that the ideas they reproduce so unreflectively, and with so little regard for empirical verification, about outlines, topic sentences, comparison/contrast essays, and the like, are as serviceable today as they might have seemed centuries ago. [3]

Knowing little of the history of rhetoric, teachers naturally could know little of its changes. They proceed from an imprecise but deeply embedded recollection of ancient views and rules of discourse, passed down through generations of their predecessors, which have little basis in fact and little support from more recent philosophical thought. By force of custom, they bring ancient rhetorical concepts to the classroom — "invention," "disposition," "elocution," "topos," "oration-form," "thesis," "enthymeme," and so on — with little or no intellectual awareness of what the concepts mean or of the long-discarded worldview from which the concepts derive. Writing is often taught as though it were a mechanical act of selecting prefabricated forms for preconceived content; as though it were nothing but a range of technical skills to be delivered by masters to apprentices through lecture, then memorized and practiced until proficiency is achieved; as though human beings lack verbal competence until teachers provide them with it; as though the surface decorum of texts were more valuable than quality of thought; indeed even as though decorum were equivalent to intellectual quality. All of these notions derive from the ancient belief that discourse merely provides a means of presenting or displaying truths which have been independently ascertained in a convenient but inessential verbal dress. Learning the forms was regarded as an optional, technical achievement, pertinent to certain occasions of public address but unrelated to intellectual growth or the quality of understanding. In the ancient world, discourse was a ceremonial exercise. And much writing instruction today, consciously or (more often) not, assumes the same perspective.

Over the past 400 years, however, profound reorientations in Western epistemology—that is, views of the nature of knowledge and the relationship between knowledge and discourse—have caused a gradual erosion of ancient belief and, with it, a repudiation of the classical rhetorical concepts on which many people continue to depend in their teaching. [4] Modern rhetorical theory, beginning as early as the seventeenth century, finds a closer connection between language and thought, discourse and knowledge, than ancient speculation had supposed. Far from serving an optional, ceremonial function, composition — the forming process at the heart of writing — is essentially related to learning, to the individual's personal search for coherence in experience. It is also, as a manifestation of human symbolic capacities, a natural endowment in essence, not a technical skill. The competence to use language to make meaning develops with application, according to modern theory, and is therefore nurtured rather than "taught." Progress toward excellence is a function of increasing experience more than objective understanding of principles. At the same time, modern rhetoric emphasizes the process of composing more than the features of completed texts, thereby distinguishing itself from both ancient rhetoric and literary criticism. It is preoccupied with the writer's choice-making in the development of texts, the exploratory movement of mind, the discovery of connections among ideas, the progressive testing and reformulating of statements.

Having had little preparation in the history of discourse theory, teachers tend to be unfamiliar with the richer concepts of modern rhetoric — "composing process," "writing-as-learning," "coherence," "revision," among others—and are therefore unaware that alternatives to their customary classroom practice are both available and preferable. Or worse, having heard about the concepts without yet appreciating what makes them modern, teachers borrow them uncertainly as new labels for beliefs or activities which remain as traditional as ever. Hence, for many, "writing-as-learning" means the prose recapitulation of what an instructor has lectured about; "writing-as-discovery" means practicing with mechanical "invention heuristics" in order to find something to say; "revising" means following an instructor's notions about *preferable* things to say or better ways to say them; and "process" means some arbitrary production formula, like "prewrite-write-revise" or "find a thesis-make an outline-fill it with language," which all writers are presumed to follow. Understanding the progress of rhetoric does not mean keeping up with the latest jargon while continuing to teach as though nothing had changed. It means achieving philosophical awareness about epistemological shifts that make the ancient and modern rhetorical perspectives incompatible. It means distinguishing the concepts of one perspective from those of the other, not as label changes but as true intellectual oppositions. And it means becoming alert and subtle about how teaching differs depending on the perspective assumed.

The effort to become more philosophical about writing instruction must begin, therefore, with knowledge of the intellectual heritage pertinent to that work: the perspectives and concepts of rhetoric as they have evolved over time. The goal is to recover for the teaching of writing as rich a theoretical context as the one so long enjoyed in literary studies. The goal is also to learn how to think about the process of composing in the context of a long history of such thinking. However, beyond this command of the evolution of discourse theory, becoming philosophical also means a willingness to be observant about how people compose—a willingness to become an active teacher-researcher in order to discover personally satisfying reasons for discarding unproductive methods and adopting more effective ones. Too many teachers proceed unreflectively from recollections of how they were taught and from hearsay about what "everybody does," supported by the outmoded premises, illusory distinctions, false claims, regimented methods, and prescriptivist emphases enshrined in composition textbooks. Eager to socialize students by enforcing "rules" for correct prose, and unaware of the folkloric derivation of so many stylistic and rhetorical prescriptions, generations of well-intentioned teachers have promoted hackneyed, "academic" writing by drilling young writers in the use of empty forms and overemphasizing the mastery of superficial editorial skills. What mainly sustains this barren school work is a powerful intellectual inertia—bred over centuries, not just years, of unreflective practice—which allows teachers to ignore, or even fail to notice, the striking discrepancies between what writers actually do and what textbooks tell us they do, or between how people develop as language users and what traditional pedagogy recommends to enhance that development. Without philosophical awareness and a willingness to act upon the results of observation, there is nothing to challenge this inertia. The teaching of writing will improve only when the motive to change inappropriate practices becomes stronger than the desire to cling to comfortable old habits.

An example of encrusted belief influencing instruction even when unsustained by observation can help to make our point about the need for philosophical awareness. Many teachers offer practice in what they regard as the rules or forms of paragraph construction, confident that their textbooks are telling them the truth and that their teaching is grounded in "common sense" about how people compose. One contemporary textbook has this to say about the paragraph:

> A paragraph is a single idea. . . . Like the essay itself, it has a beginning, a middle, and an end. The beginning and the end are usually each one sentence long, and the middle gets you smoothly from one to the other. . . . Its beginning will normally be its topic sentence, the thesis of this miniature essay. Its middle will develop, explain, and illustrate your topic sentence. Its last sentence will drive home the idea. . . . See that your paragraph is coherent, not only flowing smoothly but with nothing in it not covered by the topic sentence. . . . Make your paragraphs full and well developed, with plenty of details, examples, and full explanations.[5]

Even if these remarks were true, they would be unhelpful to students because of their vagueness about what writing paragraphs involves and even what paragraphs look like. Granting the temporal and spatial inevitability that a sentence will be found at the beginning of any paragraph, with perhaps a different one at its close and occasionally others between them, what is the use to a writer of learning impressionistic concepts like "middle" and "smooth flow" as the basis for setting out to compose? But the educational futility of these prescriptions is only their second liability. The first and more important one is that they are simply false, as even limited observation can reveal.

Here's an unexceptional paragraph from a competent adult writer, chosen at random from the middle of a book on the social dimensions of language use:

> Physicians, of course, are notoriously guilty of both mystifying and terrifying patients by using polysyllabic technical terms to denote commonplace and easily curable disorders. In fact, within the past few years, there has grown up a field known as *iatrogenics*. It is essentially the study of how doctor-talk can intensify and even induce illness. Though the term itself is unnecessarily mysterious, the idea of having a field within a field to monitor the harmful consequences of verbal mystification is, in my opinion, a splendid one, and I would urge its replication in every field. Education, for example, is a field with which I am quite familiar, and I can assure anyone who is a member of the laity that there are very few terms employed by

educators which cannot be expressed in everyday language and with admirable precision. Therefore, there ought to be a field within the field which is devoted to translating, decoding, or restating in plain language what educators are saying. If there were, educators would probably call it something like pedagantics, so that no one would know exactly what it is supposed to do.[6]

In what sense is this paragraph a "single idea"? It speaks of doctors terrifying patients with technical terms, of a field known as iatrogenics, of the importance of monitoring verbal mystification, of educational jargon, and of other matters besides. Perhaps there's a Larger Idea encompassing these—but what's the difference between a big idea and a little one? Is "verbal mystification" a larger or smaller idea than "iatrogenics"? What is an "idea" anyway? How can a paragraph be one idea and many ideas simultaneously? And what of "beginning, middle, and end"? How can one tell whether the beginning here is one sentence long or two or three? Where does the beginning become the middle? Is the beginning of this paragraph a "topic sentence"? If it were, then surely the rest of the paragraph would talk about doctors using language to terrify their patients, a tack which the paragraph evidently does not take. Perhaps in this instance the topic sentence lies elsewhere—but where then? Which sentence embraces all the rest, predicting their modifications? This paragraph appears not to have a topic sentence at all, yet if that is so, in what sense is the paragraph coherent, given the textbook writer's assumption that coherence means "flowing smoothly . . . with nothing . . . not covered by the topic sentence"? Where are the "details, examples, and full explanations" that "good" paragraphs are supposed to contain? The text contains no instances of doctors who have terrified their patients, very little explanation of iatrogenics, no details about educational jargon. Finally, consider the last sentence: what idea, systematically presented through the preceding sentences, does it "drive home"? If anything, it seems to sabotage the growing impression that the writer really believes that every professional field could, should, and would create a subfield like iatrogenics. Plainly, by *every* standard of evaluation listed in the textbook writer's definition of a paragraph, the particular paragraph discussed here is a failure.[7]

But of course it's not a failure: it makes several provocative points in a perfectly comprehensible way. Readers find it meaningful and even entertaining. The failure lies, instead, in the textbook writer's definition of rules governing acceptable paragraphs, rules which are based, not on the evidence of assorted real paragraphs, but on ancient prescriptions, which we will discuss later, too narrowly constraining the choices that writers actually have available to them in making coherent discourses. Teachers who have joined the philosophical conversation in progress in their field, who have observed their own practices and those of other writers, who know something of the history of speculation about the structual features of discourse, are aware that all formulas for paragraph design are over-restrictive half-truths: they are inaccurate as descriptions of all existing paragraphs, false as predictors of the necessary shapes of new ones, and problematic (if not downright unhelpful) as guides for the composing efforts of unpracticed writers. Observation reveals quickly enough that the formula "topic sentence + restriction + example = paragraph" is no more reliable or comprehensive than another derivable from our example—let's call it "tantalizing specific reference + plausible broadening of initial point + sabotage of developing conclusion = paragraph." In addition, the experience of writers suggests that the expertise necessary to realize this second formula in actual discourse is probably considerable, raising the possibility that following *any* formula prescribed in advance (including the popular one "topic + restriction + illustration") may, in fact, represent a complication, not a solution, of the difficulties of composing. And if that is true, then requiring unpracticed writers to follow formulas may succeed in making writing harder, not easier, at the same time as it creates an impression that all writers naturally begin their work with a clear perception of the structures their texts will eventually, and inevitably, assume.[8] Teachers' philosophical reflectiveness on these matters will not only prevent textbook lore from implicating them in its own ignorance, but it will also guide their search for teaching methods based on the soundest possible premises about how people write and how they learn to write.

For enabling the activities of observation and speculation, teachers have two excellent laboratory subjects near at hand, their students and themselves, their own composing processes and those of the writers they teach. Nothing informs so quickly about composing as watching people do it while remaining open-minded and reflective about what one sees. To illustrate, consider the following paragraph and the change of view about it that can come from knowing how the writer constructed it. The paragraph was written by a first-year college student who was also asked to compose aloud into a tape recorder so that the teacher could gain insight into the choice-making process as it occurred.[9]

Jane, I imagine, is a wonderful friend. Being her brother, I don't qualify as a friend. We have a superficial friendship only to keep our parents' sanity. (To give an example, sitting at the dinner table, she will complain about the juicy thick steak that she is not eating. I will offer to take it off her hands for her. But rather than give it to her brother, she will march into the kitchen and throw it out.) This doesn't last long though. As soon as the folks are asleep, she starts in. Monday night football will have a tied score. There is five minutes left and the Steelers are on the ten yard line and all of sudden, I am confronted with I Love Lucy. It is really too bad that she is so bright and talented and uses that as a weapon.

A traditionalist might view this paragraph in purely formal terms, regarding it not as one moment in a writer's continuing struggle to conceive and convey a personal significance but as a violation of ironclad principles of paragraph structure such as those mentioned earlier. It lacks unity, coherence, and emphasis; it lacks a topic sentence and any clear pattern of subordinations; its examples are not closely tied to the general statements they are supposed to modify. "Friendship," this teacher might say, should have been defined right at the start, since that is the broadest idea in the paragraph. Then, the writer should have explained why he and his sister could not be friends, offering an example or two—but more pertinent examples than those now included in the paragraph. Finally, since the concluding sentence introduces new information unconnected to the issue of friendship and the writer's relationship to his sister, it should be discarded in favor of a summary of the paragraph's "main points." In short, structural prescriptions might well dominate over an effort to find out what actually mattered to the writer, what the writer intended to say by means of the choices he made. Teachers commonly allow their models of the Ideal Text, their private notions of formal propriety, to deprive writers of control over their own purposes, interpreting any deviation from the Ideal Text as a "skill deficiency." These teachers might say that the writer of the statement above lacks ability to organize paragraphs correctly, with topic sentences, supporting examples, and appropriate conclusions. He should work at paragraph development drills.

But let's now eavesdrop on the writer's own process of discovering his meanings by looking at the transcript of his writing-aloud.

Talking: Now, all right, let's see.

Writing: Sister dearest, starring Jane.

Talking: You understand, the names have been changed, to protect—so she doesn't know—all right—

Writing: Jane is, I

Talking: imagine—i-m-a—you're going to have to correct the spelling, anyway.

Writing: imagine, is a wonderful friend

Talking: friend, n-d, that's right.

Writing: But unfortunately

Talking: no—I have an inescapable, marvelous invention—

Writing: I, being her brother, am not her friend

Talking: Let's see. Oh, okay—out loud

Writing: (Puts in a period) Not that we don't try to be friends

Talking: (laughter) It's just that over the years we've learned how to be enemies. Hmm. When she came back from school—she is taking a semester off from school—I figured, you know, we're both mature people, we can be friends — but, noooo. Oh, I'm not writing anymore. Gotta write, not talk. I can talk and write? Okay. But this doesn't make any sense.

Reading: Jane is, I imagine, a wonderful friend. But being her brother, being her brother

Talking: You know, that doesn't make any more sense either. Wait a minute—could I just change that around? Let's see: Being her brother, I am not her friend.

Reading: Being her brother
Writing: though
Reading: I am not her friend.
Talking: Let's see. I'll start all over again. Jesus, I've got to learn how to spell.
Writing: Is a wonderful friend.
Talking: n-d
Writing: Being her brother, I don't qualify as a friend.
Talking: period.
Writing: We have a superficial
Talking: i-c-i-a-l
Writing: friendship
Reading: a superficial friendship
Writing: Only
Reading: Only
Writing: to keep my parents' sanity.
Talking: I hope she never sees this! 'Cause even though she's smaller than me she packs a punch. Let's see. This has to be short, so I can't go into past history or anything—Oh, I can start with past history?
Writing: To give an example, sitting at the dinner table, she will complain about the juicy thick steak
Talking: e-a-k
Writing: that she is not eating. I will offer to take it off her hands for her. But
Talking: Uh, oh, you aren't supposed to start—oh, I don't know, okay
Writing: But rather than give it to her
Talking: wonderfully sweet—blow your own horn, David!
Reading: to her
Writing: brother, she will march
Talking: c-h
Writing: into the kitchen and throw it out.
Talking: Sweet girl. Hmm. Do you want me to just write what I'm thinking? Or is, do I have to write—like an essay—I should talk what I'm thinking? Okay, 'cause that's not what I've been doing. Alrighty, then, I will put a line through "sweet girl." I need a cigarette. Let's see, so...
Reading: Jane, I imagine, is a wonderful friend. Being her brother, I don't qualify as a friend. We have a superficial friendship only to keep our parents' sanity. To give an example, sitting at the dinner table, she will complain about the juicy thick steak
Talking: Well, that's not an example of keeping our parents' sanity. That's an example of her insanity. So that doesn't make any sense—um, I guess I have to, uh, give an example of what I said before that. All right.

Reading: I don't qualify as a friend. We have a superficial friendship only to keep our parents' sanity.

Talking: So, I'll put that in parentheses cause that should not follow what I just said.

Reading: I don't qualify . . . We have a superficial friendship only to keep our parents' sanity.

Writing: This doesn't last long. As soon as the folks are asleep, she starts in.

Talking: Let's see. An example of how she starts in. Let's see.

Reading: This doesn't last long. As soon as the folks are asleep, she starts in.

Talking: Mostly minor stuff—just enough to pick at you.

Writing: Monday night

Talking: g-h-t

Writing: football will have a tied score. There is five minutes and the Steelers

Talking: S-t-e-e-l-e-r-s

Writing: are on the ten yard line and all of a sudden

Talking: d-d-e-n

Writing: I am confronted with I Love Lucy.

Talking: Granted, my caring about football is as ridiculous as her caring about *I Love Lucy*, but certain things are important—But you see, writing takes an awful lot longer than the time we've been given—like most of this—if I just had longer — this would all be trashed, right off, and I would start probably in a very different way and never even mention *I Love Lucy*. Well, I would, I don't know—*I Love Lucy* is kind of interesting—I have yet to get up to the present time—she threw the steak out when she was much younger—now she is on to bigger and better things—when it comes to, like, getting money out of our parents, she's really wonderful at that—I get tipped with the terrible guilts if I feel that I want something from them—I just, if it doesn't work the first time, I give up—but she will go at it and go at it until she gets what she wants. So why don't you write that instead of Monday night football? But the folks are asleep . . . hmmm. Let's see, I'd have to work that one out later. This all has yet to be rearranged. This is only supposed to be one paragraph. If I could write a paper, I could push all of this around in different places, and by the end of the paper—or probably scratched out. Hmm.

Writing: Actually, I love

Talking: her dearly. Scratch that one out too. Let's see . . . Taping myself makes me silly. It upsets her a lot that I'm older than her and my parents always treated us a little differently—you know, I'm expected to be semi-responsible, and to be able to take care of

	things, while they really don't expect anything like that from her, you know.
Writing:	It is really too bad that she is so bright and talented but does
Talking:	e-s
Writing:	not
Talking:	Hmm. No, that's wrong.
Reading:	that she's so bright and talented
Writing:	and uses that as a weapon.

What can be learned from this narrative? Though the writer feels awkward at having to write and talk at the same time, a reader can nonetheless glimpse in it something of the true nature of composing—the messiness, the starts, stops, and restarts, the groping and tentativeness, the labored articulating of meanings and the struggle to tie them together as a coherent statement. This writer is in pursuit of a significance that matters—but that also persistently eludes him. Each assertion is a distinct effort to close on what the writer wishes to say about his relationship to his sister, but each causes dissatisfaction as well because of its inadequate or incomplete rendering of his experience. In short, the writer behaves and feels like the rest of us, like all writers regardless of their expertise, testing and reformulating ideas, following false trails, looking backward and forward in order to decide what to say next, wondering how to make connections, toying with language, getting distracted and stalling, associating freely, nitpicking over technical details, rambling, revising, and forever registering discontent with the results of his labor. Underlying all of these activities, meanwhile, giving them a sense of direction and momentum, is the writer's own growing awareness of intent: his desire, not merely to complete an assignment, or realize some formal absolute, or imitate a teacher's notion of verbal decorum, but to make valuable statements about the meaning of his own experience.

The most telling point of disjunction between this writer's narrative of his composing and the hypothetical traditionalist critique of his paragraph, offered earlier, is the fact that "the meaning of friendship" is not really what the writer set out to discuss, though "friendship" is indeed the first and most general concept he introduces. His concern, instead, is to learn about his relationship to his sister, to make sense of his feelings toward her and perhaps to ponder as well their different relationships to their parents. The teacher who allows a preoccupation with the "correct" shapes of paragraphs to dictate how writers will be required to function would surely, in this instance, have sacrificed the writer's purpose in favor of a personal agenda. The student-writer, recognizing a possible confrontation of goals, would quickly enough have capitulated to the teacher's wishes and composed the teacher's paragraph about friendship—but at what cost to motivation, to his sense of the value of composing and his own accomplishment as a writer? It's worth noting the harm already done to him by teachers who have so exaggerated formal and technical constraints that his awareness of them actually impedes his effort to pursue the meanings he values. Time and again, he worries about whether he said things the "right way": he has to "correct the spelling" — "I've got to learn how to spell"; his statement "has to be short"—"this is only supposed to be one paragraph" — so he can't "go into past history or anything"; he shouldn't begin a sentence with "but"; he's nervous about whether or not he's allowed to "just write what I'm thinking." These issues repeatedly interrupt his train of thought, betraying the tension between his desire to make meaning and an imposed requirement to follow orders of some sort. In view of his genuine inexperience at making connections explicit for a reader, the concern of his past teachers for inculcating mechanical rules seems altogether inappropriate.

There are intriguing clues in the narrative to suggest that this student-writer is becoming more aware, as he writes, of what he means and how he can convey it. And, interestingly, he is already aware that he has not yet achieved the result he is after. Far from supposing that his paragraph represents completed writing, he is quite sensitive to the evolving shape of a discourse, perhaps more so than the traditionalist instructor who views the paragraph as a "product" to be evaluated for evidence of skill deficiencies: "Writing takes an awful lot longer than the time we've been given—like most of this—if I just had longer—this would all be trashed . . . and I would start probably in a very different way and never even mention *I Love Lucy*"; "this all has yet to be rearranged"; "if I could write a paper, I could push all of this around in different places." More important, the writer really is making progress toward the coherence he seeks, although the completed paragraph does not yet reflect it. He recognizes a problem with the example of his sister's throwing out the steak: it does not effectively support what precedes it. A teacher's criticism of its lack of relevance would have minimal value for the writer, therefore, since he already understands the difficulty. He knows too that the reference to Monday night football and *I Love Lucy* should be "trashed" in favor of less superficial instances of the strain in his relationship to his sister. The example of her skill at manipulating their parents, and his resentment of her seeming freedom to be less responsible than he, is more suited to his purpose; presumably, he would exploit it if he had more space and time. The mysterious last sentence in the paragraph, which some teachers might be inclined to call irrelevant, is a reference to this unexpressed example: his sister uses her intelligence, inappropriately he believes, to get money from their parents. The writer's narrative, then, is rich in potential for more writing, and so too is his paragraph if a teacher can see it in the right light.

The teacher who has achieved philosophical perspective on composing based on an awareness of how writers actually work would be less likely to approach this student's writing in a formalistic way. Her responses to the paragraph would be aimed at assisting the writer's ongoing pursuit of his own intentions, the making and conveying of meanings that he values. She might recognize, for instance, that the writer has not yet reached the point where he can say exactly why he and his sister are not friends, but that the key to their strained relationship seems to lie in her rather selfish behavior as suggested in the writer's examples, both those expressed in the paragraph and those in the composing-aloud narrative. She might ask questions about the writer's reactions to his sister's behavior: why it bothers him so much, whether her age justifies it or not, whether he believes that there is yet some hope for the friendship he seems to wish for at least implicitly in the paragraph. Questions such as these derive from the teacher's understanding that the writer needs to do more writing, perhaps a longer statement in which he can make the connections among assertions and examples more explicit for a reader. The teacher has not assumed that she knows what the writer wants to say, nor does she have a plan to help him say it "the right way." She has simply served as a sounding-board, or an alter ego, offering the writer some strategic questions whose answers, which it is the writer's business to supply, may well enrich the writing.

There's more at issue in the practices of this hypothetical teacher than just a casual preference for having students revise earlier texts to discover new meanings as opposed to drilling them on topic-sentence paragraphs. What lies behind the practices is a philosophical perspective on how people write and learn to write, one which differs importantly from the formalist perspective encouraged in ancient rhetorical theory. Consider the traditional viewpoint first. When teachers believe, as a matter of conscious or unconscious philosophical disposition, that to write is to display ideas, that writers proceed by choosing forms — syntactic, rhetorical, logical — from an available inventory in order to slot meanings into them, and that learning to write means receiving the system of formal possibilities from a teacher and practicing their use, then certain classroom methods become more desirable than others. It becomes desirable, for instance, out of a concern for inclusiveness and clarity, to fashion curricula that separate writing into as many component tasks as possible, which can then be defined systematically in lectures, discussed until they are understood, and practiced until a test on each reveals student mastery. The way this has been done for centuries is to analyze completed texts into their constituents — words, sentences, paragraphs, essay-frames, modes of discourse — and the activity of making texts into discrete, temporal steps — finding a subject and thesis, making an outline, writing an introductory paragraph, writing a concluding paragraph, editing the text, and so on. Each of these text and activity components then becomes the basis for isolating a "skill": spelling, diction, and punctuation are skills; making correct sentences is a skill; writing general-to-specific paragraphs is a skill; argumentative writing is one skill and persuasive writing another. These skills are then sorted into units of instruction, often sequenced according to difficulty or according to a teacher's notion of their importance. The point of student writing in the context of these units of instruction is not to pursue substantial meanings but to master the skills that will enable "real" writing at some later time. The point of a teacher's commentary on student texts is to reveal the difference between what writers have done and what they *should* have done. The point of rewriting is to improve on formal propriety, to correct mistakes that represent skill deficiencies. In short, every pedagogical step assumes the philosophical perspective of ancient formalism. Attitudes, beliefs, and values consistent with a traditional outlook govern the methods.

By contrast, when teachers believe that writing is a manifestation of thinking, which depends on a natural human competence to organize experience by means of symbolic action,[10] then a pedagogy consistent with such assumptions becomes preferable to one that is not. Teaching, from this vantage point, no longer stresses giving people a knowledge they did not previously possess, but instead involves creating supportive environments in which a competence they already have can be nurtured to yield increasingly mature performance. Lecturing, which assumes that apprentices need an intellectual grasp of discrete formal principles before beginning to write, gives way before a more active context for learning, featuring repeated acts of composition, followed by responses from readers which aim to create incentives to do still more writing and thereby acquire more expertise. The exercise of isolated formal constraints becomes impertinent because writing isn't conceived of as a mere technology, a system of skills separately learned and mechanically applied; instead, as composing, it's a process of using tacit structuring capacities in the search for meaning, where form is the achievement of the search and not a preconception adopted in advance. The prescriptive rights and wrongs, the labelling of errors, the red-pencilled do's and don'ts of traditional instruction disappear with the recognition that options often have equal validity, a teacher's preference notwithstanding, and that writers, in any case, are moved to change their habits only when they notice inadequate choices negatively affecting readers' perceptions of what they are trying to say — not when they are forced to memorize abstract, unrealistic rules of performance. When teachers acknowledge and value the messiness, flexibility, and open-endedness of composing, they tolerate those features in their classrooms, encouraging writers to accept the obligation to make their own way toward coherence, stimulating and sustaining student efforts but not encumbering them with arbitrary external procedures or agendas. In other words, as in the case of more traditional pedagogy, attitudes, beliefs, and assumptions underlie teaching practices: the perspective of modern rhetoric gives an open, active classroom plausibility and direction.

A crucial fact about these differences of philosophical perspective is that the assumptions in each which give rise to alternative pedagogies also make intermingling of practices or mixing of concepts undesirable. Many teachers unfamiliar with the opposed derivations of particular activities are tempted to subscribe to what we might call a smorgasbord theory of instruction, convinced that healthy eclecticism must surely be the best policy. Textbooks, ever sensitive to shifting market demands, frequently support the theory, offering some free-writing as an appetizer, then a plateful of grammar exercises, a generous helping of rhetorical modes, and perhaps a side dish of sentence-combining. The eclecticism in these books makes them popular with teachers who like to sample a little of this and a little of that, who like to combine the practices they trust with a few new possibilities they think might be effective or at least pleasantly diverting. The smorgasbord preference is difficult to fault because it seems to support a liberal educational stance: students are individuals, they learn in different ways, they have different needs; therefore, they should be approached with flexible, customized, diversified activities. The trouble is, the variety that unreflective eclecticism appears to afford in classroom activities comes at the price of contradiction at the deeper level of intellectual perspective and instructional purpose.

⌐ Here's an example. Grammatical exercises of the sort popular in traditional handbooks assume a mechanical model of how people learn to compose: first, they come to recognize abstract grammatical forms (subject-verb-object, article-adjective-noun), then they practice the forms in uncontextualized drills, and then finally, much later, they use the forms to convey personal ideas in "real" writing. By contrast, a classroom activity such as "free writing" assumes a different view of learning: that writers already possess grammatical competence, that the best way to improve performance is to keep the writer writing, and that the pursuit of meanings is as important a growth incentive for unpracticed writers as it is for experienced writers. The more traditional, grammar-based approach values formal and technical propriety above all, regarding instruction as a process of eradicating errors. The approach that might include free writing values the writer's slow, linear, somewhat haphazard discovery of connections and implications, viewing instruction as a process of supporting the search for meaning even, at times, to the point of disregarding error as being, actually, a sign of growth.[11]

The two classroom practices, in other words, clash at the level of theoretical perspective even though they appear as merely two of many equally useful teaching possibilities. The approaches are incompatible because they assume opposed philosophical premises. The teacher who combines them in one syllabus might be likened to the hypothetical doctor who treats patients with antibiotics one week and then bleeds them the next for a change of pace. Students are different, to be sure, and should be approached in flexible ways. Variety *within* a unified instructional setting is laudable. But diversity of approach to the point of intellectual contradiction only results in confused pedagogical goals and mixed instructional messages to students. The teacher who tells students that writing is exploratory, full of false starts, dead ends, and new directions, and who recommends free writing and journal keeping, but who simultaneously insists on formal outlines and requires only single drafts of essay assignments is working from confused pedagogical goals. The teacher who encourages students to "think for themselves," to take risks in their writing in order to discover new significance, but who then faults their subsequent discourses mainly for tense shifts and spelling errors is delivering contradictory messages (ideas are nice, but it's really form that counts). Of course, more than mere consistency is at stake here: the smorgasbord approach is indeed inconsistent, but another approach which adheres faithfully to a unified philosophical perspective that also happens to be outmoded or problematic is not necessarily more admirable. The major problem with a pedagogical smorgasbord is its failure to distinguish plausible ideas about writing and learning to write from those that are implausible, mixing them in the interest of variety with no consideration of their intellectual validity or methodological pertinence. Ancient rhetorical theory is too limited in certain crucial respects to be an adequate foundation on which to base teaching practice, as we will show. Under the circumstances, eclecticism is not a virtue when it involves a discontinuity of worldviews. Astronomers don't blend Ptolemaic with Copernican cosmology, and teachers of composition should be similarly wary of blending the epistemologies of ancient and modern rhetoric.

In short, to the extent that writing instruction still relies on ancient assumptions about knowledge, learning, and discourse, we see a debilitating philosophical confusion that superficial broadmindedness only intensifies. Some people argue, in a spirit of compromise, that "bridging the gap" between classical and modern rhetorical perspectives is preferable to turning away from one in order to embrace the other.[12] Doubtless, compromise is an effective solution to many problems, and gap-bridging is often a worthy effort. The gap between literature teachers and writing teachers, for instance, deserves to be bridged, and the sooner the better. But the process of merger or bringing together is not always as well-suited to intellectual progress as it is to political negotiation, and the distinction between ancient and modern epistemologies is chiefly an intellectual issue, though it has political implications. Intellectual consolidation is possible whenever concepts or problems can be interrelated within a single line of reasoning. But what if two lines of reasoning oppose each other, and what if evidence supporting one is stronger than evidence supporting the other? This, we will argue, is the case in discourse theory. Efforts to bring together opposed perspectives on discourse only invite the formation of pseudoconcepts, purchasing accommodation at the price of intellectual confusion. There is already much unintentional confusion in writing instruction resulting from philosophical uncertainty. Hence, a recent textbook celebrating "the process approach" offers a six-step recipe as its version of "process": first, the writing of a declarative sentence, then the making of three more sentences about the sentence in step one, then the making of a paragraph for each sentence in step two, and finally in steps four to six, the developing of each paragraph with details and examples![13] But the situation will surely worsen if teacher-researchers consciously endeavor to create pseudoconcepts out of an ill-considered desire to preserve antiquated ideas. Simplified schemas of the aims of discourse, for instance, are pseudoconcepts, we believe, to the extent that they are regarded as motivationally significant in writers' choice-making. Recent attempts to define three or four generalized "intentions" parallel Aristotle's ancient effort in their emphasis on completed discourses which can be catalogued according to presumed effect—informative, suasory, argumentative, poetic, and so forth. When these categories are then regarded as aims shaping writer's decisions, that is, controlling the process of composing, the notion of generic intent is a pseudoconcept. And when that pseudoconcept finds its way into teaching, the result is a pedagogy based on false premises about how writers compose. We do not regard such pseudoconcepts as a beneficial form of intellectual accommodation.

At this point, teachers may (indeed should) rightly ask, by what authority do we claim that classical rhetoric is inadequate and modern rhetoric more promising as a ground for instruction? The answer brings us full circle in the argument we have sketched here and will elaborate later. We claim it by the authority of continuing observation and speculation, the slow, careful, incomplete but on-going process of research in which teachers ought to be playing their parts. Classical concepts do not retain the same intellectual validity today that they enjoyed hundreds of years ago, nor have they ever achieved teaching validity either in available research or in the experience of teachers. They are flawed because they do not accord with the evidence of observation and because they are rooted in an epistemology which is itself insufficient, as more than three centuries of accumulated insight have come to reveal. Naturally, there is still much to learn about the nature and operations of discourse and about the best means of teaching writing. But if the destination has not been reached, at least the journey is underway; its starting place, the contributions of ancient rhetoric, has been left behind. If researchers don't yet know everything, they know more than they once did. Teachers must become philosophers if they are to differentiate ideas or methods that lack support in experience from those that have support. They must become philosophers in order to carry out the work of improving instruction by first improving the theoretical underpinnings of instruction.

We'd like to forecast a central argument of later chapters by recourse to two examples of what we mean to say, one personal experience of the learning process conspicuously short-circuited and another of learning going on. Early on a summer morning, gloriously indifferent to our book-writing responsibilities, we decided to escape to the neighborhood tennis courts for some diversion. On arrival, we noticed two young boys trudging courtward, rackets dragging behind them. They seemed oddly unenthusiastic in light of the fact that tennis is a game, after all, and should therefore have a different sort of appeal for young boys than that of, say, taking out the garbage or scrubbing behind the ears. The appearance of their tennis coach, however, and his subsequent teaching practices, quickly explained the boys' lack of interest (perhaps also their lack of ability). The coach immediately lined them up parallel to a fence over in a corner of the court area and began lecturing them on the fine points of an Eastern forehand—grip, angle of the racket, position during backswing, position after followthrough, location of the feet. He spoke with authority and obviously knew what he was talking about. He was clear and thorough—and a perfectly reasonable disciplinarian whenever the children's attention wandered (which was frequently). After twenty minutes of shaping hands to rackets, moving feet about, and talking, talking, talking, he asked the boys to begin practicing what they had learned. They were to bounce tennis balls in front of them and then hit the balls with the proper forehand finesse—into the fence! For half an hour the two boys hit balls at that fence, with the instructor offering well-meant and almost certainly incomprehensible corrections of their technique. The boys never came onto a court, never felt the excitement, the satisfaction, of hitting a forehand successfully toward an opponent or chasing after a shot hit in return, never learned the deeper lesson that success in tennis mainly means hitting a ball over the net more times than the other person does. To be sure, before leaving, the coach recommended that the two boys practice their new "skill" by playing tennis for awhile. And for awhile they did—very badly, very self-consciously, very disinterestedly. In ten minutes they left the court, happy to be free of such complicated, unrewarding labor. We doubt they were looking forward to the next day's backhand lecture.

Meanwhile, next to us on another court two somewhat older players were engaged in a match with all the trimmings—serving, rallies, smashes at the net, scoring of games and sets. One player was a good deal better than the other and giving the other an informal lesson. She didn't have to spend much time telling her partner that his technique was poor because the proof of it was evident every time the ball plopped in the net or sailed out of play. Her response to "error" was to call 15-love and serve again, recognizing that more playing experience, not detailed postmortem analysis, was the key to improvement. (Besides, she was no Billie Jean King herself and understood that error is a natural part of the game.) From time to time, she did introduce a technical matter, as when she suggested that her partner keep his elbow a little higher while serving—which brought success on the next serve and, predictably, failure on the one after that. But mainly the two just played tennis, and whatever advice the better player offered was received and understood in the context of playing the game. The two seemed to be enjoying themselves; more important, they both seemed to have clear images of themselves as tennis players and therefore some motivation to keep working at their abilities. After ten thousand more forehands and ten thousand more backhands in the process of playing tennis, they would both be better players, provided they kept picking up helpful tips along the way from other performers with outside vantage points.

Notes

[1] Teachers should know, for example, about the journals that can help them keep abreast of recent thinking in their field, especially those published by the National Council of Teachers of English. They should also know about collections of articles that will give them ready access to broad lines of argument in their profession, as well as current research trends and practical ideas for their teaching. These collections include: Gary Tate and Edward P.J. Corbett, eds., *The Writing Teacher's Sourcebook* (New York: Oxford University Press, 1981); Richard L. Graves, ed., *Rhetoric and Composition: A Sourcebook for Teachers and Writers,* new edition (Upper Montclair, NJ: Boynton/Cook, 1984) and Patricia L. Stock, ed., *fforum: Essays on Theory and Practice in the Teaching of Writing* (Upper Montclair, NJ: Boynton/Cook, 1983).

[2] When we speak of "composing" here, we refer to composing in the written language but we are also mindful of the larger sense of "composing" as the forming/ shaping process in numerous media. In other words, composing is a richer concept than "writing," and wherever we use the term we mean to designate the forming/ shaping activities of mind, not merely the learned behaviors associated with writing in the narrowest sense—using a pen or pencil, making the letters of

written discourse, using the technical conventions of the written language, and so on. The distinction is crucially important because "composing" is a natural human endowment while "writing" is learned. Yet "writing" means next to nothing if divorced from the larger concept of "composing." For stimulating discussions of these issues, see Ann E. Berthoff, *The Making of Meaning* (Montclair, NJ: Boynton/Cook, 1981) and Janet Emig, *The Web of Meaning*, eds., Dixie Goswami and Maureen Butler (Boynton/Cook, 1983).

[3]Janet Emig's criticisms of the poverty of writing textbooks are well known and well worth reading. See *The Composing Processes of Twelfth Graders* (NCTE Research Report, No. 13, 1971), Chapter 1. See also Donald C. Stewart, "Composition Textbooks and the Assault on the Tradition," *College Composition and Communication*, 29 (May 1978), 171-76.

[4]The irreparable epistemological disjunction between ancient and contemporary thought is fundamental to our argument because it accounts, in our judgment, for the infertility of classical rhetorical concepts in modern discourse theory as well as in the modern writing classroom. The work of Michel Foucault is especially important to our position, in particular, *The Archaeology of Knowledge* (New York: Harper and Row, 1972) and *The Order of Things: An Archaeology of the Human Sciences* (New York: Pantheon Books, 1970). Foucault describes the epistemological shift with great subtlety, and the excitement of his arguments repays attentive reading despite their complex form.

[5]Sheridan Baker, *The Practical Stylist*, fourth edition (New York: Thomas Y. Crowell, 1977), pp. 16-22.

[6]Neil Postman, *Crazy Talk, Stupid Talk* (New York: Delacorte, 1976), pp. 228-29.

[7]For extended discussion of the Postman paragraph, see C.H. Knoblauch, "The Rhetoric of the Paragraph: A Reconsideration," *Journal of Advanced Composition*, 2 (1981), 53-61.

[8]Obviously, mature writers can work very productively within unusual constraints, such as the sonnet form. But handling the sonnet form well presumes a developed ability to write: imposing the form on unpracticed writers, far from supporting their efforts to organize, only increases their anxiety and the likelihood of failure. Mike Rose offers an argument parallel to ours about the difficulties students have in following artificial performance recipes; see Mike Rose, "Rigid Rules, Inflexible Plans, and the Stifling of Language: A Cognitivist Analysis of Writer's Block," *College Composition and Communication*, 31 (December 1980), 389-401.

[9]The "composing-aloud protocol" is explained as a research tool in Linda Flower and John Hayes, "Plans That Guide the Composing Process," in *Writing: Process, Development and Communication*, Vol. II in the series *Writing: The Nature, Development, and Teaching of Written Communication*, eds., Carl H. Frederiksen and Joseph F. Dominic (Hillsdale, NJ: Lawrence Erlbaum Associates, 1981). See also Hayes and Flower, "Uncovering Cognitive Processes in Writing: An Introduction to Protocol Analysis," in *Methodological Approaches to Writing Research*, eds., P. Mosenthal, L. Tamor, and S. Walmsley (New York: Longman, 1983).

[10] We will speak in Chapter 3 of "symbolic action" or "symbolic representation" as an innate human capacity or disposition to make meaning—that is, to fuse mind and experience—through the medium of signs, including language, and interpretive behavior. We depend on Ernst Cassirer, *Philosophy of Symbolic Forms*, especially Volume I, "Language" (New Haven: Yale University Press, 1955) and Susanne K. Langer, *Philosophy in a New Key* (Cambridge:Harvard University Press, 1957) for the theory of symbolic form.

[11] The concept of "error" in student writing is currently undergoing an important transformation, mistakes no longer regarded as proof of incompetence but as a symptom of growth. See, for instance, David Bartholomae, "The Study of Error," *College Composition and Communication*, 31 (October 1980), 253-69. "Intellectual growth and language development are monuments to the efficacy of error. In the development of language and thought, we see a chain of 'mistakes' that begins in infancy . . . and continues through adulthood. The cognitive-developmental position values error, viewing it as a 'window' into the mental processes involved in language use," Loren S. Barritt and Barry M. Kroll, "Some Implications of Cognitive-Developmental Psychology for Research in Composing," in *Research on Composing: Points of Departure*, eds., Charles R. Cooper and Lee Odell (Urbana, IL: NCTE, 1978), p. 53.

[12] Edward P.J. Corbett's well-known *Classical Rhetoric for the Modern Student*, second edition (New York: Oxford University Press, 1971) is the noblest effort to bridge the gap between ancient and modern worlds, and also by far the most accurate rendering of classical concepts. We do not fault its descriptive adequacy but only its philosophical assumption about the contemporary relevance of the ancient perspective. More problematic, in our view, is Erika Lindemann's recent book, *A Rhetoric for Writing Teachers* (New York: Oxford University Press, 1982), which intermingles classical and modern thinking as though the differences were not serious enough to elaborate. Since different attitudes about discourse arise from different rhetorical traditions, and since the teaching of writing is affected by those attitudes, we regard the blending of ancient and modern concepts as confusing and unproductive.

[13] William J. Kerrigan, *Writing to the Point: Six Basic Steps*, third edition (New York: Harcourt Brace Jovanovich, 1983). This text seems to us a perfect example of mistaking some arbitrary performance recipe for the idea of "composing process."

Chapter 2

Ancient Rhetoric
in Modern Classrooms:
That Old-Time Religion

Many things have come and gone in the world since the Greek sophists inaugurated composition instruction by hiring out as masters of the subtle arts of persuasion 2500-odd years ago. These days the citizens of Athens are no smarter than the rest of us and struggle with the same pollution problems. The Roman Empire has retreated to the modest boundaries of Italy, and Latin, once the language of the world, to the boundaries of a few high-school and college classrooms. Zeus and Jove have been demoted to mythological figures. Almost no one assumes that the earth is the center of the universe, or that animal entrails can be read to foretell the future, or that electricity can cure warts. People have given up, reluctantly, on centaurs and dragons, on the Great Chain of Being, on alchemy, on phlogiston and the "ether," on witches (for the most part) and on the punitive value of drawing-and-quartering. Of all the intellectual systems that once animated the classical world, only the concepts of ancient rhetoric, preserved in the hearts if not quite consciously in the minds of traditional writing teachers, seem to have survived so vigorously the ravages of time and the usually inexorable processes of evolution. For better or worse, the writing classroom, even when superficially modernized by audiovisual aids and computer programs, more faithfully sustains the worldview, the attitudes, assumptions, beliefs, and values, of antiquity than perhaps any other twentieth-century educational enterprise. We think it's mainly for the worse.

This is by no means to belittle the extraordinary achievement of ancient rhetorical speculation. From the fifth century, B.C. to the middle of the seventeenth century, A.D., over 2000 years, the systems of Greek and (later) Roman discourse theory dominated Western thought, profoundly influencing law, politics, education, literature, and other social institutions. The major documents of the tradition, Aristotle's *Rhetorica*, Cicero's *De Inventione* and *De Oratore*, the *Rhetorica ad Herennium*, and Quintilian's *Institutio Oratoria*,[1] rank with the Bible in their influence on European intellectual history, especially in light of their importance to the education of youth until well into the Renaissance. Our insistence on the conceptual inadequacies of the classical tradition doesn't imply a lack of admiration, nor does it derive from a knee-jerk preference for modernism. It's based on the progress of rhetorical thought resulting from more extensive observation and less prescriptive speculation in the four centuries following the Renaissance, a period we'll discuss later and one which has seen numerous ancient institutions, political, theological, legal, and scientific, reorganize themselves for similar reasons. It isn't accidental that so many disruptions of time-honored structures and beliefs have occurred in the same 400 years. Beneath them all, and influencing them, revolutions in epistemology and in the methods of acquiring and validating new knowledge have been at work to reconceive the very foundations, dimensions, and aspirations of intellectual inquiry. Rapid advances in the natural sciences have been the most visible signs of these revolutions, but they affect every aspect of modern thought. They have significantly altered the assumptions and concepts of discourse theory, which has evolved well beyond the still classical premises implicitly directing traditional writing instruction. And that's the problem: classrooms continue to attempt artificial resuscitation of a view of composition long ago separated from the epistemological atmosphere that had once supported it.

Consider the many remarkable resemblances between ancient epistemology and the modern but traditionalist writing class. In the ages when Aristotle, Cicero, and Quintilian first described the principles of rhetoric, human knowledge — in the sense of conscious, reasoned judgments about experience — was regarded as essentially complete and stable, a mirror of the way things "really are," a system of revered truths and connections among truths which manifested the harmony implicit in a universe created and governed according to rational plan.[2] The world's harmony existed prior to and independent of human perception, a fact of Nature. It was a harmony regulated by certain unchanging relationships beneath the flux of everyday experience: matter and form, substance and accident, being and becoming, genus and species, cause and effect.[3] The truth was the truth; error was demonstrably error; the knowledge derived from experience and tradition was as substantial and sufficient as the world itself, an equivalent intellectual image of Reality. The purpose of discourse in this ancient epistemological context was very simple: its moral imperative was to convey the truth in a verbal dress that would make it attractively visible to particular audiences on particular occasions. Knowledge did not depend on this "articulation" for its existence: the "substance" of ideas preceded the "form" of their expression.[4] The point of expression was to preserve and celebrate and communicate the truth by decking it in ceremonial garb, the various formulas and ornamental designs of public discourse, whether spoken or written. For the developed logical mind, according to Aristotle, a purer rational representation of truth in the form of propositional and syllogistic knowledge was sufficient. But for weaker minds, verbal artifice made the truth comprehensible by first making it simple and appealing.[5]

For many contemporary teachers of writing, we suspect, much of this thinking, especially the relationship between knowledge ("content") and discourse ("form"), is familiar, not as an outmoded view dispassionately recollected but as commonplace truth taken uncritically for granted. Many writing teachers still believe, or at least appear from their practice to believe, that ideas exist prior to language, that the content of a discourse is wholly independent of its form, that knowledge is fixed and stable, the possession of a master who passes it on to students, and that writing is largely a ceremonial activity. The artificial progression of stages, which many teachers recommend, from selecting a subject to finding a thesis to building an outline to "fleshing it out" with prose, surely implies that writers first assemble and arrange ideas before clothing them in a suitable language — that ideas are found, somehow, outside language and then shaped into discourse. The traditional practice of making writing assignments with reference chiefly to some idealized formal constraint — the "five-paragraph theme," the general-to-specific paragraph frame, the cause/effect essay — which students are to "fill up" with matter surely indicates that many teachers differentiate form from content, what students say from how they say it, even to the point of grading each separately. The typical practice of assigning conventionalized subjects drained of energy — abortion, capital punishment, summer vacation — surely suggests that writing is a perfunctory, ceremonial exercise, not designed to discover new learning but only to recapitulate in decorous prose what people already know — or at least what teachers know better than students so that they can confidently "correct" students' ideas.[6] Finally, the very format of the traditional classroom, the teacher-as-boss dispensing information from the front of the room, only occasionally allowing students to guess the "right" answers in class discussion, surely demonstrates that knowing how to write, as well as other kinds of knowledge, is regarded as the possession of masters who grasp it fully and bestow it on students.

These customary teaching attitudes and practices all reflect ancient beliefs that knowledge (in the sense of conscious, connected thinking) is separable from as well as prior to discourse (some means of expression), that a privileged class possesses, safeguards, and conveys the truth, and that writing is merely a vehicle for transmitting the known to those who don't yet know. The beliefs are part of the philosophical perspective of antiquity concerning the nature of discourse, a perspective which gave meaning and definition to the concepts of classical rhetoric. To examine the Greco-Roman rhetorical tradition, therefore, is to discover the deepest, earliest underpinnings of conservative writing instruction.[7] We'll discuss some important principles of ancient discourse theory, relating them in turn to contemporary-traditional teaching, with reference to concepts in four categories: those related to occasions for composing, those related to compositional genres, those related to modes of argument, and those related to the actual making of texts. In the first category, rhetoricians distinguished a variety of situations in which discourse might occur (such as Aristotle's three occasions for oratory: deliberative, forensic, and epideictic), and therefore, implicitly, a variety of intentions for writing (to advocate, to defend, to praise, and so on). In the second, they differentiated the shapes or forms available for discourse (the

Ciceronian six-part oration, the five-act tragedy, the periodic sentence). In the third, they examined alternative methods or modes of argument (including syllogism, enthymeme, and example, in Aristotle's system, or deduction versus induction, in Cicero's). Finally, in the fourth category, they considered the procedures for crafting particular discourses and the order in which they should occur (as described in the five parts of Ciceronian rhetoric: invention, arrangement, style, memory, and delivery). Still popular teaching practices derive from the concepts in each of these categories, and indeed the concepts themselves are sometimes as actively influential in the minds of many teachers as they were 2,000 years ago. However, as we will show, they are no longer supportable in terms of the epistemological assumptions of the modern world.

Let's look, first, at the occasions and idealized aims of discourse. In the *Rhetorica* Aristotle defined three circumstances calling for suasory discourse. Deliberative oratory was the mode of discourse appropriate to political assemblies: the orator's "purpose" was to advocate or dissuade from a course of action. Forensic oratory was appropriate to the law court: its concern was to accuse or defend. And the third oratorical mode, the epideictic, was suited to ceremonial occasions, such as marriages, funerals, and testimonials: its purpose was to praise or blame (*Rhetorica*, 1358b3). Elsewhere, Aristotle distinguished certain non-rhetorical modes as well, including scientific discourse, which aimed to explain the truth, and poetic, which aimed to instruct by pleasing. In all these cases, and throughout ancient discussions of the matter, "intention" receives only schematic treatment: it is presented as a generalized, static concept and associated with highly formal settings, ritualized styles of speaking or writing, restrictive forms of presentation, and simplified, equally schematic effects on readers.[8] Little thought was given to the complexities of purpose and reader response encountered in actual discourse, the motivations underlying choices, the multiple ends often at stake, the infinitely subtle and diverse reactions of individual readers, the variable strategies by which the same or different effects are achieved in myriad concrete circumstances. The ancient concern was not to portray individual situations with empirical detachment but to prescribe the right conduct for certain *types* of situations, based on appeals to traditional practice. The concern was to outline ideal intentions as prelude to an equally abstract — and absolute — differentiation of genres (scientific, political, legal, poetic, and so on), stipulating for each the kinds of performances suited to the occasions for which discourses in that genre were prepared. Often, for example, the public oration resembled a gymnastic event, where judges know the range of acceptable behavior (say, the routines of the parallel bars) and evaluate, not chiefly what is done, but how well a performer does what is supposed to be done.[9] The stipulated "aim" of the speech established the terms for its evaluation as an instance of praise, defense, or advocacy (just as in many writing courses, where ritualized composing still goes on). It was a feature of the performance, in other words, not a sophisticated psychological motive for creating discourse. In light of these classical attitudes, we see a problem when contemporary researchers and teachers adopt the ancient habit of taxonomizing ideal types or modes of intention. James Kinneavy, for instance, has subdivided writing into expressive, literary, persuasive, and referential kinds. James Britton subdivides it into expressive, poetic, and transactional. Richard Lloyd-Jones has distinguished expressive, persuasive, and explanatory modes.[10] Textbooks often taxonomize writing along the lines of persuasion, exposition, and argument. In both method and content these modern taxonomies resemble the ancient ones: texts are differentiated according to presumably distinctive features, then ordered on the basis of shared features into a small number of groups typically regarded as exhaustive. In our view, to the extent that the taxonomies also preserve ancient assumptions about discourse, or are used by teachers in the context of those assumptions, they are misleadingly reductive and artificial.

What's wrong with distinguishing general aims of discourse? Up to a point, nothing is wrong — as long as the goal is only to sort completed writing in a way that allows discussion of some range of interesting features or effects. It's a kind of literary critical procedure, designed to identify and comment on distinctive features of texts as some reader perceives them. Its value lies, then, in offering a lexicon for studying some range of samples from a certain angle, and the lexicon may be more or less sufficient depending on its ability to represent the full extent and variety of observed linguistic experience. Historically, however, taxonomies of the aims of discourse have given rise to some damaging misconceptions: that the aims are as truly distinct in actual writing as they appear to be in the theoretical oppositions of a taxonomy; that each aim is realized or embodied in a particular mode or manner of writing which is different from the mode or manner associated with a different aim; and that each aim predicts a range of strategies for effective composition, so that knowing the generalized aim is equivalent to knowing how to make choices while writing (Quintilian, *Institutio*, X, ii, 21-22). For the ancient rhetoricians, conviction was philosophically different from persuasion, and therefore "argumentative discourse" must be similarly different from "persuasive discourse," featuring a distinctive style of reasoning as well as manner of expression. And if the modes are distinct, then so too must be the strategies for composing in each of them.[11] This highly schematized way of thinking about discourse encouraged a dogmatic rather than speculative attitude, exaggerating boundaries of intention and therefore also boundaries of genre, boundaries of acceptable performance, and boundaries of effect. Unfortunately, much writing instruction today is compromised by the same overrestrictiveness — and largely because of the same tendency to schematize, then draw conclusions about performance from the apparent oppositions in the scheme. For that reason, we regard taxonomies of ideal aims as problematic whether the theorists who have devised them support the misconceptions surrounding them or not.

Consider, first, the classroom misconception about discourse "modes" related to the broad intentions sketched in various taxonomies. Teachers regularly assign "persuasion essays" and "argument essays" as different writing tasks. They often assign "expressive writing" early in a term and then "expository writing" later, regarding these "modes" too as distinct. Expressive writing, they often reason, is easier than expository because it doesn't have to be well-organized — as though disorder were somehow appropriate because it is a feature of one mode. Ancient assumptions underlie these assignments: first, that distinctions among the modes are real and reliable (if not absolute); second, that different strategies are associated with each; third, that resulting texts are supposed to present necessarily different shapes or features. But how well do these assumptions stand up in the face of actual writing? For instance, is the Declaration of Independence persuasive or argumentative? Does the decision depend on features of the text or only on a reader's frame of reference? Of course, some will argue that modes can be mixed occasionally, which preserves the view that they are objectively distinct to begin with and may be joined by extremely clever writers to form exotic hybrids. But why is it more sensible to suppose a mixing of modes than to suppose that the modes are actually artificial distinctions, of limited descriptive value since they seem to merge so often in actual discourse? It seems as plausible to claim that *all* discourse is argumentative, and also persuasive, as it is to discriminate modes. All writing entails making choices about what to say (and therefore what to leave out) as well as where to say it. Since any text could have been shaped otherwise, it's "argumentative" in the system of choices it represents as correct and sufficient: it argues its way of looking at a subject. Meanwhile, writing also anticipates the needs and expectations of projected readers in attempting to communicate something of value: therefore, it always aims to persuade readers that its statements are true and worthy. Whether a given text is regarded as argumentative or persuasive in purpose is surely less a matter of its objective features than a matter of the situation in which it was composed and the disposition of its readers to react in certain ways. Hence, a letter to a congressional representative is persuasive in aim, not because of the strategies used in its preparation, and not because of its distinctive shape or features, but because of the context in which it occurs and the representative's inclination to take it seriously. Once the letter is divorced from that context, judgments of its persuasiveness become arbitrary. At the same time, the determination that it's persuasive given the circumstances of its creation by no means precludes its being argumentative as well, not because modes can be mixed but because distinctions of mode are relative to begin with.

More contemporary taxonomies of intention do not escape the same relativity, the same dependence on readers' perceptions for judging the significance of textual features. As a result, they too must not be regarded as distinguishing modes of writing, with separate strategies of realization and necessarily different shapes. Which of Britton's ideal aims, "expressive," "poetic," "transactional," best characterizes John Dryden's *Essay of Dramatic Poesy*, a work of literary criticism (transactional) which conveys a sense of the writer's personal involvement with his subject (expressive) and which attracts aesthetic attention to its form and features (poetic)? The fact is, calling it an example of one mode would highlight one range of characteristics, while calling it an instance of another would simply emphasize a different range. The judgment in any case is a reader's to make, since the discourse can support alternative responses and since Dryden was surely unconcerned about "being literary critical" or "being artistic." Ultimately, Britton's spectrum of ideal aims for completed writing, like the similar spectra of Kinneavy, Lloyd-Jones, and others, is a characterization of reader response and should not be mistaken for a description of types of writing or (still less) ways to write. This certainly does not mean that there is no use for taxonomies of general aims. It is only important to realize what they do and what they are not designed to do. They offer tools for analyzing texts in usefully contrastive ways. But their contrastive distinctions do not identify modes such as "persuasive writing" or "expressive writing." There is nothing intrinsically or identifiably "persuasive" about one range of textual features as opposed to another and therefore no persuasion essay.

Just as there is no persuasion essay, no ideal text that all readers would characterize as persuasive on the basis of its properties, neither is there a ready-made strategy for making writing persuasive (or for causing it to embody any other such generalized aim). Both errors derive from the ancient habit of looking at existing texts, a collection of venerated works by poets, tragedians, great orators, and others, and then describing their characteristics in ways which implied that other writers should produce similar-looking discourses. In ancient rhetorical theory "being persuasive" assumed a ceremonial context: it was tied to a ritualized speech situation with specified rules of conduct. Hence, from the classical perspective, knowing that persuasion was called for did imply knowledge of an expected kind of performance, a stipulated textual shape, based on traditional practice, and a stipulated way of achieving it. But once a generalized aim such as "persuading" is divorced from the highly determined circumstances of ancient oratory, as it is in most contemporary writing, its usefulness as a guide to making choices is, at best, extremely limited. *Operational* purposes rather than idealized aims are what really motivate writers to make choices while composing.[12] These purposes exist in writers' minds as dispositions to communicate particular information to particular readers in specific situations. They are not broad decisions to "be transactional" or to "be scientific," but are rather concrete reactions to single occasions for discourse, representing the desire to affect readers in certain ways.

Usually, a writer proceeds with numerous operational purposes in view, and strategy arises out of the effort to coordinate them and the choices they propose. A writer who wishes, for example, to compose a letter seeking employment may ultimately produce a "persuasive" statement. Certainly, the writer wants to. But a desire to be persuasive is far too generalized to direct the writing: there is no inventory of choices which is tailored exclusively to such an end. Rather, operational purposes guide the writing: the intent to offer a self-description that will maximize the chances of getting a job; the intent to represent credentials according to an estimated sense of what the prospective employer needs to know; the intent to create a favorable impression without exaggerating; the intent to demonstrate serious interest without appearing overaggressive or desperate; the intent to suggest a certain salary range without implying that a somewhat lower salary would be unacceptable; the intent to force a speedy decision without pushing the reader into a rejection. Choices arise out of these aims as educated guesses about the best things to say and the best ways to say them. The writer will include school or professional background because an employer would probably like to know something about it. The writer will explain why the job seems attractive in order to signal a serious interest. The writer will choose a tone that communicates professionalism, confidence, and amiability (though, of course, different writers would feel that different tones achieve these ends). The writer might suggest that another job offer has already been received, and at a certain salary, in order to influence the reader's response. Given the concrete, operational purposes that influence real composing, as in this example, writing teachers who set students to producing "persuasive essays" and "argumentative essays" on the classical model of ceremonial discourse are actually leading students away from the recognition of motive that serves most directly to guide choices. They are misleading students by attaching an inappropriate importance to certain preferred textual features — let's say, topic-sentence paragraphs, the use of examples, and a "personal" tone of voice — as though these constituted being persuasive. And they are confusing them as well by implying that a knowledge of the features leads to an ability to compose "persuasion essays" — which is like asking someone to bake a cake by pointing to a finished cake and explaining that it is devil's food rather than angel and two-layered rather than three.

After distinguishing occasions and aims of discourse, classical rhetoric discriminated a variety of acceptable forms or shapes for texts, compositional genres such as oration, tragedy, epic, satire, ode, and epistle. Among ancient theorists, the genres were regarded as fixed and eternal, possessed of a reality quite independent of any particular discourse and ranked by order of importance (epic at the top and lyric at the bottom). The concept of "genre" both emphasized the distinction between form and content and also exaggerated the ceremonial nature of writing, its presentational function, its role in displaying the truth in one costume or another. Cicero and Quintilian are precise in specifying the constraints of an oration, for instance, just as Aristotle had been precise in describing the conventions of tragedy — the number of acts, the order of the plot and subplots, the correct stylistic choices, and so on. A writer was expected to follow the rules — like the gymnast displaying interpretive gifts only within the rubric of acceptable parallel-bars routine.[13] Since composing had a ceremonial, at times even a liturgical, import, honoring the constraints had ethical, not merely aesthetic, significance (*De Oratore*, III, xlv, 178-83): mismanage the form and the magic is dissipated; err and the gods are distraught.[14] Immediately, one sees a connection to some contemporary writing classrooms. How many teachers run their students through the ritual constraints of The Business Letter, The Book Report, The Critical Essay, and — holiest of holies — The Research Paper? Each is defined in its pristine generic integrity; the rules for responsible behavior are carefully depicted; the consequences of disobedience are ominously foretold — violate footnote conventions and generations of scholars will groan from their graves. Students whose sincerity has the better of their judgment might feel somewhat like the altar boy at a Catholic mass of thirty years ago: one misstep and who knows what angry powers may be unleashed? Violate conventions of The Business Letter, and the corporate gods will not be pleased. We have spoken before of the socializing concern of writing teachers: their eagerness to introduce students to polite, socially acceptable linguistic behavior, either because that behavior is intrinsically edifying or because it is economically advantageous. Probably, this commitment to socialization has largely taken the place of an earlier feeling of moral responsibility to preserve the forms of language that guarantee the efficacy of ceremonial composition. But writing teachers, whatever their motives, continue to safeguard the integrity of their most valued genres, the inviolability of generic constraints.

Cicero and Quintilian discuss the features of the oration-genre in ways that would touch the heart of the traditional writing teacher (*De Inventione*, I, xv - lvi; *Institutio*, IV - VI). For Cicero, there are precisely six parts to an oration: the content of each part and the order of parts are fixed, though in certain circumstances one part or another might be omitted from a particular oration. Notice the similarity to classic term-paper format, a similarity which is far from accidental. First comes the "exordium" where the orator arouses the interest of an audience through an introduction to the "theme" of the oration, just as the opening paragraphs of The Term Paper are supposed to "hook" the reader by laying out an enticing thesis statement. The "narrative" comes second and corresponds to the "background" section of The Term Paper, where a context for the thesis is provided through a review of relevant issues. The "partition," located third, sets out the order of arguments, offering a preview of coming attractions, just as the early paragraphs of The Term Paper declare that the writer will argue some given sequence of issues in order to reach a particular conclusion. The "confirmation" then rehearses the pro arguments of the case: "capital punishment is a terrific idea because it deters would-be criminals." The "refutation" introduces the meager position of one's opponent: "some will say that capital punishment is a terrible idea because it is ineffective and inhumane." The "rebuttal" of the opposing position follows, thereby strengthening the orator's case: "actually these arguments are utter rubbish because...." Finally, the "peroration" concludes the oration by summing up what has come before, satisfying that most ancient of teacherly admonitions: "first, you say you're going to say something; then, you say what you said you'd say; and finally, with appropriate flourish, you say you said what you said you'd say."

But what could be wrong with teaching the formal conventions of the term paper, the business letter, or the critical essay? After all, many writers use these forms; indeed, one mark of a professional in some field is the ability to write according to the constraints of an appropriate genre: business people write business letters; English professors write critical essays; scientists write lab reports. We don't oppose an emphasis on the superficial shapes of discourse because we question the use of genres in professional circumstances. We oppose it because it's unhelpful in the classroom. We oppose it because of the ways in which many writing teachers regard generic constraints, even to the point of making up pseudo-genres, like the five-paragraph theme, out of preoccupation with form for form's sake. Too many teachers, like their ancient predecessors, view genres as rigid structures that must be learned precisely and then never violated if writing is to be coherent, organized, and effective. Too many believe that learning to write is equivalent to learning these structures, that teaching writing means insisting on formal correctness, that tidying up the surface of discourse causes the maturation of writers. The consequence has been to promote a ceremonial view of discourse among students, a belief that writing is mainly a process of honoring the conventions that matter to English teachers rather than a process of discovering personal meanings, thinking well in language, or achieving serious intellectual purposes. Students know well enough that their "business letters" are fake, even if the real world produces them. They know that their "research papers" are frequently rote recapitulations of readings and lecture notes, possibly never found in the real world. They know that their school writing is, on the whole, a ritual performance, like the ancient declamatory exercises, produced chiefly to be evaluated for technical error and then discarded. As a result, their motivation to write often, earnestly, and well is adversely affected, so that the emphasis on superficial form which had been supposed to accelerate growth actually serves to impede it.

Our main point, here, is that the classical genres, as well as their modern successors, really *are* superficial shapes — not unimportant, but just superficial. It is certainly true that numerous Ciceronian orations have been composed over the past 2000 years: writing can assume that form any time the writer chooses. But we would distinguish between what writers *may* do and what they *must* do in order to achieve coherence in discourse. The skilled writer who can produce a six-part Ciceronian oration could as easily produce the five-part oration of Quintilian, or a business letter, or a research essay, or a lab report, or a periodic sentence, or a paragraph that proceeds from general to particular, if it were important to do so. However, what makes that writer skilled is not an ability to reproduce these shapes; what makes the writing intelligible and effective is not chiefly its reliance on these shapes. Coherence comes from the ability to make sensible statements and to interrelate them in ways that achieve one's purposes, regardless of the public form of the discourse. Genres, meanwhile, are neither eternal nor inflexible, as the ancient rhetoricians tended to suppose. Writers and readers invent and follow them; they are not gifts from the gods, to be honored scrupulously or venerated across the generations. Some genres, such as the epic, are nearly extinct, while others have come into existence long after the heyday of orations and encomiums, for example, the novel, the periodical essay, the argumentative historical narrative, and the biography. Writers violate generic constraints every day with striking results in the generation of new meaning. Doctorow's *Ragtime* is a celebrated recent instance, intentionally confusing fictional and historical constraints in order to discover more rather than less significance. Genres are convenient public conventions enabling writers and readers to adjust quickly to each other for the sake of communicative efficiency. They facilitate conversation, but they do not create the very possibility of conversing.

Teachers err, we believe, when they assume that teaching generic constraints, the formal propriety of discourse, is the way to develop writing ability. We take this position even when real genres are at issue, but we take it more strongly when teachers create phony genres such as the five-paragraph theme, assuming that nonsense written down in the authorized shape of five paragraphs is somehow preferable to nonsense written down in three or seven—or assuming, even more naively, that nonsense will eventually turn into sense if only the five-paragraph format is practiced long enough. The five-paragraph essay pushes the classical view of genre to a point beyond all rationality, one instance of how modern composition textbooks pervert the ancient rhetorical tradition in the process of adhering to it. Some textbooks present the model as though it were the very foundation of meaningful discourse, the deep structure of thought itself. Even those teachers who are cynical about its eventual value beyond the classroom argue that its artificial regimen will support the efforts of unpracticed writers, showing them how to manage and organize their ideas. We submit, however, that human thought does not more naturally accommodate itself to one discourse structure than it does to another: all structures are equally contrived and the problem of working to realize any one of them is essentially the same as working to realize another. Futhermore, asking students merely to slot information into prefabricated boxes, regardless of the number of boxes, does not represent a first step toward improved organizational ability. Ordering ideas in discourse depends on the ability to see connections, to work them out, to experiment with alternatives, to think clearly and well. Giving students the chance to struggle with language, to fashion their own shapes, to make their own connections with the help of a discerning teacher-reader, will be more helpful to their development as writers than following a needlessly restrictive convention masquerading as a real constraint on discourse. Painting-by-the-numbers, though it guarantees a reasonably tidy product, has never yet served to make a painter. The chance to experiment with colors and combinations of colors, with brush strokes and free shapes on canvas, is messy and chaotic, but it allows for the gradual accommodating of creative energy to form that *can* make a painter.

Then what about those real genres, the ones that professionals know how to use: shouldn't students learn to write in those forms? We would say yes, provided that they have a developed capacity to write in the first place, an ability to think well in language, and provided they have some reason to learn a particular form. The unpracticed writer may take a whole semester to master the constraints of a business letter while the skilled writer can learn them in five minutes. The first writer will have trouble, not because the business letter as a genre is difficult to manage, but because thinking in writing is difficult. Our argument is simply for first things first: writing becomes superficially difficult when teachers insist that it be done *this* way rather than that; it also becomes a merely ceremonial exercise when its formal appearance is given a higher priority than what it says. The unpracticed writer is unlikely to discover much motivation to write in circumstances where meanings are valued only to the extent that they are delivered in the teacher's prescribed format. By contrast, the second writer may have good reason to learn the form of the business letter, and, if so, the teacher may well wish to take five minutes to explain its conventions. But we would add that the best place to offer experience in professional genres may not be the writing class at all—where a professional constraint must be taught in the absence of the modes of thought and the kinds of problems that animate discourse in a given field. Instead, a course *in* that field may be the place to introduce the pertinent genre—the lab report, the legal brief, the critical essay—because there the constraint has obvious value as a communicative ritual among professional equals. A better activity in the writing classroom seems to us to be a freer pursuit of meanings and a less restrictive experimentation in form without much regard for the proprieties of public discourse. In fact, we might call this freer pursuit of meanings the appropriate "genre" for writing classes—a true-to-life formal expectation in *authentic* school discourse.

The trouble is, many teachers are unwilling to tolerate such freedom for young writers (they would call it a relaxation of rigor) because they are committed to socializing their students. Generic constraints enforce verbal decorum — they represent a correct way of behaving in the world. Teachers, like their predecessors, the ancient rhetoricians, attach not only aesthetic but also moral significance to well-wrought prose. Decorum is an ancient ideal, related to civility, obedience to authority, good citizenship, and other social virtues (*Institutio*, I). Generally, today, young children are taught tidiness in their classroom writing — a polished hand, a blotch-free manuscript — before they are encouraged to think well, and long before they are encouraged to be imaginative. Adherence to genre may be to the college classroom what nice round letters are to the elementary — an exercise in good breeding which leads ultimately to responsible citizenship. These deep moral and political values often find voice in teachers' arguments that they are preparing students to gain entrance into desirable socioeconomic groups and preferable occupations. Up to a point, we do not dispute these arguments, or the deeper values that support them, or the socializing responsibility of the writing teacher. But we suggest that, in each case, their exaggeration and overemphasis have led to teaching practices which enforce unproductive, even damaging, priorities. The relentless concern for socialization, unbalanced by an equal concern for nurturing individual creative ability, has caused a stilted teaching emphasis on decorum, manifested in tedious, uncompromising lectures on the modes and forms of discourse, leading to sterile exercises in their applications which result in hackneyed, pointlessly conventionalized writing. The grim, resolute argument about "making it" in social and professional life, so often used to explain the need for this sterile classroom, overlooks the fact that humanity, imagination, flexibility, and intellectual self-reliance have more value in life (and learning) than codes of formal behavior. It also overlooks the fact that a preoccupation with the codes cannot instill these personal virtues or create the motivation to prepare for the social group or profession in which the codes are meaningful.

The concepts of classical rhetoric which come closest to an actual model of writing behaviors are those related to the methods of argument and the procedures for crafting particular texts, the two latter categories in our brief review of ancient theory. Cicero has been the most influential classical source for those concepts, outlining five stages in the composing of an oration (*De Inventio*, I, vii and following). The first stage is "invention," where arguments on a thesis are retrieved from a store of available possibilities. The second stage is "arrangement," where the arguments are placed in an acceptable order. The third stage is "elocution," or simply "style," where the arguments are clothed in an appropriate dress of words. The order of these activities was presumed to be fixed: find ideas, arrange ideas, express ideas. The last two stages were important to orations as oral performances, but are not relevant to written composition: "memory" concerned the mnemonic devices which enabled an orator to recall the parts of an argument in correct sequence, while "delivery" concerned the gestures, body movements, and facial expressions accompanying the performance. The first three parts of Cicero's scheme have haunted Western discourse theory, solidifying the distinction between thought and language, or content and form, while offering a mechanical model of how one is joined to the other. It should strike the modern mind as curious that anyone could talk about two of three presumed stages of the writing process without reference to the fact that language is, after all, intimately involved (though the outliners and "prewriters" still afoot in the world might find it less so). But, for Cicero, thinking and argument preceded words, knowledge preceded articulation, so that it seemed only natural to discuss what was prior and more important (invention and arrangement) before attending to subordinate issues (correct style).

And don't many composition instructors agree? Cicero's stages precisely parallel the sequence of steps conventionally described for the writing of a term paper. First, the writer settles on a thesis and searches for some ways to support it—just the business of invention. Quintilian offers some helpful advice about the initial framing of a question, recommending such powerful general questions (called "theses") as "Should a man marry?" and such powerful specific questions (called "hypotheses") as "Should Cato marry?" (*Institutio*, III, v, 5-8). The idea, especially in the case of students training to become orators, was to rehearse a question that everyone already knew about, a traditional issue with a ready store of familiar arguments, so that the oratorical performance could be judged in the context of accumulated wisdom about the subject and with primary reference to the orator's skill in handling his (moribund) case. Quintilian suggests a few favorites for students at different "skill levels." An easy one for beginners is to "discuss the credibility of the story that a raven settled on the head of Valerius in the midst of a combat and with its wings and beak struck the eyes of the Gaul who was his adversary" (*Institutio*, II, iv, 18). For intermediates, there was the old favorite, "Which is better, town or country life?" (II, iv, 24). And for the advanced, a real teaser: "Should a man disinherit his son born of a harlot because that son has married a harlot?" (XI, i, 82). Modern theses and hypotheses have changed somewhat beneath the pressure of issues more relevant to the past 500 years or so—people now ask students to write about "capital punishment," a matter the ancients would not have thought sufficiently provocative to warrant declamation. But teachers still ask their students for the same sorts of mind-numbing truisms, on well-rehearsed subjects, so that they can more easily scan the ritualized products for presentational flaws.

After finding a thesis and recollecting some worn-out arguments about it, the next step is to put them into an outline — roughly corresponding to the rubric of classical "arrangement." The idea here is to predict an order of ideas without actually *writing* too much (since it isn't time yet to "use" language). In ancient rhetoric the pure logical proposition, or the argument comprised of such propositions, was not perceived to be a linguistic entity: it enjoyed a kind of preverbal, austerely rational integrity. It could be clothed in the ornaments of style, but its existence and intelligibility did not depend on stylistic representation. It was substance awaiting verbal form (Aristotle, *On Interpretation*). Contemporary teachers often insist on the outline stage of composing as though it embodied just that pure, preverbal arrangement of ideas that ancient theory described. Some textbooks celebrate outlining, not as an occasionally helpful, informal jog to a writer's memory while composing, but as a substantive activity which produces an artifact valuable and formally complete in itself. Finally, according to the ancients, after finding a thesis, recalling arguments for it, and arranging the arguments in convincing order, the orator/writer resorts to language in order to "flesh out" the vital outline which conveys a text's essential meaning. With the manufacture of appropriate stylistic effects, an apostrophe here, an asyndeton there, a metaphor or two, preferably unmixed, the oration — and the term paper — stand forth fully realized.

Each of Cicero's stages of composing has its parallels in the beliefs and practices of traditional writing teachers. Invention is the most interesting because it is the least understood of the ancient processes, the one most often garbled in composition textbooks. According to the ancients, arguments were not so much created by individual human imagination as recovered from traditional lore: the concern of invention theory was to tell orators where to look. Rhetoricians offered a variety of "locations" in which to find materials, which they called, in Greek, *topoi* (*topos* = "topic") and in Latin *loci* (*locus* = "place"). The "topics" or "places" included both purely formal patterns of argument, such as "definition," "classification," and "illustration," and also actual, but generalized and abbreviated, lines of reasoning, such as "showing the relationship between Socrates and his wife as an instance of the dubious rewards of marriage."[15] The generalized lines of argument come down to (relatively) modern times in the so-called "commonplace books" of the sixteenth and seventeenth centuries, and perhaps also in the writers' journals and notebooks occasionally popular today. The formal patterns have also come down to the present day, but in a peculiarly fragmented and misunderstood condition, thanks to the historical naiveté of textbooks. According to the ancients, an orator reviewed the *topoi* as a means of recollecting the best arguments for a case: Cicero called the "topic" literally "the region of an argument," which can yield various concrete lines of reasoning. As such, the *topoi* perfectly manifest both the static character of knowledge as conceived in the ancient world and the focus of classical discourse theory on completed texts. For they were not meant to describe activities of the mind in coming to new ideas but only to characterize an inventory of stored-up argumentative strategies and plot-lines derived from a recollection of past arguments and stories sifted from the venerated texts of the classical tradition. Arguments in antiquity were not "invented" in the modern sense but only retrieved; they were not created but simply remembered and reapplied.[16]

For many contemporary writing teachers, assisted by their bizarre books, the *topoi* are a central instructional concept. But it is at best an imperfectly understood concept. To begin with, the *topoi* have lately come to be thought of as "cognitive activities,"[17] whereas the ancients regarded them essentially as mental storehouses. Modern theorists and teachers should at least pause to wonder how well the topics — as mechanistic subdivisions of memory — can be expected to function after this unanticipated metamorphosis into organic intellective processes. Then, adding incompleteness to improbability, most teachers work with (and most books mention) only five or six of the *topoi*, typically definition, classification, comparison/contrast, identification, illustration, and cause/effect. Yet Aristotle alone lists nearly thirty topics, including opposites, part to whole, more and less, proportional results, incentives and deterrents, conflicting facts, meanings of names, and so on. And both Cicero and Quintilian add to these. Why the same five or six? We needn't go into all the historical reasons, but an important reason is that textbooks are mainly written with reference to other textbooks, which also listed only those five or six: thus does folklore perpetuate itself. Finally, adding error to incompleteness, some textbooks have promoted their favorite *topoi* to the status of forms or structures for discourse — creating "the extended definition essay," "the cause/effect essay," and perhaps most famous of all, "the compare/contrast essay," strange mutants of the latter-day classical mind, pretending to an organizational function they do not have and were never intended to have.

A writer's decision to compare one thing to another offers no help at all with the basic organizational questions of what to say, where and how to say it, and what to say next. It simply yields a certain range of information and a possible way of seeing that information. Yet teachers readily assign the "comparison essay" or the "definition essay" as though it promised a helpful structural constraint, insisting, for example, that a definition first presents the object or idea to be defined, then the class to which it belongs, then the characteristics which place it in that class, and finally the characteristics separating it from other members of the class. But a teacher who requires such a sequence is indulging in wholly arbitrary law-making, reducing composition to a narrow, formalist ideal almost never discovered in real writing. Certainly, writers can create discourses following such a sequence, just as they can make perorations follow exordia, but these artificial orders do not represent constraints on coherence: other sequences are equally possible, and so are other ways of defining. Moreover, when teachers assign "definition essays" they imply that the point of some writing is to define for its own sake, that such writing is generic. In fact, however, defining is nothing more than one of many strategies available to writers for accomplishing their purposes.

But then, some instructors may say, why not teach the *topoi* as strategies — perhaps as "prewriting heuristics" (according to one popular jargon) reflecting mental processes natural to us all? Of course, there is nothing wrong with such a practice if by "wrong" one means that students would fail to develop as writers if teachers asked them occasionally to compare one thing to another, or define or illustrate or identify. Any writing could improve the capacity to write, even writing the "definition essay." The trouble lies mainly in what students infer about the nature and value and purpose of writing when teachers isolate heuristic "strategies" outside the context of writers' primary concerns — which are to make significant meanings and communicate them to others. One implication is that the discovery process is a collection of such strategies (often called "skills" or even "subskills") and another implication is that each lies initially beyond the writer and so must be mastered as a strategy, perhaps best by drilling, before it can be applied to the making of meaningful statements. It is conceptually wrong, we suggest, to regard inventiveness as a collection of skills and strategies, and pedagogically inappropriate to make them a focus of attention. Breaking the composing process into skills parallels in method the ancient subdivision of mind into reason, imagination, and emotion — fictional constructs which have the effect of mechanizing an organism that functions more integrally and complexly than isolated parts suggest. The fact that different rhetoricians located different ranges and numbers of *topoi* should be enough to suggest the fictional nature of the analytical distinctions that *topoi* represent. At best, they are reductive models of human intellective action, implying that the whole is merely the sum of its parts. At worst, they deceive people about the limits of writers' inventive powers by implying the necessity of thinking in certain fixed and predetermined ways. Furthermore, even granting some analytical plausibility to the *topoi*, their connection to the performance of writers seems remote. What writer actually sets about composing by first inventorying the stock of available ways to think? Writers in action look to their purposes, not to their tools, so that highlighting "strategies," particularly when writers already "know" them in the sense of knowing their use, seems more distracting than helpful.

According to the classical rhetoricians, arguments derived from *topoi* can take only a couple of possible forms. For Aristotle, they were enthymeme and example (*Rhetorica*, 1356b); for Cicero, induction and "ratiocination" (*De Inventione*, I, xxxi, 51 and following). Example, which corresponds roughly to Cicero's *inductio*, is an argument which progresses from an instance, or succession of instances, until a probable conclusion can be inferred: Agamemnon had a terrible time with his wife; Socrates had his problems too; and then there was Macbeth. . . . Enthymemic arguments, which approach Cicero's concept of *ratiocinatio*, proceed from general, well-established convictions to locally applicable versions of them: Socrates is rational because he is a human being. The preferred type was, naturally, this latter, deductive mode because of ancient confidence in the stability of general truths: given the reliability of the broad assertion that human beings are rational, the weaker claim that Socrates is rational enjoys a comfortable inevitability, though it isn't particularly enlightening. Deductive argument sustained the Age of Belief for many centuries, but it also made the advance of knowledge in a modern sense all but impossible because the general assertions from which argument proceeded lay beyond intellectual scrutiny themselves. "God made the earth the center of His universe; denying God's plan is heresy; God disapproves of heretics; Galileo denies God's plan. . . . " During the seventeenth century the rise of modern science, especially the development of empirical method, brought about a shift of preference from the deductive to the inductive mode, which has been sustained into the twentieth century. But the essential opposition of argumentative modes which Aristotle distinguished remains plausible in modern rhetoric and anyone inclined to look can indeed discover both modes working deep in the methodological fabric of modern, no less than ancient, arts and sciences.

The trouble is, Aristotle's venerable and simple distinction functions at too high a level of abstraction to have much relevance even for the analysis of discourse, let alone for developing facility in argumentation. As an analytical differentiation, it resembles the separating of physical reality into animate and inanimate, or food into raw and cooked: no one denies the legitimacy of the opposition or its generative power, but it only creates a frame of reference for analysis without explaining very much in itself. At the same time, from a teaching point of view, it describes something that does not require description. Writers do not set out to "be inductive" anymore than they set out to "be grammatical." Rather, the process of making any line of reasoning necessitates a shaping of argument which retrospective study can reveal to have been inductive and deductive. Hence, it is more than a little silly to have writers practice "deductive argument" as though it were something they needed to learn—as though it were one of several important but optional approaches to organizing their thoughts. The fact is, they couldn't escape being inductive and deductive even if they tried. What matters to a writer on the level of conscious choice is how to connect one assertion to another on the basis of some perceived proximity between the two, and then how to make a chain of such connected assertions which accomplishes his or her purposes. The local decisions about proximity have nothing to do with an understanding of the difference between deduction and induction. They depend on the writer's knowledge of a subject, awareness of purpose, and estimation of the needs and expectations of an audience. Teaching the concepts of deduction and induction is misleading, therefore, as well as trivial. It conveys a false promise to writers that they will have solved intellectual or organizational problems merely by deciding which mode to employ. Instructors would be well advised to consult their own experience as writers, and that of others, to determine how functional the concept of argumentative mode really is in their performance.

According to Cicero, the second compositional task, after locating arguments by means of the *topoi* of invention, is arranging the arguments in some sequence. This activity corresponds to present-day outlining and includes both an anticipation of the proper order of "parts" in an oration from exordium to peroration (which, as we suggested earlier, strikingly resembles the order of a research paper in contemporary traditional instruction) and also a judgment about which of two possible strategies to select for presenting the line of reasoning. "Synthetic" arrangement displays general propositions or conclusions first, followed by specific statements about their meaning and implications. Among modern discourses, the textbook typically favors a synthetic arrangement, and so too do many newspaper articles and business memos. As a rhetorical option, synthetic arrangement depends on the recognition that a reader who is either ignorant of a subject or impatient to learn the writer's most important information will find it more satisfying to see generalities first. The alternative style of display, "analytic" presentation, moves gradually through a succession of specific statements until a larger inference comes into view. Analytic arrangement requires more work from readers and is considered a more sophisticated style of presentation; its strength lies in engaging readers' interest by giving them some responsibility for anticipating where the writer is headed. Literary criticism tends to proceed analytically, as do many periodical essays and, of course, mystery stories.[18] From ancient times to the present there has been some confusion about the relationship between analytic/synthetic arrangement and deductive/inductive argument, a confusion that one often finds in composition textbooks. The argumentative modes refer to deep processes of reasoning, while the two basic types of arrangement represent presentational alternatives, given audiences with different needs and capabilities. A writer might well make a conscious decision about arrangement strategy but would rarely, if ever, make such a decision about "how to think" regarding a subject.

Two points deserve to be made about classical arrangement theory as it bears on the contemporary teaching of writing. One has to do with teachers' tendency to tell only half the story about arrangement alternatives, to labor the advantages of synthetic order as though no other option existed while ignoring the rich potential in analytic arrangement. The second, larger point concerns the serious inadequacy of classical arrangement theory for representing the actual complexity of organizing ideas as discourse. Consider the lesser point first. Most teachers and nearly all textbooks insist that essays should begin with thesis statements and that paragraphs should begin with topic sentences. The implication is that only synthetic order, and indeed the most highly restricted version of it, can be coherent. The ancients were smarter than that, realizing that the gain in clarity from synthetic arguments was offset by the loss in reader interest, not to mention a loss in the intellectual subtlety of one's line of reasoning. Analytic arrangement is no less coherent than synthetic, though it requires more discernment in readers, and it is a good deal more flexible and adaptive to a writer's process of intellectual discovery. It is not less controlled but only less stilted and formulaic. Teachers often mistrust and denigrate students' attempts to order analytically, but the source of their mistrust is by no means an empirical awareness that writers fail in that method more often than in the other (no such evidence exists or could exist). It is instead their conviction, which not even the ancients would have supported, that the essence of "organization" is a movement from general statements to more specific ones. It is true that ancient rhetoricians tended to favor synthetic arrangement. But their motive was not a fear that writers were unable to manage analytic method or, still less, that the method entailed an inherent risk to coherence. Rather, it was their pragmatic belief that uneducated audiences would find synthetic order easier to follow. If teachers wish to locate themselves in the class of "uneducated audience," their prescriptions about synthetic arrangement have a rhetorical justification. But a restrictive connection between that mode and the nature of coherence is unsupportable.

A larger point about classical arrangement theory, however, is that it finally has little to offer us about what organizing discourse really involves. Except for the broad discrimination of synthetic and analytic methods, it fails to explore up close, one assertion at a time, the nature of *consecutiveness* in discourse. It speaks formulaically of large boxes containing different sorts of information — the exordium, the partition, and so on — just as composition textbooks speak of "introductory paragraphs" or "conclusions." But it does not talk about connection or entailment, the perception that one thing follows from another, or that this assertion stands in some intellectual proximity to that one, or that one idea precedes or anticipates another. It does not talk about what matters most to writers as they strive to organize their discourses: how to get started, what to say next, when and how to stop, how to create the vector of an argument (the sense of its forward movement), how to create the rhetorical illusions of wholeness, appropriateness, and sufficiency. It may be that no theory will offer generic answers to these questions because, in fact, their answers are largely discourse-specific, a function of the writer's intent, understanding of a subject, and awareness of an audience. But ancient theory failed even to ask the questions, content instead to label large subdivisions of discourse as though an orator's honoring of the sequence of those subdivisions were equivalent to "being organized." To be sure, organization involves overall impressions of design, a sense that one area of discussion will precede or follow another, a judgment about the most effective distribution of controlling ideas. But *composing* entails the making of consecutive assertions, connecting them to and modifying them with other assertions, groping toward larger meanings by experimenting with the more local significance of word combinations, phrases, clauses, and clause relationships. Broad prescriptions about arrangement tend to be as unhelpful as they are arbitrary. For instance, the "rule" that a first paragraph must introduce a thesis and "hook" the reader is both overdetermined (because first paragraphs can do lots of things and are "first" only in a temporal, not a qualitative, sense) and also uninformative (because it doesn't explain how to proceed but only what the product looks like). Alas, many writing teachers mistake such "rules" as true and useful statements about organization because of the influence of ancient arrangement theory on their textbooks and their own habits of mind.

The third, and for our purposes the last, compositional activity in Cicero's scheme is "elocution" or style, the clothing and adornment of arguments in verbal dress. For the ancient rhetoricians, argument and expression were distinct, and expression was by far the subordinate concern. Aristotle asserts, in fact, that putting arguments into words is nothing more than a concession to weak minds, to "the sorry nature of an audience," which would be unnecessary if only human beings could discipline themselves to pure rational inquiry (*Rhetorica*, 1404a5-10). The "proposition" was the essential unit of logical thought. Language served to mark it, to render it visible, but it was not regarded as a linguistic entity. It was a rational sign, which could be verbally conveyed in different ways but which enjoyed a separate and prior reality beneath any verbal representation (Aristotle, *On Interpretation*, 16a5-10). Arguments were composed of strings of propositions and were therefore also conceived as rational, not linguistic, structures. Ideally, Aristotle insists, "the case should . . . be fought on the strength of the facts alone" (*Rhetorica*, 1404a1), and "when a matter is plain, piling up words only dissolves the clearness and beclouds the sense" (1406a3). To be sure, as Cicero points out, the beauties of oratory have their place: periodic style, felicitous phrasing, words well-suited to the sense, figurative ornaments of expression, all reflect the harmonies, balances, and rhythms implicit in the world (*De Oratore*, III, xlv-xlviii). But for Cicero no less than Aristotle "elocutio" only embellishes argument: there is scarcely a suspicion prior to the Renaissance that linguistic choices might have greater impact on the quality of thought than merely to enhance or obscure it. From the ancient perspective, language communicates ideas in ways suited to different occasions, but it is not yet implicated in the very shaping of those ideas, nor is the process of articulation as yet substantially related to the process of conception. The ancient rhetoricians regarded language as a mere clothing of ideas and postponed commentary on language until a remarkably late stage of their review of the activities of composition. They also regarded stylistic options and figurative language as mere ornaments of discourse, the jewelry on the clothing of argument.

A paradox in the historical study of style, however, is that, although it has always, until very recently, been regarded as a subordinate issue, it has, at the same time, received more attention than any other rhetorical concern, far more attention than either invention or arrangement. Hence, many rhetoric manuals throughout the centuries have contained nothing more than catalogues of tropes and figures of speech, with no mention of the larger composing issues discussed by Cicero or Quintilian. The resolution of the paradox is instructive for teachers of writing. It lies in the historical view of rhetoric itself as a handmaid to logic, whose proper domain was stylistic analysis while the more exalted business of logic was to attend to the features and rules of argument. Rhetoricians conceded the subordinate status of language while also conceding the primary responsibility of logic for the invention and arrangement of arguments, thereby leaving themselves sole jurisdiction only over the forms and strategies of expression, which they then studied intently. As time went on, but particularly after Boethius installed logic as the principal discipline in medieval education, teachers of the merely verbal arts sank into disrepute, regarded with suspicion or disdain by all who aspired to more respectable intellectual pursuits.[19] The very word "rhetoric" began accumulating the pejorative associations it has retained to the present time. A student of rhetoric might find this gradual process of trivialization regrettable, but the fact is, ancient assumptions about the subordinate status of expression surely made it inevitable. What seems to us far more unforunate is the extent to which contem-porary writing teachers seem willing to accept the same trivial view of verbal composition and therefore a similarly marginal role for themselves in the develop-ment of intellectually mature human beings. It's more unfortunate because it's unnecessary: the ancient perspective on discourse is no longer supported in modern epistemological theory, while the perspective that has arisen to take its place, one which accentuates the relationship between discourse and knowledge, could offer teachers a central role in the nurturing of intellectual development if only they were philosophically alert to its implications.

Unfortunately, many of them are not. Of course, nearly all writing teachers will concede that "ideas" are what really matter in writing. But they will then add that their job is not mainly to evaluate thought in student composing, for that is the province of experts in other disciplines. Instead, their business is to attend to expression, grammatical and technical correctness, formal and stylistic decorum, the "mechanics," the "basics," the verbal "subskills," as though ideas really were one thing and expression another. To be sure, society at large and colleagues in other fields look to writing teachers to deal with precisely these issues, hiding their contempt for the enterprise because they know "someone has to do it" and delighted that they have not been fool enough to volunteer themselves. But what other academic craft besides the teaching of writing looks so timidly beyond its own expert practitioners for a definition of its task? Writing instructors largely deserve their diminished regard in schools because they have allowed emphatic but unenlightened public pressures, together with their unfamiliarity with the evolving philosophy of their own discipline, to dictate the nature and scope of their work — in the process suffering additional abuse for failing to accomplish even the minimal objective they have been "assigned," namely, the development of so-called "basic literacy." The ultimate irony in all of this is the fact that the very perspectives and methods which writing teachers have forced themselves, and allowed others to force them, to accept are what prevent them from achieving the goals that they and others have proposed. By restricting their focus to linguistic propriety, instead of the much broader value of "literacy," and by doing so in a context where verbal skills are tacitly regarded as a subordinate intellectual competence in the first place, they make failure all but inevitable. What, after all, could motivate students to prize literacy when it is defined as avoiding comma splices and mixed metaphors?

The ancient rhetoricians planted the seeds of this awkward and unproductive contemporary situation by fixing their attention so relentlessly on what they themselves understood to be the least important aspect of composing, the dressing of arguments in language. Under "elocutio" the ancients discussed all the technical concerns so familiar to writing teachers: in general, the rules governing linguistic choices. Grammatical correctness went without saying, but beyond that certain constraints of usage and style were also enforced. Verbal decorum was a paramount concern and included rules of purity, propriety, and perspicuity (Quintilian, *Institutio*, I). "Purity" referred to the pedigrees of words, their domestic or foreign derivation (native stock has generally been preferred over imports through the ages, the former associated with simplicity and directness, the latter with obfuscation and posturing). "Propriety" referred to the choice of the "right" word for a given context (Samuel Johnson once noted, for instance, the impropriety of Shakespeare's choice of the word "knife," a mere kitchen instrument, to describe the murder weapon in *Macbeth*; kings are slain with daggers, not knives). "Perspicuity" concerned the clarity of word choice, which, though no one ever thought to explain exactly what it meant, basically had to do with employing only those words that most directly evoked the "things" for which they were intended to stand. Clarity, unclear as its own reference has always been, remained from Aristotle onward the most vital feature of linguistic representation.

Beyond the decorum of individual words, rhetoricians also distinguished varieties of sentence structure — typically, periodic versus "loose" — and varieties of style — plain versus ornate, or "high," "low," and "middle," each suited to different situations. The making of sentences was viewed in mechanistic terms: words were simply strung together one at a time like beads, subject to laws of concord and government. Language was made up of bits and pieces: the parts of speech (nouns, verbs), each naming something in the "real world," and grammatical signs (defined in the declensions and conjugations of Latin, for example) to show how they fit together. Style was not so much a natural or distinctive feature of an individual writer's practice as a ceremonial garb stipulated for all writers by context: tragedy required "high" or elevated language, comedy a lower style. Tropes and figures, finally, were thought to enhance certain types of style. They were seen as overlays on "ordinary" sentences, deliberately chosen (often from available lists of metaphors, metonymys, synecdoches, and the like) for artistic effect, and simply slotted in place of "normal" words and expressions. Hence, the writer who found "youth" too prosaic for his taste could substitute "the dawn of life" in order to make a more ornate sentence. Such ornaments were to be carefully applied, however, so as not to jeopardize clarity. If verbal expression was the least important aspect of composing, figurative language was the least well-regarded and potentially the most unreliable, even dangerous, variety of expression. Accordingly, given the perverse talent for self-abasement that has long typified rhetoricians, figurative language received by far the most extensive treatment in rhetoric manuals, sometimes, indeed, constituting the only subject of discussion.

Obviously, the parallels between the concerns of ancient elocution and the practices of contemporary but traditional writing instructors are close and numerous. Grammatical correctness and verbal decorum are essential preoccupations of both. Teachers prefer diction to be pure, no two-syllable, flowery Latin words when one-syllable, plain Anglo-Saxon words are available. They want it proper as well, certainly no slang or colloquial expressions. Above all, they want it "clear," though clear to whom or in what sense it not always explained: presumably, language is either clear or it isn't, and teachers know the difference. Sentences, they imply, come in precut pieces called parts of speech which are to be strung together according to rules that children need to learn. Hence, students are asked to identify the parts in existing sentences and then to practice joining them in their own. Drilling in the use of assorted small chunks of language — prepositional phrases, adverbial clauses, and the like — is designed, supposedly, to teach students how to string them together; and the drilling often goes on without reference to meaning or any sense of a rhetorical context, as though language were merely a formal veneer independent of thought. Style, ideally, should be simple rather than complex ("Simple," like "Clear," is a Platonic reality, it would seem, which does not require explanation), and "smooth" or "flowing" rather than "awkward." Writers should avoid metaphors in "expository prose," teachers say, but can use them, sparingly (and as long as they are not mixed), in other, less important kinds of writing. Often, in fact, writing courses include a unit on "the metaphor," and even some practice in making metaphors, just in case writers should one day have opportunity to insert one in place of a more mundane expression. The other twenty-five, or fifty, or one hundred tropes and figures (depending on which classical rhetorician one consults) are not usually mentioned because of limited class time, but it is apparent that some teachers believe that figurative language actually comes in pieces called tropes and figures, just as normal language comes in nouns and verbs, because they occasionally select a handful for illustration of poetic effect. They may even drill students in their use if more important matters — correctness, clarity — have been dealt with. Finally, underlying and energizing the teaching of grammar and verbal decorum are the same social, ethical, and aesthetic imperatives so powerfully attached to linguistic behavior in antiquity. Students must learn to write properly, whether they actually say anything significant or not, because their teachers, their parents, and perhaps even heavenly forces value the self-discipline, obedience to authority, and above all, good breeding of which polite discourse is the visible sign.

All of these traditional attitudes, beliefs, and concepts have been repudiated, not in the past ten years or the past fifty, but gradually over a period of hundreds of years. The intimate relationship between language and idea, or discourse and knowledge, has been recognized since the seventeenth century. The organic nature of language as a system of "plastic" structures rather than isolated bits and pieces, and the organic way in which people develop as language users without conscious training, have been ackowledged since at least the eighteenth century. The psychological origins of style as an expression of the individual writer, and the deeply creative power of metaphor, not as an artificial overlay on the prosaic but as perhaps the most fundamental of all language acts from infancy onward, have been explored thoroughly in the eighteenth and nineteenth centuries. Yet the teaching practices of unreflective instructors lag far behind these awarenesses. Teachers continue to separate thought from language, knowledge from articulation, content from form, ostensibly conceding the priority of thought but then vigorously enacting their own limited roles as guardians of superficial expressive decorum. They do not view language as symbolic action, the very essence of intellective life, a natural, organic, human, meaning-making capacity well-developed long before the intervention of any teacher and far more flexible and powerful than any artificial rule could characterize. Instead, they seem to regard it as an alien instrument, unusable until its use is taught, a "skill" acquired only through repetitive drilling, an unnatural mechanical device, full of obstinately uncooperative gears and wheels, which only the most persistent application can enable us to control. And all the while, as though to contrive an importance for language that it otherwise would not possess, they tie its correct use to values — discipline, obedience, good breeding — which certainly sound admirable but which can only be regarded as superficial themselves if so superficial an attainment as, say, proper spelling is sufficient to manifest them. Many teachers remain trapped today in the paradoxical attitudes about discourse in which the ancient rhetoricians first trapped themselves.

We think a fitting climax to our review of classical rhetorical theory and its impact on traditional writing instruction would be to show that misgivings about rhetoric, as defined in antiquity, are not mere demons of our own fevered brains, and not even peculiar anxieties of the late-twentieth century, but in fact have been pervasive in Western intellectual history right from the beginning. The most eloquent critic of the inherent inadequacies of the ancient model is surely Plato, who by accepting the rhetoricians' own views of their work demonstrates how trivial and even pernicious a business they had undertaken. In Plato's dialogue, *Gorgias*, Socrates takes the sophists to task for having mastered, not a true art like politics or medicine, which is grounded in learning and moral commitment, but only a "knack," like food preparation or personal adornment, where a pleasing appearance is valued over substance. The rhetorician, he says, deals only with empty forms and strategies of persuasion, regardless of the content of a given argument or the justification for seeking to persuade in the first place. Potentially, the rhetor is a charlatan who cares nothing for the truth, who pretends to a knowledge he does not have by sounding more convincing in debate than the truly knowledgeable. For the orator, Socrates says, "there is no need to know the truth of the actual matters, but one merely needs to have discovered some device of persuasion which will make one appear to those who do not know to know better than those who know" (459c).

Rhetoricians attempted to defend themselves from Plato's attacks by arguing, as Aristotle does, that orators must be philosophers as well, seekers of the truth, and by insisting with Quintilian that good orators must first be good human beings who join learning to ethical understanding in the service of responsible conduct. But Plato's arguments are difficult to oppose as long as one accepts their basis: his assumption, taken from the sophists themselves, that rhetoric defines nothing more than a system of optional communicative vehicles for ideas that have been independently ascertained; that it offers a catalogue of all-purpose, ready-made structures available to good and evil alike for conveying truths — or errors or lies — on any occasion. Our point here has been that many writing teachers do, in fact, still tend to accept these beliefs about discourse; and having done so, they are as vulnerable as the sophists to Plato's censure. The teaching of writing is still dominated by a concern for modes and forms of discourse: description, narration, exposition; five-paragraph themes; comparison/contrast essays; topic-sentence paragraphs; plain versus elevated, or correct versus incorrect, style. Rhetoric textbooks talk about these forms as though they really existed out there in Plato's Ideal Space, labelling and taxonomizing them as though writers really did select them in advance from an inventory that the rhetorician/writing teacher is responsible for stocking. "Rhetoric readers" offer presumably typical samples of the modes and forms, though with a revealing cautionary note that — awkwardly — the models seldom demonstrate a single option but instead merge several in curious hybrids. Many teachers still seem to believe, whether they say it out loud or not, that what students say matters less than how they say it, that learning to manipulate strategies and genres is more important than thinking well in language or discovering personal stances and values. Writing in the classroom still tends to be conventionalized and ceremonial, a reiteration of dead issues solely for the purpose of demonstrating mastery of formal or technical constraints.

To the extent that writing teachers continue these practices, write and teach from these books, accept these beliefs, Plato's attacks should be ringing in their ears, a constant reminder that the divorce of verbal form or rhetorical skill from a sense of intellectual and moral integrity can easily turn discourse into an exercise in posturing or, worse, a weapon for the unscrupulous. Plato shows why teaching by the ancient prescriptions is inappropriate, despite some teachers' insistence that students nonetheless "learn to write" in traditional classrooms. Granted that any writing may improve writers' competence, even the mechanistic exercises that ancient rhetoric encouraged, still some attitudes toward the nature and value of writing are less productive than others for stimulating writers' growth. Everyone knows stories of the ferocious piano teacher who drills students so relentlessly in the scales that they learn to hate the instrument even as they labor toward its mastery. Technical skill is barren if unaccompanied by a motivation to learn piano and some eagerness to play. Classical writing instruction exaggerates formal and technical awareness, as Plato long ago pointed out, with little regard for the potentialities that make composing a valuable activity in the first place: its power to make new meaning and to convey meaning to others. The consequence is that writing becomes a ritual behavior, which many writers find puzzling and eventually frustrating: for to struggle with the mastery of formal conventions without the opportunity to make personally valuable meanings is like having to learn table manners before getting the chance to eat. Indeed, worse than that, when those conventions are idiosyncratic — the five-paragraph theme — they make writing not merely trivial but also pointlessly difficult — like learning to play tennis in leg-chains. One might learn to play tennis eventually, but it is perverse to credit the chains for the accomplishment. Finally, and this is Plato's most serious concern, an emphasis on conventions instead of meaning implies that the conventions matter more than anything else, that manipulating audiences through technical virtuosity is the ultimate purpose of learning to write. From such a viewpoint, writing becomes more than trivial and difficult: it becomes potentially unethical as well.

Fortunately, however, teachers are not without alternatives to the perspectives and assumptions of the classical tradition, and therefore not without defense against Plato's charges of their vacuity and lack of integrity. Rejecting his assumptions about rhetoric, they can deny that writing teachers care nothing for ideas or the pursuit of knowledge. But first, of course, those assumptions must be explicitly set aside: teachers must acquire the philosophical reflectiveness needed to perceive the limits of traditional instruction and to discover more promising conceptual underpinnings for their work. Preferable theoretical assumptions are available, indeed have been for centuries — altered views of the nature, functions, and operations of discourse, the relationship between language and thought, the role that discourse plays in enabling and advancing knowledge, and the ways in which people grow as language users. Our next chapter will review some crucial historical modifications of ancient discourse theory in the context of what writing teachers need to understand in order to adjust their classroom practice. But we can only recapitulate the arguments. It is for teachers themselves to discover the measure of intellectual commitment necessary to make the theory come alive in their own attitudes toward effective instruction.

Notes

[1]Our references to these works are from the following English translations: Aristotle, *Rhetoric*, trans., Lane Cooper (Englewood Cliffs, NJ: Prentice-Hall, 1960); Cicero, *De Inventione*, trans., H. M. Hubbell (Cambridge: Harvard University Press, 1968); Cicero, *De Oratore*, 2 vols., trans., E. W. Sutton and H. Rackham (Cambridge: Harvard University Press, 1976-77); and Quintilian, *Institutio Oratoria*, 4 vols., trans., H. E. Butler (Cambridge: Harvard University Press, 1969). Though we do not refer to the *Rhetorica ad Herennium*, because it reiterates Ciceronian concepts, the work has great historical importance and deserves reading. Its best English translation is H. Caplan (Cambridge: Harvard University Press, 1954).

[2]Cicero writes: "all this universe above us and below is one single whole, and is held together by a single force and harmony of nature" (*De Oratore*, III, v, 20). And later: "the whole of the content of the liberal and humane sciences is comprised within a single bond of union; since when we grasp the meaning of the theory that explains the causes and issues of things, we discover that a marvellous agreement and harmony underlies all branches of knowledge" (III, v, 21). For ancient arguments about the nature of knowledge, see also Plato, *Republic*, especially Parts 7 and 8, Aristotle's *Metaphysics*, and the books of his "Organon," *Categories, On Interpretation,* and *Prior Analytics.*

[3]For Aristotle's four causes, efficient, formal, material, and final, see the *Metaphysics*, Book I. For the predicaments and predicables, see *Categories.*

[4]Aristotle insists that words denote our conceptions of things for purposes of communication, while "the mental affections themselves, of which these words are primarily signs, are the same for the whole of mankind, as are also the objects of which those affections are representations or likenesses, images, copies." See *On Interpretation*, trans., Harold P. Cooke (Cambridge: Harvard University Press, 1973), 16a5-10. See also Aristotle's *Rhetoric* on the character of the truth and "the natural and universal notion of right and wrong," which, he says, is "one that all men instinctively apprehend, even when they have no mutual intercourse nor any compact," *Rhetoric*, 1373b13. Cicero observes: "A full supply of facts begets a full supply of words, and if the subjects discussed are themselves of an elevated character this produces a spontaneous brilliance in the language" (*De Oratore*, III, xxxi, 125).

[5]See Book III of Aristotle's *Rhetoric*, "Lexis," and also Cicero, *De Inventione*, I, ii, 3.

[6]The origin of the classroom practice of assigning standardized subjects about which to make decorous, conventional statements is the ancient "declamatory exercise" which advanced students were set to performing as the final test of their oratorical skills. Over centuries, declamation came more and more to exaggerate formal and technical virtuosity with little or no regard for serious intellectual engagement — leading nearly in a straight line to the ceremonial writing assignment of contemporary instruction. For description, see Donald L. Clark, *Rhetoric in Greco-Roman Education* (New York: Columbia University Press, 1957), Chapter VII.

[7]We can do little more here than whet teachers' appetites for learning about ancient rhetoric. Excellent full-scale reviews include George Kennedy, *Classical Rhetoric and Its Christian and Secular Tradition from Ancient to Modern Times* (Chapel Hill: University of North Carolina Press, 1980); Kennedy, *The Art of Persuasion in Greece* (Princeton: Princeton University Press, 1963); and Charles S. Baldwin, *Ancient Rhetoric and Poetic* (New York: Macmillan, 1924).

[8]Douglas Ehninger has pointed out that ancient rhetoric was essentially a "grammatical system" in the sense that it offered schemes and taxonomies, categories and parts, all derived from retrospective analysis of existing texts, as its theory of discourse. He writes: "in their desire to draw lines between phenomena which by nature blend into another — to divide, compartmentalize, and name — the ancients gave if not a false, at least a painfully oversimplified picture" of discourse.

See "On Systems of Rhetoric," in *The Rhetoric of Western Thought*, eds., James L. Golden, Goodwin F. Berquist, and William E. Coleman (Dubuque, IA: Kendall/ Hunt, 1976), p. 11.

[9] To be sure, in the golden age of Grecian oratory (c. 5th cent., B.C.) public address had a crucial practical function in the democratic assembly and the law court. But very early in the classical tradition, with the decline of Grecian democracy (which removed the public voice from government) and with the school emphasis on declamation (which made oratory into an intellectual game), the formulaic and ceremonial aspects of oratory began to dominate its once practical uses. See Baldwin, *Ancient Rhetoric and Poetic*, especially Chapter 4. Also, page 71, where he notes that, after Pericles, public address "narrowed more and more toward an artificial combination of forensic ingenuity and dramatic imagination." Reading ancient orations is the best way to become sensitive to their ceremonial, ritualized flavor. Some instructive examples are found in J. F. Dobson, *The Greek Orators* (New York: Books for Libraries Press, 1919; rpt., 1967).

[10] See James Kinneavy, *A Theory of Discourse* (Englewood Cliffs, NJ: Prentice-Hall, 1971); James Britton, *Language and Learning* (London: Penguin, 1970), p. 174; and Richard Lloyd-Jones, "Primary Trait Scoring," in Charles R. Cooper and Lee Odell, eds., *Evaluating Writing: Describing, Measuring, Judging* (Urbana, IL: NCTE, 1978), p. 39.

[11] Compare, for instance, Aristotle's discussion of suasory discourse in the *Rhetoric* with his discussion of scientific discourse in the *Prior Analytics*, including the difference between syllogistic and enthymemic reasoning, or the different attitudes toward appropriate language in each mode. See also the *Poetics* for a third genre.

[12] For clarification of the difference between ideal and operational purposes, see C. H. Knoblauch, "Intentionality in the Writing Process: A Case Study," *College Composition and Communication*, 31 (May 1980), 153-59.

[13] Dobson writes: "Greek oratory was much bound by conventions from which even the greatest speakers could not altogether escape. ... Athenian audiences expected it," *The Greek Orators*, p. 32. See also Kennedy, *The Art of Persuasion in Greece*, pp. 266-67.

[14] It is important to understand the connection between discourse and magic in the ancient world, the extent to which the power of language was seen to influence people and events *provided* that formal correctness insured its efficacy. See Jacqueline diRomilly, *Magic and Rhetoric in Ancient Greece* (Cambridge: Harvard University Press, 1975). See also Kennedy on the ancient belief that formal integrity assured truth-value: *Classical Rhetoric*, pp. 15, 38, 56-57, and *passim*; also see Kennedy on the connection between magic and speech in the works of the orator Gorgias, pp. 29-30.

[15] See Aristotle, *Rhetoric*, 1358a; Cicero, *De Inventione*, II, xiv, 47 — xv, 48; *Topica*, II, 8 and XIX, 72.

[16] See Kennedy, *The Art of Persuasion in Greece*: "The traditional quality of rhetoric discouraged novelty in thought, style, and treatment by implying as time went on that all the answers were known and that the problems now discussed by orators

had been perfectly treated in the past," p. 25. And later: "The development of rhetoric into a closed system was the prelude to a concept of life and thought as a closed system," p. 124. On the point that "truth" in the ancient world is rather recollected than discovered, see Kennedy, *Classical Rhetoric*, pp. 46, 65, and *passim*.

[17] See, for instance, Frank D'Angelo, *A Conceptual Theory of Rhetoric* (Cambridge, MA: Winthrop, 1975), pp. 38 ff. We would not deny D'Angelo's point that the mind can act on experience in ways that the ancient *topoi* predicted. We only suggest the philosophical inadequacy of subdividing imaginative activity in the artificial ways that the classical rhetoricians did, as though the whole were equivalent to the sum of its *topos*-parts.

[18] See Cicero, *Partitiones Oratoriae*, trans., H. Rackham (Cambridge: Harvard University Press, 1977), XIII, 46.

[19] For the later history of the classical perspective, see Kennedy, *Classical Rhetoric*, especially; also, W. S. Howell, *Logic and Rhetoric in England 1500-1700* (New York: Russell and Russell, 1961) for a detailed look at the fortunes of Ciceronian rhetoric in a single later time and place.

Chapter 3

Discourse as Knowledge/
Knowledge as Discourse:
Modern Rhetoric for Writing Teachers

The origins of modern rhetoric lie in the epistemological crisis of the seventeenth century, when ancient faith in the probity and completeness of traditional lore about the world gave way before a newly skeptical habit of mind, a preference for empirical, "scientific" investigations of experience, a recognition of the open-ended, but always ultimately limited, character of human knowledge, and a new dependence on discourse for shaping and extending that knowledge.[1] The fulfillment of modern rhetoric lies in the gradual articulation of the concept of "symbolic representation," the organic coalescence of mind and nature through symbols, which began in Kant's *Critique of Pure Reason* and which has culminated in such generative twentieth-century statements as Ernst Cassirer's *Philosophy of Symbolic Forms*, Ferdinand de Saussure's *Course in General Linguistics*, and Alfred North Whitehead's *Process and Reality*, all arguing a way of thinking about language, discourse, and knowledge which Susanne K. Langer, herself a major contributor to the theory of symbolic forms, has memorably termed "philosophy in a new key."[2] The tenets of modern rhetoric have formed haphazardly and incrementally through diverse, often conflicting schools of thought, French rationalism, British empiricism, Scottish common-sense philosophy, French and British romanticism, German idealism, and European phenomenology and structuralism, among others. Its earliest spokesmen, Descartes and Antoine Arnauld; Francis Bacon, Locke, Berkeley, and Hume; Giovanni Vico; Condillac and Rousseau; Kant, Herder, Coleridge, and Nietzsche, to name a few, are figures perhaps as distant from the minds and practical activities of most writing teachers as are the classical rhetoricians of Greece and Rome. More contemporary thinkers in the "new key" may be only slightly more familiar. Yet these architects of modern rhetoric have shaped a new intellectual world, one which writing teachers, knowingly or not, willingly or not, inhabit with everyone else, however successful some of them have been in separating their classrooms from it.

Unlike the ancient intellectual world, which it has permanently displaced, this new world features a perpetual search for knowledge, where learning is an endless adventure in making sense out of experience, an exploratory effort in which all human beings are both teachers and students, making and sharing meanings through the natural capacities for symbolic representation that define their humanity. It is a world founded on this perpetual search, not on the authoritarian premises and unassailable dogmas of antiquity, not on the passive veneration of conventional wisdom or the declarations of privileged ministers of the truth. And it is a world in which discourse — writing as well as other modes of symbolic action — constitutes simultaneously the means of learning and the shape of knowledge, so that creating discourse is equivalent to the process of coming to know, whether it happens in physics laboratories or law courts, legislative assemblies or corporate board rooms, the academic offices of historians and literary critics, the artist's garret or the stage — or in writing classrooms full of eager minds whose nourishment is serious intellectual effort, not ceremonial exercises. We believe teachers of writing can derive valuable concepts from modern rhetoric, which can lead to more effective instruction because they provide, where classical formalism did not, a view of the activities that deeply characterize writing and that developing writers are striving to bring under their control. Specifically, they convey, as ancient rhetoric could not, a portrait of the mind in process, coming to understand its experience, and of composing *as a process*, manifesting the mind at work. Though we can hardly begin to offer a full description of the evolution of the modern perspective, we are persuaded of the advantage teachers gain from recognizing certain of its crucial principles. We intend, therefore, to introduce those which most clearly reveal its divergence from ancient discourse theory, its own theoretical frame of reference, and its explicit relevance for composition instruction.[3]

The place to begin is with the first challenges to ancient epistemology, directly related to the emergence of empirical science, which developed over the course of the seventeenth century.[4] For as Ernst Cassirer pointed out in his famous study of the Enlightenment, what matters most about the revolution in science during the period between Galileo and Newton is not the fact that so much new detail about the physical world came to light, but rather the fact that philosopher-scientists, in the process of comprehending that mass of detail, reached a new awareness about the nature of scientific inquiry — the ways and means by which the mind perceives, acts upon, and comes to understand the "data" of experience.[5] The real achievement of the scientific revolution is its conception of scientific method — scrupulous observation of the world and equally scrupulous testing of successive generalizations designed to account for what is observed — which had the effect of focusing attention on the active, interpretive powers of mind and the various instruments, especially language and mathematics, by which the mind carries out interpretive functions. According to the empiricist psychological theory which developed concurrently with speculation about the nature of scientific method,[6] the mind works toward understanding, toward "knowledge," by striving to integrate sensory data it receives from prior acts of perception. The mind asserts connections among the data, grouping them in classes, relating one class to another, building chains of "associations," as they were called, into composite pictures which could tentatively represent the "coherence" of experience. The principal tool for this activity, philosophers of the age quickly realized,[7] is language, because words and word combinations, sentences and strings of sentences, forge the connections that mental activity strives to intuit: they provide structures by means of which orderly, connected thinking can occur. Making verbal statements, therefore, is equivalent to carrying out intellectual investigation — or generalizing linguistically to comprehend experience. It is a heuristic process whereby the effort to assert connections and array them as integrated verbal patterns — texts — yields new understanding: in effect, new knowledge. Discourse, then, far from having the restrictive presentational function that the ancient rhetoricians supposed, actually has a central, generative role in the pursuit of knowledge.

Descartes' *Discourse on Method* (1637) is an instructive and representative early challenge to ancient theory, as well as a herald of the new science.[8] It begins by declaring Descartes' mistrust of the traditional knowledge stored in all the books he had read as a student, books which in ages past had preserved and venerated the supposedly unchanging wisdom of the world, books which had been endlessly studied and annotated, searched for secret meanings, carefully copied and passed across generations, demonstrating what seemed to him the undynamic and restrictive character of ancient thought (page 5). Descartes also attacks the perpetuator of traditional lore, the stylized, ultimately tautological methods of classical reasoning: "as far as logic was concerned, its syllogisms and most of its other methods serve rather to explain to another what one already knows, or even, as in the art of [Cicero], to speak freely and without judgment of what one does not know, than to learn new things" (page 14). In place of the "speculative philosophy now taught in the schools" he recommends a "practical one" concerned with discovering the nature and behavior of the physical world (page 45). In short, Descartes is arguing the collapse of a worldview, assuming that knowledge is not a gift from the gods, or a fully achieved inheritance from the past, but a gradual accumulation of insight from a search continuously in progress, and assuming that the means of acquiring knowledge is personal observation of experience, not consultation with sacred books, followed by intellectual judgments of its significance. Aristotle's favored method of reasoning had been deductive, where particular conclusions derive from general premises. The direction of investigation, therefore, had been downward rather than outward, clarifying and elaborating *a priori* axioms but neither extending not reconceiving those axioms in a search for fundamentally new knowledge. Descartes offers, in place of classical method, a more dynamic, "scientific" method, emphasizing the mind's active tendency to construe order from empirical examination of the data derived from sensory experience.

The prototype for orderly inquiry of the sort that "scientific method" espoused was, according to Descartes, the analytical procedures of mathematics, especially geometry. "Those long chains of reasoning, so simple and easy, which enabled the geometricians to reach the most difficult demonstrations, had made me wonder whether all things knowable to men might not fall into a similar logical sequence." Beginning with the simplest, most fundamental assertions, and carefully following "the order necessary to deduce each one from the others," Descartes reasons that "there cannot be any propositions so abstruse that we cannot prove them, or so recondite that we cannot discover them" (page 16). Later philosophers will challenge Descartes' optimism about achieving intellectual certainty, and they will fault other problematic Cartesian assumptions as well. But the point here, for our purposes, is two-fold: that Descartes makes "knowing" into a process — a connected chain of reasoning which represents the open-ended struggle to discover new data from experience and new ways of organizing them; and also, as important, that he equates the struggle to know with the making of discourse — technically the fashioning of mathematical demonstrations, but by extension, as he and others readily perceived, the use of some language. For him, learning and composing are inseparable; knowledge and discourse are inseparable; the operations of mind, through the media of its composing instruments, are inseparable from the perceiving and judging of experience — which is to say that any order proposed for experience is an order of mind, not an order intrinsic to things themselves. Hence — the final extension of French rationalist skepticism — the world is only knowable (in the sense of "rendered intellectually coherent") through the operations of mind — that is, through discourse, linguistic or otherwise — because the "meaningfulness" which human beings value is exclusively a function of discourse, not an embedded feature of some Reality that people apprehend directly. Granting these conclusions, the disintegration of ancient epistemology, and with it ancient rhetorical theory as well, becomes unavoidable.

Although Descartes' arguments are broadly challenged by British empiricist and later philosophers, they nonetheless convey to the newly scientific seventeenth century some radical premises about the nature of composing: that it is an endlessly renovative process, that any achieved coherence is necessarily partial and tentative, carrying a latent potential for its eventual "revision," and that composing is as open-ended as the search for knowledge itself. Having decided, for example, to devote himself to medicine, Descartes acknowledges both the power of his method for medical investigation and the impossibility of completing that investigation by himself. He sees a tension in his frame of reference: the promise of his discovery procedure is that it enables the formulating of new and reliable insights, one upon another through the consecutive reasoning of discourse; but its paradox is that it never ceases to generate, that it is inexhaustible in its construing and reconstruing of experience. Every insight leads to others; each proposition in the chain of argument implies more to follow. Hence, there can be no ultimate destination in the search for truth, no conclusive "text" that will, once and for all, convey the fully perceived significance of things. Knowledge for Descartes is an activity, not a state: it can never be freed from the process of articulation. This fact has implications for his own composing and also for that larger composing effort of many minds which finally enables scientific progress. Since writing is a learning process for the writer, restatement is required until a satisfying coherence emerges. Hence, he resolves to "continue to write everything that I consider important . . . as if I intended to publish it. In this way I will have additional opportunities to examine my ideas." In other words, the effort to articulate is what creates potential for new learning. And the resulting text should be of publishable quality — that is, as connected and orderly as possible — because "we always scrutinize more closely that which we expect to be read by others than that which we do for ourselves alone." He does not imply, however, that everything will be published merely because it is written. Instead, he knows that "frequently the ideas which seemed true to me when I first conceived them have appeared false when I wished to put them on paper" (page 48). Writers perpetually confront error, imprecision, and incompleteness as new assertions are posed and tentatively related to any developing chain of reasoning. They grope for meanings, test them for plausibility, learn what they want to say by repeated efforts at formulation. And what is kept, the resulting discourse, though coherent is not itself free of uncertainty: there will always be more to say and more precise or comprehensive ways to say it. Recognizing the limits of his own capacity, Descartes frames his obligation in narrow terms: "to publish faithfully to the world the little which I had discovered and to urge men of ability to continue the work." He trusts the future to the community of scientists, through the generations, who will sustain the search for knowledge, expecting each one "to publish whatever he had learned, so that later investigators could begin where the earlier had left off. In this way mankind would combine the lives and work of many people, and would go much further than any individual could go by himself" (page 46).

Writing a half-century later, and from the opposed perspective of British empiricism, John Locke nonetheless asserts many of the same opinions as Descartes about the limits of ancient epistemology, the new scientific method, and the active character of mind in interpreting experience. In the *Essay Concerning Human Understanding* (1690), he makes his famous declaration about the indissoluble relationship between discourse and knowledge: "there is so close a connection between ideas and WORDS . . . that it is impossible to speak clearly and distinctly of our knowledge, which all consists in propositions, without considering, first, the nature, use, and signification of Language" (II, xxxii). Unlike Aristotle, Locke perceives that propositions are linguistic acts rather than preverbal rational signs. Knowledge consists of these propositions, related to form arguments about the signifigance of experience, and therefore knowledge is a linguistic construction, a "discourse." Knowing is an activity of creating and shaping "texts," just as Descartes had implied, not an absolute state or condition. It is a perpetual struggle to make coherence by ordering sensations, insights, scraps of information, feelings, impressions, imaginative intuitions, partly formed and unconnected ideas within (and by means of) the structures of language. Locke agrees with Descartes that mathematical argument is the purest example of discourse enabling new knowledge, because it proceeds by "a continued chain of reasonings . . . to the discovery and demonstration of truths that appear at first sight beyond human capacity" (IV, xii). This "chain" is both open-ended, hence genuinely exploratory, and rigorously controlled, since each statement in the chain depends on those coming before. The two intellectual faculties guiding the creating of text, whether in mathematics or in verbal discourse, Locke calls "sagacity" and "illation" (IV, xvii). By recourse to these concepts he develops a basic model of composing, emphasizing as the ancients never had done the *consecutiveness* of assertions in discourse rather than merely some system of formal boxes such as those represented in the Ciceronian oration.

By means of "sagacity" the mind "discovers" ideas relevant to a particular line of argument, while by "illation" it "so orders the intermediate ideas as to discover what connection there is in each link of the chain." The first may be said to govern "invention" and the second "arrangement," but in each case Locke's sense of the activities of composing differs dramatically from Cicero's. Invention is no longer a matter of retrieving arguments by recourse to *topoi* but of finding information through empirical search and making assertions that express relationships the mind perceives in or imposes on that information in order to render it coherent. In other words, invention is a creative act, involving the making of new meaning, not a recall of preconceived lines of argument or ways of arguing. Eighteenth-century rhetoricians will regularly attack Aristotle's or Cicero's views on invention because of their realization that the ancient perspective denied the personalized, creative nature of thinking in discourse, Hence, Joseph Priestley, one important mid-century theorist, insists that "rhetorical topics are most useful in the composition of *set declamations on trite subjects*, and to *young persons*, than in the communication of original matter, and to persons much used to composition."[9] Another eighteenth-century rhetorician, Hugh Blair, agrees, noting that "the study of common places might produce very showy academical declamations," but could "never produce useful discourses on real business." For the writer who has no other goal but "to talk copiously and plausibly" with "none but the most superficial knowledge of his subject," the *topoi* can be helpful. But "such Discourse, could be no other than trivial. What is truly solid and persuasive, must be drawn . . . from a thorough knowledge of the subject, and profound meditation on it."[10]

Arrangement, for Locke, is not a matter of choosing a prefabricated formula that predicts where different arguments are to be displayed, but rather a problem of contriving a sequence of assertions according to successive inferences about how any two might be connected. Indeed, Locke equates "illation" with inference, which, he says, "consists in nothing but the perception of the connection there is between the ideas, in each step of the deduction." By making progressive and cumulative inferences about relationship, "the mind comes to see, either the certain agreement or disagreement of any two ideas, as in demonstration, in which it arrives at *knowledge*; or their probable connection, . . . as in *opinion*." By repeating the processes of finding information, asserting its significance through propositional statements, and then fashioning the statements into plausible sequences based on entailments inferred from the evolving chain, any composer sustains a developing discourse in order, eventually, "to draw into view the truth sought for" (IV, xvii). Numerous eighteenth-century rhetoricians, following Locke's lead, join in filling in this primitive scheme of how writers make choices while composing.[11] But what is important for our purposes here is the perspective motivating their effort: because of Descartes and Locke, among others, theorists over the next century assume from the start that discourse makes knowledge, that it is an open-ended, creative process involving repeated formulating and revising, that it manifests the dynamic action of the human mind in shaping experience, and that the truly interesting question for rhetoric is not what completed discourses look like or ought to look like, but rather what the composing process itself is like, how the operations of language, reflecting the powers of mind, work to create meaning. This perspective is fundamentally opposed to that of ancient rhetoric, and writing teachers can profit from realizing that it is not only more useful for their purposes in the classroom but also a long-time intellectual development, no passing fad of the twentieth century but a serious reorganization of discourse theory that has permanently altered the way contemporary rhetoricians view composition.

The eighteenth and nineteenth centuries are an exciting period of moving outward from the essential, although in many ways still primitive, insights about language and mind, discourse and knowledge, deriving from the epistemological upheaval of the preceding century.[12] We cannot begin to cover the breadth or complexity of that evolving thought, but certain highlights are important. Language theorists gradually come to realize, for example, that linguistic capacity is innate, part of the definition of "human," the possession of even very young children who have not yet received formal training in grammar and therefore know nothing of the "rules" that ancient speculation had supposed must be consciously learned on the way to becoming literate. Even as early as 1668 a French school teacher had observed: "No man is ignorant, that since the beginning of the world unto this day every one hath learnt his mother-tongue *without Rules*, and spoken it better than any other." Children, the writer is persuaded, "understand all that (namely, the rules) even from the age of 6 or 7 years," without grammatical instruction.[13] Theorists also realize that language is better conceived as an organism than a mechanism both in form and function, that it is comprised of "plastic" structures implicit in particular instances of use rather than bits and pieces to be bolted together in narrowly prescribed ways. As a manifesting of mental processes, it reflects, as the Scottish critic William Duff writes in 1767, the mind's "plastic power of inventing new associations of ideas, and of combining them with infinite variety."[14] One consequence of this organic view of the relationship between mind and language is a loosening of classical rules of style and a subtler awareness that style is the mark, the expressive signature, of the individual creative intelligence.[15] And just as style is linked to creative activity, rather than to ceremonial decorum as in ancient theory, so metaphoric expression is an organic feature of language, vitally involved in the creation of new meaning. Hence, Hugh Blair comments that all language, not just the language of poetry, is "tinctured strongly with Metaphor. It insinuates itself even into familiar conversation; and, unsought, rises up of its own accord in the mind" (*Lectures*, I, 296). Tropes and figures, according to the later eighteenth century, are generative language acts, associated with the very origins of language as a medium which fuses mind and nature through *expression*, possessed of connotative as well as denotative significance. Metaphor in its largest sense, a coalescence in verbal form of feeling with perception, proliferates in the animated speech of savages, in the talk of children, in everyday conversation, and in the most philosophical discourse (though there sometimes encrusted with years of conventionalized use). It generates new meaning by revealing unexpected connections in the most compressed, evocative form. And since connection-making is intrinsic to knowledge, metaphor is the most dynamic, imaginatively explosive means of knowing.

These late eighteenth century views of figurative language as a verbal intermingling of feeling and perception, or a fusion of "mind" and "nature" in expressive acts, have historical importance because they anticipate the culmination of modern discourse theory in the concept of "symbol" or "symbolic representation." The tendency in seventeenth- and most eighteenth-century thinking about mind, language, and knowledge was to create unnatural distinctions — subject/object, mind/nature, inner experience/outer world, private reality/actual fact — which led to false conclusions about how processes of mind, and therefore processes of language, work to shape awareness. Empiricism supposed that the world is comprised "in itself" of sensory impressions and experiential "data" which the mind takes in and organizes as "ideas" signified by words. The mind is, then, initially a receiver and only subsequently an active agency: it is *reactive* rather than *formative* or creative. Composing, then, is tied restrictively to a process of "fact-finding," or gathering the "hard data," as some would put it, and "associating" facts through a rather sterile process of sorting experiential atoms into verbal compounds, then making statements about the world, the validity of which is to be determined solely by repeated appeals to empirical verification. Knowledge, then, comes to be equated with only the most restrictively "scientific" (in the sense of positivistic) discourse, all other acts of language regarded as a falling away from knowledge into fantasy, illusion, subjectivity. What is exaggerated in empiricist discourse theory is the concept of "reference," the denotational accuracy of statements according to empirical test. And what is finally lost in that theory is the concept of *meaning*, that fundamental human process which manifests itself in empirical reasoning but also in a host of other ways to produce knowledge in the richest sense. Scientific discourse is an example of meaning-making; it is not the standard by which meaningfulness is to be evaluated. Indeed, the ultimate irony of scientific discourse is that the supposedly objective "materiality" to which it applies its statements is *already* a context of meaning which shapes the character and value of scientific arguments.[16]

This is the stunning insight of Kant's *Critique of Pure Reason*, which states in the very first sentence of its introduction: "Experience is without doubt the first product which our understanding brings forth. . . ." For Kant, according to Charles

Hendel, "instead of human knowledge being shaped to reality, it is our human judgment which determines whatever is to have the character of being reality for us. The roles are reversed — the judgment conditions reality."[17] The atoms of experience, in other words, that Locke posited as the starting point of knowledge are themselves already artifacts of mind, interpretations rather than perceptions of the world. Discourse, than, the embodiment of the mind's activities, is generative in a far more fundamental way than Descartes or Locke had imagined, for it gives rise to these artifacts within the rhetorical context called "empirical science." Ernst Cassirer points out, for example, that the concepts with which a physicist operates, space and time, mass and force, atom, energy, and so on, "... are free 'fictions.' Cognition devises them in order to dominate the world of sensory experience.... Each particular concept, each special fiction and sign is like the articulated *word* of a *language* meaningful in itself and ordered according to fixed rules."[18] This does not imply, of course, that science is "fictitious" in the popular sense, or that it is purely "subjective," which would be to perpetuate the stark empiricist duality — either "real" or fanciful — that Whitehead has called "the bifurcation of nature." The statements of science are correct within the discourse of science, assuming they conform to the rules of verification which science proposes. But stipulating the truthfulness of scientific discourse does not have to come at the price of denying meaning to other forms of discourse, as empiricist thought had tended to suppose. The point is that the conditions for meaningfulness reside *within* particular discourses and need not be the same for all of them. Hence, the truth of a statement in one discourse — say, "men can be fathers of children" — does not deny the meaningfulness of an opposite statement which occurs in an alternative discourse: "the child is father of the man." Seventeenth- and early eighteenth-century theory discovered that scientific inquiry is a discourse. But Kant, and those who follow him, discovered that it is one of many, a species rather than a genus, and that the sources of meaningfulness lie deeper than the notion of "correspondence between mind and experience" can suggest.

What Kant essentially grasped is the fact that language — or mathematics, or some other system of signs, any of which is a discourse — does not constitute a window through which to view "the world." It is rather a mediating — an enveloping — reality in itself, where "sensation" and the forming capacity of mind coalesce in representation. Kant referred to this representation as the "transcendental schema," a melding of the sensuous and the abstractive which defines — not just the substance of knowledge — but the conditions of knowing (*Critique*, A137-38; B176-77). Hence, Samuel Coleridge, following closely in Kant's footsteps, observes: "We learn all things indeed by occasion of experience; but the very facts so learnt force us inward on the antecedents, that must be presupposed in order to render experience itself possible."[19] These "antecedents" are the conditions of meaningfulness which accompany the mind's variable modes of perception. And it is their priority that Coleridge has in mind in his famous definition of the primary imagination — "the living power and prime agent of all human perception," a "repetition in the finite mind of the eternal act of creation in the infinite I AM" (*Biographia*, XIII). A century later this recognition of the creative primacy of imagination will lead to the theory of "symbolic forms" as Cassirer and others elaborate it. The discourses which manifest the human process of making meaning — language, art, myth, mathematics — are modes of symbolic action or symbolic representation. They do not "interpret" our experience of the world but instead *constitute* that experience — as the living power of all human perception.

Here is Cassirer's monumental statement of the pervasiveness of symbolic behavior, including language preeminently but also more than language, as the source and content of meaningfulness:

> Every authentic function of the human spirit has this decisive characteristic in common with cognition: it does not merely copy but rather embodies an original, formative power. It does not express passively the mere fact that something is present but contains an independent energy of the human spirit through which the simple presence of the phenomenon assumes a definite "meaning," a particular ideational content. This is as true of art as it is of cognition; it is as true of myth as of religion. All live in particular image-worlds, which do not merely reflect the empirically given, but which rather produce it in accordance with an independent principle. Each of these functions creates its own symbolic forms which, if not similar to the intellectual symbols, enjoy equal rank as products of the human spirit. None of these forms can simply be reduced to, or derived from, the others; each of them designates a particular approach, in which and through which it constitutes its own aspect of "reality." They are not different modes in which an independent reality manifests itself to the human spirit but roads by which the spirit proceeds toward its objectivization, i.e., its self-revelation. If we consider art and language, myth and cognition in this light they present a common problem which opens up new access to a universal philosophy of the cultural sciences (*The Philosophy of Symbolic Forms*, p. 78).

Discourse enacts the world: its knowledge is not "about" the world but is rather constitutive of the world, the substance of experience, an explanation of the self. Discourse represents, not an accumulating of facts or even of arguments, though it encompasses these. Essentially, it represents the contexts of meaningfulness that human beings create for themselves and inhabit. Because discourse is manifold, the experiences it generates, the worlds it articulates, are manifold as well. And because it is a process, it represents the growth of mind, the expanding of imagination and the maturing of intellect.

Heady stuff! What does it all have to do with the teaching of writing? Our point chiefly is that to understand the character of modern rhetoric is to discover richer attitudes toward and motivations for teaching than a classical perspective provides. Writing is the making of meaning, first, last, and always: it is other things only because it is this. Writing is the expression of human intelligence and imagination, not merely a convenient packaging of preconceived thought, and certainly not a mere social grace or job skill. It is one of several ways in which people act upon their perceptions in order to express personal significance — and the activity matters fundamentally to the health and growth of mind, not to mention the functioning of society and the perpetuation of culture.[20] All human beings share and apply the competence to make meaning through symbolic representation, including language. It isn't a competence that "bright" people have but not "slow" ones; or that the educated possess but not the uneducated; or that "older, more experienced" people have but not younger ones. It isn't a gift that teachers bestow on students. Rather, it is a *power* that students bring with them to classrooms, hoping they might learn to use it more effectively for their own purposes. To be sure, creating written discourse involves the learning of certain skills pertaining to the technology of the medium and some of its distinguishing conventions: children learn over time to grasp a pencil, to form letters, to display statements graphically on a page, to shape verbal patterns adapted effectively to existing (albeit ephemeral) genres. But before and during the mastery of these technical facilities, not just afterwards, children are making meaning through language — by talking and listening initially, from which they acquire a complete functional knowledge of the grammar of their language, including dialect features; by "pretend writing," a potentially beneficial simulation of verbal composing; by drawing letters of the alphabet; by composing parts of sentences, broken sentences, disorganized paragraphs, and rambling texts.[21] The making of meaning suffuses these activities and makes them valuable, whatever the writer's experience or technical skill. Adeptness at managing the medium will grow with application, as long as the learner sees reason to continue developing. And teachers can certainly assist that growth. They can also impede it by making writing so uninviting and pointless that students prefer to forgo the opportunities it can offer them — in which case, their "inability to write" is mainly a function of their attitude toward the medium, not their competence to make meaning through language.

Modern rhetoric offers concepts related to the essential activities of verbal composing which can help teachers understand how and why writers perform as they do. Insight into the process can lead to teaching that encourages writers' growth by emphasizing sensible priorities — freeing writers to pursue meanings because that is what matters, at the same time supporting their efforts through attention to the most important concerns that preoccupy writers — finding and managing information, making and connecting assertions, planning and reshaping, gradually coordinating intentions to effects, struggling messily toward coherence. We'll sketch some broad features of the process, not presuming to offer anything as descriptively adequate as a "model," but only wishing to show how the philosophical vantagepoint of modern rhetoric can lead teachers to regard composing as a form of symbolic action. Later, we'll suggest some implications for teaching. A good place to start is with the idea of "coherence," because that is what writers are after: it is the goal that energizes the activity, no less for students than for experienced writers. In an essay titled "Reflections on Writing," which appears in his book *The Wisdom of the Heart*, Henry Miller, certainly an experienced writer, offers a subtle and revealing intuition about the effort to achieve verbal coherence and the quality of the resulting artifacts:

> I began in absolute chaos and darkness, in a bog or swamp of ideas and emotions and experiences. . . . I am a man telling the story of his life, a process which appears more and more inexhaustible as I go on. Like the world-evolution it is endless. It is a turning inside out, a voyaging through X dimensions, with the result that somewhere along the way one discovers that what one has to tell is not nearly so important as the telling itself. . . . From the very beginning almost I was deeply aware that there is no goal. I never hope to embrace the whole, but merely to give in each separate fragment, each work, the feeling of the whole as I go on, because I am digging deeper and deeper into life, deeper and deeper into past and future.

What we find striking in these remarks is Miller's sense of the partial and fragmentary quality, and therefore, the insufficiency, of any "finished" writing, any achieved coherence. The process of discovering significance, he has learned, is finally more valuable than any pattern of meanings preserved as "text." The process has about it an inexhaustible energy that forever denies closure, while the texts that derive from it are static artifacts, complete but flawed, permanent but merely historical, left behind as the writer proceeds to further discourse in search of a more satisfying or more comprehensive rendering. This mixture of creative jubilation and denial of ultimate attainment is characteristic of the modern rhetorical perspective, where discourse is seen to be purposeful but unbounded, orderly but always, in a sense, inadequate. Coherence, in Miller's intriguing phrase, is that "feeling of the whole" which a discourse conveys as its record of a struggle to encompass all the dimensions of meaning evoked but never fully embraced in its pattern of statements. Coherence, we might say, is what a writer settles for at that point where the promise of exploration is abandoned to the expediency of circumstance. Its achievement is to render articulate, and therefore intelligible, the welter of images, thoughts, and experiences that comprise a writer's awareness. Its limitation, however, lies in the misleading quality of its permanence: for the writer's intent is both realized and betrayed in the process of articulation. The coherence of a text conveys a fiction about its certitude and sufficiency: it's a trick that writers play on readers, enticing them to actualize meanings which are endlessly partial and potential.[22] It stimulates a desirable impression of finished business, causing readers to forget that the writing has started and ended strategically (if not quite arbitrarily), that something more, or less, or different could easily have been said. A discourse implies, therefore, by means of its pleasingly contrived and interrelated assertions, a plausibility that conceals its own necessary tentativeness — this is precisely the achievement of rhetorical and linguistic shaping. All texts, to the degree that they achieve coherence, offer their writers both more than they started with and less than they were after.

It is important to emphasize, as Miller does, the strategic and unstable nature of coherence in order to account for some basic features of composition. The impulse to reformulate, to qualify and extend in response to a perception of insufficiency, is crucial to all writing (indeed, all composing). It motivates the elaboration of successive sentences in a paragraph or assertions in a line of reasoning. It prompts the revision of earlier drafts and leads to the generation of new texts. In broader terms, it stimulates the "rewriting" of philosophy and literature and law, the movement of any cultural institution created by language (and, more broadly still, the movement of all cultural institutions — science, religion, art — as "composed" by means of symbolic action). Writing is eternally renovative, progressively shaping, testing, and revising its statements. It's intrinsically subversive as earlier coherences are sabotaged in the context of additional information and insight. Writing aspires to fullness but it settles for comprehensibility. Choices must be made about what to include and what priorities to enforce. The saying of one thing constrains the saying of something else; one focus of attention precludes another. Some assertions must occur first, some later, in the linear sequence that writing requires, and there is nothing inevitable about the hierarchies and emphases established. The laws of the medium shape the options for expression: their effective application yields coherence and a practical adequacy. But the making of meaning is inexhaustible because it never closes on something extrinsic to itself which limits its scope. It is its own end and therefore endlessly in progress. The paradox of verbal expression is that the very activity which enables coherence works simultaneously to undermine texts the moment they appear to achieve it.

Recent scholarship has made it fashionable to call the laws of the medium "constraints," without which discourse could not occur. The writing process is a system of constraints that define strategies and predict the shapes of texts. That is to say, they prescribe the limits of coherence, the range of intelligible options, linguistic, stylistic, logical, and rhetorical, from which a writer can make choices. Some of them are deeply embedded and resistant to change, for example, the syntactic patterns of a given language. These patterns require the distribution of information in certain modes of relationship: subject-object, agent-action, cause-effect, primary-subordinate, past-present-future, among others. They restrict the movement of discourse to recurring cycles of predication (where one thing is said of another) and inference (where one thing is shown to follow from another), because the function of syntax is precisely to infer relationships and represent them as predications. Other constraints are less implicit, artificial and subject to ready evolution with shifting fashions or individual predilections, for instance, the structures of the periodic sentence, or the six-part Ciceronian oration, or the form of a business letter. Such constraints may broadly be called generic: they signal the public, formal rules a writer intends to follow when making predications and inferences. Still other constraints affect writing from without, for instance, the interaction between a writer's controlling sense of purpose and an estimate of the needs and expectations of some intended reader. This rhetorical sensitivity importantly influences choices about what to say and where and how to say it, though it does not predict those choices as restrictively as do the conventions of syntax. In a moment, we will show how these constraints and others work together during composing.

But first let's be precise about what constraints do. We do not want to say carelessly that they "regulate" the writing process, for this would introduce a problematic conception of writing-in-itself as something that exists prior to any constraint. Obviously, one could not describe verbal expression apart from the phonological, syntactic, semantic, logical, and rhetorical conventions that cause it to be what it is. Diary writing and so-called "free writing" are as fully constrained as any other kind of composing. It is truer to say, therefore, that the network of interrelated constraints serves to characterize writing as a process, accounting for its features and differentiating it from composing in other modes. If one were to press further and ask, "what is it, then, that is constrained?" we'd have to answer, "the same thing that is constrained by the conventions governing painting or dance or any other symbolic behavior, namely, the semiological and structuring capacities — the meaning-making abilities — definitive of our humanity." At this point, we've reached the conceptual limit of the physicist who seeks the fundamental materiality of things: just as the physicist knows about elementary particles through their effects rather than "in themselves," so we know the processes of thinking and feeling and imagining by their dramatization in different media. Remember that "writing process" is a concept within a symbolic field, and that "meaning-making" is a concept in still another symbolic field. No "fundamental materiality" is reachable in discourse theory any more than it is reachable in physics. The symbolic field constitutes the experience: "fundamental materiality" is itself a concept.

The interesting question is, what happens when the human capacities to think and feel and imagine are manifested as writing? That is, how are they shaped within the constraints of verbal composition? For simplicity's sake, we'll consider only a few of the most rudimentary operations that enable verbal discourse. One we can call the conceiving of information. A second is the making of assertions, where one thing is predicated of another as a declaration of relationships the writer sees amidst the information. A third is the connecting of assertions, both within syntactic units and across syntactic boundaries, on the basis of inferences the writer makes about their entailment — that is, the ways in which any one of them might necessitate or follow from the others. Importantly, all of these operations occur in and through language: we may call them logical activities or rhetorical or imaginative or whatever; but they do not precede verbal representation as the ancient rhetoricians supposed. They are all linguistic acts, the manifesting of intellective action within verbal constraints. Importantly, too, they do not follow any fixed priority or sequence: contrary to the classical belief in steps, parts, or stages of composition, modern rhetoric assumes a plasticity in verbal acts (to continue using one of Coleridge's favorite metaphors) — not just a complex reciprocity among discrete operations, but an organic wholeness, distinguishable into parts (as a plant is) but not "made up" of parts. In fact, there is a danger in distinguishing "operations" in the first place, a danger of viewing them in mechanical and regimented ways. This we do not intend. Still less would we wish to encourage teachers, even accidentally, to have students practice such discrete "operations" in contrived drills. The only value of discriminating them lies in the opportunity it provides to make statements about how composing occurs.

One task a writer engages in is conceiving information. But what is "information," where does it come from, how is it "found," and what makes it pertinent? Even saying what it is becomes difficult in the modern epistemological climate. Locke was incorrect, as Kant suggested, in supposing that the world actually comes in empirical bits and pieces, fragments of sensation, experiential atoms which the mind then pieces together. Experience may be *construed* as discrete bits, or it may be viewed as a continuous process, for instance, as atomic particles from one perspective or as fields of force from another. Let's say simply that "information" is a product of the mind's habit of differentiating in order to synthesize, a procedure that language peculiarly enables through its capacity to represent experience "grammatically" — as aspects, alternative modes, hierarchies of abstraction, and so forth. Language represents differentially, portraying a dialectical relationship between analysis and synthesis (Coleridge refers to secondary imagination as a process which "dissolves, diffuses, dissipates, in order to recreate" [*Biographia*, XIII]). It constitutes the perception of experiential multiplicity, in order to establish the conditions for inferring order, reducing the multiplicity to unity. The need to discover a coherence amidst diverse information causes the stating of assertions and thereby initiates the process of composing.

Our point is, "information" is a useful fiction, allowing a writer to get about the business of making connections — which is the essence of composing. In the writing of this book, for instance, we have chosen to "decompose" a particular subject — the rhetorical tradition — into certain kinds of information: "classical rhetoric" names one subdivision, within which we include assorted smaller conceptions: "topos," "discourse as ceremonial display," "monolithic, absolutist tradition," "static view of knowledge," and so forth; "modern rhetoric" names another subdivision, which includes additional conceptions: "the rise of empirical science," "composing as learning," "epistemological crisis," "model-building," "mind in process," and the like. Other writers would surely see our subject differently, and would therefore decompose it differently in order to make statements about it. Their notecards and tentative outlines would label different stores of information. Even their definition of what counts as information might change: as in the case of a crotchety classicist who believes that there is no such thing as "new rhetoric" but only a historical succession of footnotes to Cicero. Information itself lies as much in the mind of the writer as the connections asserted within it. This is not to say that there are no limits to what can be regarded as information, that anything goes, that all is relative. There are rules governing the valid conception of materials for composing in different circumstances. The writing of our book, for instance, acknowledges the scientific convention of appealing to "sources" as a demonstration of our reliability. We are obliged to make use of other texts pertinent to our subject and to borrow the conceptions of other writers as part of the process of making meaning in our own text. Doing so insures a continuity of understanding (even for our statements of disagreement) that is desirable in academic discourse. Ignoring or rejecting without cause the information of major historians of rhetoric, such as W.S. Howell, would not be regarded as a sign of creative independence by our anticipated readers; it would simply be thought ignorant and foolish. We certainly also conceive our own information relevant to the subject through our own intellectual analysis or imaginative intuition. But that information must be such that interested readers could retrace our steps, read what we have read, confirm the judgments we have made: our authority in readers' eyes for declaring our information to be true and significant depends on this possibility of independent verification. Other modes of discourse, however, need not enforce the same constraints.

Having said what information is, we can more easily explain where it comes from, how it is found, and what makes it pertinent. It comes out of the perspective a given writer applies to a subject; it is located through a process of coming to know that subject — thinking, making observations if possible, reading, talking, wondering, asking questions, seeking answers; and its pertinence is estimated from a writer's own sense of intention and audience, the impression of what needs to be said in order to accomplish a particular end. Now, perhaps, it is possible to see the pointlessness of the ancient *topoi* of invention, especially as self-conscious and uncontextualized formal exercises in discovering ranges of information. Rhetoricians such as Blair and Adam Smith attack classical invention theory during the eighteenth century on the grounds that it is ritualistic and mechanical, but more importantly on the grounds that it offers superficial technique as, seemingly, a substitute for serious thinking about a subject. Writers find their materials through working to understand the issues and ideas that concern them. They apply deep processes of mind to achieving that understanding — comparing, defining, changing focus, opposing, categorizing. But these activities go on in the midst of an effort to learn about a given subject for a given reason. They are rarely consciously and almost never systematically reviewed; indeed, ritual review of "all" the possible ways of creating information is more distracting than helpful to a writer. Still less do they need to be "learned" before their use is possible, as when students are set to uncontextualized exercises in defining, contrasting, and so on, apart from the purposes and contexts that make such activities meaningful.

We discussed the concept of "purpose" or "intention" briefly in Chapter 2, but it is worth an additional word here, along with the concept of "reader," in connection with the search for what to say.[23] Some student writers, even graduate students if dissertation performance is any guide, tend to think that information is hard, fixed, and permanent, that it lies "out there" and needs to be gathered up completely before writing can occur. Because they do not appreciate the rhetorical nature of information, they allow themselves to be intimidated by its apparent bulk. They amass boxes of it — often finding subsequently that they are unable to cope with what they have so meticulously gathered because they have failed to control and shape the search for it. The fact is, information is limitless: there is no end to it because it is an intellectual construct to begin with. It depends on a writer's perspective and mode of analysis for its very existence and on a writer's sense of purpose and audience for its value as pertinent writing material. It becomes meaningful to a writer only through its potential to assist the achieving of some goal. Recall from Chapter 2, though, that by "purpose" we do not mean the generic purposes emphasized in classical rhetoric, which are too generalized to be useful for writers' performance. Instead, writers evolve and invoke operational purposes in the course of writing, specific and localized motives for choosing one sort of information over another. In the writing of this chapter, for instance, we have chosen not to include information about the biographies of modern rhetoricians (though it "exists" in great quantities) because one of our operational purposes is to offer a coherent intellectual overview of modern rhetoric with a minimum of distracting historical or other scholarly detail. We have also chosen to include information about writers' purposes and the making of assertions while excluding much available material on "deconstruction theory" and structural semantics, even though all of these categories belong equally under the subject of modern rhetoric, because another operational purpose is to establish connections between modern discourse theory and the teaching of writing — where, we believe, the latter two categories are less relevant.

Besides a writer's operational purposes, the sense of an intended reader serves also as a constraint on what to say. The shape and direction of writing always depends to a degree, and sometimes depends crucially, on its being said *to someone* as well as for some reason. For example, our choice to omit biographies and a great mass of other historical as well as scholarly detail depends on our decision to conceive a teacher-reader whose principal interest in this book will be to see relationships between its theoretical information and personal teaching practices, not to learn the intellectual history of the past four centuries. An important point here, however, is that "the reader" as a constraint on discourse does not mean any one individual who actually reads a text. A writer's intended reader is always imaginary.[24] This fact remains true at either extreme of the composing situation: when a writer knows an actual reader for whom the text is intended, the conception of that reader is no less a fiction; and, when a writer is composing highly personal discourse, seemingly directed at no one, the conception of an intended reader is nonetheless actively present. In the first instance, a writer makes choices based on the kind of response desired; and those choices then define the role any actual reader is expected to play as a participant in the discourse. The writer may well try, where possible, to anticipate real needs based on any information available about a potential reader's experience of the subject, age and education, likes and dislikes, and so forth. But the writer's anticipation of that reader nonetheless constitutes a strategic impression, narrowed for its explicit usefulness to the writing, and not a concrete image of some external personality. Meanwhile, in the second instance, a person who intends a more private or self-referential statement, say a diary entry not intended for public view, still retains a construction of the "intended reader," even if it is only a projection of some version of the writer's own personality. For example, the person may project a reader who is very sympathetic and tolerant of shortcomings; or the writer may imagine a reader who is going to be very uncompromising, reluctant to accept maudlin language or self-justification. Even in the case of private writing, without some reader projection, choice-making would be motiveless and therefore, in effect, impossible. Words could appear but coherence could not.

So far, we have spoken of the conceiving of information and the constraints governing it. A second basic "operation" in composing is the making of assertions which reflect a writer's understanding of relationships inferred amidst the information. Making assertions from successive inferences is the central activity of written composition, for it involves discovering and articulating connections — and establishing connections is the motive for creating discourse, as well as the basis of the knowledge that discourse makes.[25] What is an "assertion"? Let's say that it's the most rudimentary verbal expression of a relationship, a topic and a comment. Two examples of the assertion are the logical proposition and the elementary independent clause from transformational-generative grammar: each conveys a basic predication, a conclusion that one thing may be said of another through minimal syntactic structure. Assertions are implicit in syntactic relationships. They are simpler than typical sentences, which include qualifiers and subordinations that serve to embed several assertions in a single, but complex, syntactic pattern. "Discourse is knowledge" is one of our most important assertions in this chapter. "Conceiving information is one aspect of the composing process" is a sentence which contains several assertions, interrelated within its syntax: "information is conceived," "composing has aspects," "generating information is one aspect," "composing is a process." Human beings naturally make assertions in order to conceptualize experience and render it coherent. To this extent, composing is an inherent capacity which requires no teaching — at least if we define "teaching" in the classical sense of giving students something they did not have before. To say that a person "can't write" is always false to one degree or another: at most, the expression may signify that a writer has not yet gained sufficient control of all the conventions by which written discourse achieves and communicates extended patterns of meaning. More often, the expression refers to something astonishingly trivial — the writer doesn't spell accurately or can't use commas or has not attended to the agreement of subjects and verbs or lacks a "pleasing" style. But the radical capacity to assert connections in language is species-specific to human beings, a mode of symbolic action. It is the competence that empowers writing. Teachers should be clear about their relatively humble role in writing instruction: they help to nurture composing ability by helping students gain control of writing as a medium, but they do not bestow that ability upon students as a gift from the advantaged to the underprivileged.

Making verbal discourse, then, is a process of asserting connections among the ideas, impressions, images, bits and pieces of recollection or research, insights, fragmentary lines of reasoning, feelings, intuitions, and scraps of knowledge that comprise a person's experience of some subject. Writers infer these connections according to what they find valuable or important or suggestive in their materials, and they express them within syntactic and rhetorical constraints just as they conceive information within those constraints. Of course, composing does not usually stop with a single assertion. A third operation essential to the process is the connecting of assertions to form lines of reasoning, the larger patterns of meaning that represent developed understanding and generate new knowledge. Typically, a writer fashions consecutive statements in order to come to terms with a range of ideas and insights that is too broad or various to be adequately integrated all at once. Since an individual assertion is limited in scope, its formulation invariably raises questions. Our assertion that "knowledge is discourse" raises such questions: What does "knowledge" mean? What does "discourse" mean? What does the assertion itself signify? How can it be exemplified? What are we to conclude from it? The questions may concern the relationship of any one assertion to those preceding, or the implications for others to follow, or simply the clarity or adequacy of the assertion itself. Whatever their focus, the questions give rise to new information which in turn stimulates new inferences: "'knowledge' is a pattern of connections perceived as coherent"; "discourse conveys such a pattern"; "to make discourse is to discover connections, therefore new knowledge"; "the patterns of relationship within discourse constitute knowledge." In this fashion, a system begins to develop, expanding gradually as additional assertions, necessitated by the perception of unassimilated insights, are joined to the evolving sequence.[26] The three operations continue to work reciprocally: the perception of a range of information creates the need to order it as a pattern of assertions; making any one assertion creates the need to make more; the evolving pattern reveals a need for, and the availability of, new information, which can be incorporated into still more assertions to clarify or expand those already derived. The tendency of the process is to go on indefinitely, but in actual writing it continues until all the pertinent questions have been answered within the rhetorical limits of the writer's purpose.

In other words, the central problem of composing is never finding something to say but rather finding a means of regulating, and eventually halting, the process of making connections. Any range of information could enable an unlimited number of assertions; the last paragraph of any discourse could easily become the first paragraph of another; any statement can give rise to an infinity of other statements, which are related to it through more and more distant, less and less pertinent avenues of conceptual interrelationship. The consequence for a writer, in the absence of some control, might be either an aimlessness derived from the unresisted temptation to sample diverse possibilities at random or, more seriously, frustration and even paralysis in the face of so many alternatives. Writing teachers recognize these consequences in the rambling, disjointed efforts of some students and in the writer's block of others. Laurence Sterne's novel, *Tristram Shandy*, which all writing teachers should read for hilarious profit and profitable hilarity, perfectly demonstrates the incoherence that results from random inferential activity. Tristram's autobiographical writing expands exuberantly in myriad directions but ultimately fails to accomplish its stated purpose, which was to articulate and render coherent his own life history. Tristram associates freely, not rigorously, and is finally tyrannized by the flood of unintegrated experience that competes for equal attention at the close of each sentence. He has proceeded hundreds of pages into his narrative before managing even to describe what he'd promised at the start: his birth and christening. His description of his own composing process will strike familiar chords among writing teachers: "of all the several ways of beginning a book which are now in practice throughout the known world, I am confident my own way of doing it is the best — I'm sure it is the most religious — for I begin with writing the first sentence — and trusting to Almighty God for the second."

The question that needs resolving is how to regulate the process of making and connecting assertions to achieve a coherent, even if necessarily inadequate, finished discourse. At the extreme, for example, it is possible to relate assertions on the basis of all sorts of associative principles or possibilities, giving rise to a string of statements in which any one follows somehow from the one before and leads to the one after, but without any sense of orderly direction or movement: "oranges are fruit; fruit is good for you; medicine is also good for you; the sick require medicine; flu is a sickness; I had the flu once; I have had numerous unpleasant experiences. . . ." Even the constraint of a writer's purpose, let's say it is to talk about oranges, is not sufficient to control the movement of assertions within an evolving statement, because there are many more assertions pertinent to that intent than the writer could possibly use and many more varieties of connection than could be explored in the available space and time: "oranges are fruit; they are in the same class as pears and apples; they grow on trees, while other fruit grow on vines; they have a spherical shape; they can be used to make orange juice; some people believe oranges taste better than other fruit; they contain vitamin C; an orange a day keeps the dentist away. . . ." Tristram Shandy knows his purpose well enough: it is to tell his life's story. But knowing the goal does not by itself help him to progress in an orderly fashion toward it. What is lacking in the list of assertions about oranges, and what is lacking in Tristram's text — or rather what Sterne intentionally suspends to serve a subtler artistic purpose — is the constraint of "entailment," that constraint beyond syntax yet still within the organizational structure of the discourse which insures its integrity *as* discourse.

Viewed from the standpoint of product, entailment describes a pattern of interrelated assertions perceived to be coherent as a line of reasoning, an orderly movement of mind. Viewed from the standpoint of process, it represents an intuition that something *ought* to follow, not merely from the preceding assertion, but from the context of related assertions which has developed up to the point of making the next one. While the process of inferring/asserting connections moves writing forward sentence by sentence, the constraint of entailment insures that the whole discourse is animated by its own distinctive logic of interconnection.[27]

What the sense of entailment ordinarily contributes to the process of making inferences is a pragmatic, if not absolutely rigorous, definition of relational proximity, boundaries of relevant inferential action within the limits of a writer's intent and the increasingly insistent, emerging shape of the discourse. What ought to follow at any point in an evolving text depends, in other words, on a writer's awareness of what may be best suited both to achieving the purposes of the writing and to furthering the organizational logic already implicit in the partly elaborated pattern of assertions. Interestingly, in all writing, at a certain point, the system of assertions itself begins to require the kinds of choices that are relevant for completing it. Also, at this point, some new insights, even if pertinent to the subject, even if superior to those already conveyed, may have to be suppressed if they compromise structural integrity. Or, alternatively, some substantial portion of the existing text must be abandoned to allow the new insight to assert its influence over the logic of interconnection. When writing teachers tell students that a statement "doesn't follow," or that two assertions aren't yet closely enough related and need others between them, they are responding to the impression of coherence that the student's writing has already created up to the point of the offending or missing assertion. They are commenting on the importance of entailment to the coherence of a text.

Given an awareness of entailment, any writer feels more and more pressure to end a discourse as the range of assertions congenial to an evolving system begins to narrow. There are many more possibilities, many more options to evaluate, at the start of a discourse than later: there is at once more pure potential at this stage and also more anxiety to realize it, more difficulty in deciding what to say first. As the writing proceeds, choices grow more restricted and are, in a sense, easier to make: the range of plausible inferences is diminished and the sense of entailment is more sharply focused. Hence, the end of a discourse often seems to arise out of necessities in the writing itself. But it is the *system* that exhausts itself, not the subject of which assertions are being made. We sense at this moment, for example, that Chapter 3 has come to define itself clearly enough so that we could not now introduce a great many potentially relevant assertions, simply because doing so would violate its existing integrity. It would be fun to show how poem writing or novel writing manifests the various constraints we have described just as surely as expository writing does. But it is not sufficiently proximate to our line of reasoning to justify inclusion. It would distort the structure of our argument. Inevitably, too, we are suppressing some of those more troubling, more provocative insights which would place an inappropriate pressure on the coherence we have striven to create. It seems to us, for instance, that the sort of judgment, or the mode of connection-making, involved in asserting that "mortgage rates are too high for middle-class house buyers" is quite different from that involved in the statement, "like a running grave, time tracks you down." But pursuing this insight might jeopardize simpler, yet currently more useful, directions to our argument. Indeed, it might even sabotage the argument and necessitate a new, more sophisticated formulation. We propose to bury the insight in order to conceal the ragged edges and tears and strains common to all discourse, in order to sustain the illusion of complete-ness and sufficiency that all texts depend on, including our own.

This unavoidable deceptiveness is worth an additional comment. Co-herence results from the strategic manipulation of constraints as manifested in the effort to devise plausible sequences of assertions. A writer or reader recognizes the coherence of a discourse when he or she perceives the force of its entailments, when the logic of its interconnected statements appears self-evident, conveying a believable fiction about the integrity of its interrelationships. But the measure of its inadequacy lies just beneath the surface, in many possibilities of connection that have been deliberately eliminated to preserve intellectual, imaginative, and structural consistencies. Unwritten texts inhabit the spaces between assertions and threaten to sabotage the discourse. The ability to discover new connections holds a promise that keeps every writer looking beyond previous sentences and previous ways of seeing things. In the repudiation of earlier statements lie the insights which will re-energize the process of stating inferences and conceiving new entailments. What we celebrate in any achieved coherence, therefore, is its implicit suggestion of new, still broader patterns of interrelationship to be ex-plored. For it is in the creative rewriting of past discourse that we witness the progress of learning; and it is the progress of learning that insures individual growth and the perpetuation of culture.

"Creative rewriting" is an essential concept, the last we will include as representative of the vantage point of modern rhetoric. The natural tendency of discourse is to explore, to progress from what is known to what is not yet known. The process of stating and interrelating assertions eventually takes the writer into new intellectual territory because it forces experiments in the making of connec-tions that have not been made before. The assertion "knowledge is discourse" is an instance of powerful imaginative insight. It derives from an extended line of reasoning evolved not just within a single text by a single writer, but within a succession of texts by many writers and over a period of centuries. Previous discourses had to be "rewritten" — in the sense that previous connections representing an earlier state of understanding had to be questioned and aban-doned — in the struggle to articulate the insight. Then, through powerful intuition, a few writers — Locke, Kant, Cassirer — created progressively subtler formulations. "Creative" writers are creative because they retain the imaginative flexibility needed to abandon earlier discourses in order to see things in new ways. The most powerful learning comes, not from the effort to validate some existing state of knowledge (though that is a useful activity), but from the discovery of a new conception which changes the very dimensions of knowledge. It is *helpful* to know that two toy cars with rubber bumpers, made to collide with each other in an experimental setting, will rebound precisely as Newton's law said they would. In this instance, one statement has extended another by verifying it. But it is *stunning* and life-enriching to learn that energy is equivalent to mass multiplied by the square of the speed of light, for this assertion has interrupted one discourse — that of Newtonian physics — and introduced another — that of Einsteinian physics —

with a potential for entirely different kinds of connection-making. In the process, it has altered the dimensions not only of physics but of modern civilization.

Coleridge recognized the creative power of discourse at the start of the nineteenth century, and Nietzsche developed the same perception at its close.[28] Both understood that there are two sorts of knowledge available from composing. The more typical new knowledge is corroborative, a useful, if rather domesticated, extension or qualification of a current line of reasoning. The discourse of physics from the late-seventeenth to the late-nineteenth century was largely devoted to elaborating, clarifying, or showing the validity of the "text" of Newton. Its knowledge was of a corroborative nature. But the rarer and more valuable kind of knowledge entails an imaginative reconstruction of the very terms of connection-making within some developing discourse, a new orientation for more composing, a new system of entailments. It is not a consequence of what has preceded but a creative rewriting of the past in new dimensions. Einstein's assertion is not essentially corroborative but is, let us say, "reconstitutive." It promises fundamentally altered directions of inquiry; it is powerfully generative, where the preceding discourse — Newtonian physics — had begun to lose its creative energy, saying more and more about less and less, fine-tuning its own system of assertions but tending toward imaginative entropy. The altered discourse in physics represents rejuvenation in its provocative reconstituting of physical knowledge.

To be sure, such dynamic moments in the history of knowledge occur only occasionally despite the most intensely concentrated artistic and scientific efforts in poetry, philosophy, mathematics, and other enabling discourses. But for teachers, an important implication of modern rhetoric is that what is true of composing on the most sublime cultural heights has relevance down in the valleys as well. *All* human beings share in the creative ingenuity which is supremely articulated by Shakespeare, Kant, or Einstein: we value the achievement of these minds precisely because they *are* human — the best versions of ourselves. More metaphors are expressed on street corners than in poems, and each metaphor is a creative insight, a new connection. The most mundane revision effort of an inexperienced student writer shares in the spirit of the progress of knowledge provided its emphasis is on the making of meaning, the achieving of richer coherence, the deeper penetration of a subject. That effort has its place, however rudimentarily, in the larger cultural struggle to reconceptualize experience in order to advance understanding. Teachers willing to accept the premise that students can take responsibility for serious thought and imagining will find the writing classroom an exciting workshop for the making and sharing of meanings, a legitimate instance of the intellectual interchange that sustains culture. Chapters to follow will suggest ways in which teachers' awareness of modern rhetoric can make instruction richer and more productive by focusing attention on students' intellectual and imaginative capacities. Specifically, they will show how engaging those capacities in the shaping of worthwhile discourse can strengthen students' writing as a vehicle for discovering new knowledge and thereby promoting personal growth.

Notes

[1]Our argument about the epistemological shift in this period is related most specifically to changes in rhetorical theory in Wilbur S. Howell, *Logic and Rhetoric in England 1500 - 1700* (New York: Russell and Russell, 1961) and Howell, *Eighteenth-Century British Logic and Rhetoric* (Princeton: Princeton University Press, 1971). Its larger intellectual contours are fully explored in Michel Foucault, *The Order of Things: An Archaeology of the Human Sciences* (New York: Pantheon, 1970). A comprehensive overview of changes in rhetoric from ancient to modern times is *The Rhetoric of Western Thought*, eds., James L. Golden, Goodwin F. Berquist, and William E. Coleman (Dubuque, IA: Kendall/Hunt, 1976).

[2]Langer is perhaps the most readable modern philosopher of symbolic form, and she extends the tradition established by Kant and Cassirer, as well as by Whitehead. See, especially, her *Philosophy in a New Key* (Cambridge: Harvard University Press, 1957) and *Philosophical Sketches* (New York: New American Library, 1962). Another important resource connecting symbolic theory specifically to rhetoric is I.A. Richards, *The Philosophy of Rhetoric* (New York: Oxford University Press, 1965).

[3]For an overview of the significance of seventeenth- and eighteenth-century rhetorical theory for modern composition theory and pedagogy, see C.H. Knoblauch, "Modern Composition Theory and the Rhetorical Tradition," *Freshman English News*, 9 (Fall 1980), 3-17. See also Edward P. J. Corbett, "John Locke's Contributions to Rhetoric," in *The Rhetorical Tradition and Modern Writing*, ed., James J. Murphy (New York: Modern Language Association, 1982), pp. 73-84. See also Donald Stewart, "Some Facts Worth Knowing About the Origins of Freshman Composition," *The CEA Critic*, 44 (May 1982), 2-11. For the connections of nineteenth-century theory, see, for example, Robert J. Connors, "The Rise and Fall of the Modes of Discourse," *College Composition and Communication*, 32 (December 1981), 444-455.

[4]For background on the philosophical underpinnings of the new science, see Herbert Butterfield, *The Origins of Modern Science 1300-1800* (New York: Macmillan, 1957), and E. A. Burtt, *The Metaphysical Foundations of Modern Science* (New York: Doubleday, 1932). For a general epistemological argument about the nature of change in scientific "paradigms," itself an important contribution to modern rhetorical theory, see Thomas Kuhn, *The Structure of Scientific Revolutions*, second edition (Chicago: University of Chicago Press, 1970).

[5]Cassirer's study is as readable as it is classic: *The Philosophy of the Enlightenment* (Boston: Beacon, 1951).

[6]Cassirer reviews "associational theory" in Chapter 3 of *The Philosophy of the Enlightenment*. A more thorough study is Martin Kallich, *The Association of Ideas and Critical Theory in Eighteenth Century England* (The Hague: Mouton, 1970).

[7]It is no accident that the period from 1660 to 1800 features such a profusion of new studies of language, producing more philosophical discussions of the connections between language and mind than in any historical period preceding. A review of the catalogue of the Scolar Press series of facsimile reprints, *English*

Linguistics 1500-1800, will illustrate the point.

[8]We cite from René Descartes, *Discourse on Method*, trans., Lawrence J. Lafleur (Indianapolis: Bobbs-Merrill, 1960).

[9]Joseph Priestley, *A Course of Lectures on Oratory and Criticism* [1777] (Yorkshire: Scolar Press, 1965), p. 24.

[10]Hugh Blair, *Lectures on Rhetoric and Belles Lettres* [1783], ed., Harold F. Harding (Carbondale: Southern Illinois University Press, 1965), II, 181-82.

[11]In addition to Priestley and Blair, see also, among many others, Adam Smith, *Lectures on Rhetoric and Belles Lettres*, ed., John M. Lothian (London: T. Nelson, 1963); George Campbell, *Philosophy of Rhetoric*, ed., Lloyd F. Bitzer (Carbondale: Southern Illinois University Press, 1963); and Henry Home, Lord Kames, *Elements of Criticism* (Edinburgh, 1762; rpt. 1967), 3 vols. esp. Volume I.

[12]The best short general review of eighteenth-century developments is Douglas Ehninger, "Dominant Trends in English Rhetorical Thought, 1750-1800," *The Southern Speech Journal*, 17 (September 1952), 3-12. See also Vincent Bevilacqua, "Philosophical Influences in the Development of English Rhetorical Theory, 1748 to 1783," *Proceedings of the Leeds Philosophical and Literary Society*, 12 (April 1968), 191-215. The nineteenth century lacks the vitality of the eighteenth in rhetorical theory as such, but its contributions to discourse theory are interwoven in its literary criticism, psychology, and general philosophy, including works by such figures as Goethe, Coleridge, Keats, DeQuincey, John Stuart Mill, Alexander Bain, Marx, Nietzsche, and others. An overview of nineteenth-century "rhetoric" remains to be written.

[13]*An Examen of the Way of Teaching the Latin Tongue* (Yorkshire: Scolar Press, 1969), p. 7.

[14]William Duff, *An Essay on Original Genius* [1767] (Gainesville, FL: Scholars Facsimiles and Reprints, 1964), p. 267.

[15]Blair, Priestley, and Kames all pursue these issues in depth. By the 1760s arguments about the psychological origins of style and the primitive origins of figurative expression are commonplace.

[16]The clearest expression of this insight is Langer, *Philosophy in a New Key*, pp. 12-21. For the limitations of Cartesian and empiricist epistemology, see Cassirer, *Philosophy of the Enlightenment*, Chapters 2 and 3.

[17]Hendel's review of the relationships between the thinking of Kant and that of Cassirer offers an excellent introduction to the evolution of the theory of symbolic form. See Ernst Cassirer, *The Philosophy of Symbolic Forms*, Vol. I, "Language" (New Haven: Yale University Press, 1955). Introduction by Charles W. Hendel.

[18]Cassirer, *The Philosophy of Symbolic Forms*, p. 85.

[19]Samuel Taylor Coleridge, *Biographia Literaria*, ed., George Watson (New York: Everyman's Library, 1965), p. 79. A difficult but important and provocative modern statement of the idea of conditions of meaningfulness and the nature of our "experience of the world" is Alfred North Whitehead, *Modes of Thought* (New York: Macmillan, 1966).

[20]For discussion of the socio-cultural significance of language uses, see Peter L. Berger and Thomas Luckman, *Social Construction of Reality: A Treatise in the Sociology of Knowledge* (New York: Doubleday, 1966). For the power of language in the personal construction of "reality," see Lev Vygotsky, *Thought and Language* (Cambridge: MIT Press, 1962), and Michael Polanyi, *Personal Knowledge* (London: Routledge, 1962).

[21]For arguments about children's development of language abilities, see Margaret Donaldson, *Children's Minds* (New York: Norton, 1979), and Glenda Bissex, *Gnys at Wrk: A Child Learns to Write and Read* (Cambridge: Harvard University Press, 1980).

[22]Reader response theory describes the dynamic relationship between texts and readers. See Louise Rosenblatt, for example, *The Reader, the Text, the Poem: The Transactional Theory of the Literary Work* (Carbondale: Southern Illinois University Press, 1978). Later chapters will rely significantly on this aspect of modern rhetorical thought.

[23]Wayne Booth's concept of "rhetorical stance" may be helpful in understanding how the creation and shaping of materials is carried out: situation determines the relevance and use of information. See "The Rhetorical Stance," *College Composition and Communication*, 14 (October 1963), 139-45.

[24]See Walter Ong, "The Writer's Audience Is Always a Fiction," *PMLA*, 90 (January 1975), 9-21.

[25]For discussion of the "assertion" in composing, see Josephine Miles, "What We Compose," *College Composition and Communication*, 14 (October 1963), 146-54.

[26]Several modern rhetoricians have described the process of composing and interrelating successive assertions (a view sometimes referred to as "linear rhetoric"). See, for instance, Robert Gorrell, "Not by Nature: Approaches to Rhetoric," *English Journal*, 55 (April 1966), 409-16, 449; Richard L. Larson, "Toward a Linear Rhetoric of the Essay," *College Composition and Communication*, 22 (May 1971), 140-46. For a different perspective on the same issues, see James Britton, "Shaping at the Point of Utterance," in *Reinventing the Rhetorical Tradition*, eds., Aviva Freedman and Ian Pringle (Conway, AR: L & S Books, 1980).

[27]W. Ross Winterowd describes some, but probably not all, of the possible varieties of entailment in "The Grammar of Coherence," in *Contemporary Rhetoric: A Conceptual Background with Readings*, ed. Winterowd (New York: Harcourt Brace Jovanovich, 1975).

[28]Nietzsche's *Use and Abuse of History* is a provocative examination of the perpetual reconceiving or reconstituting of history. Adrian Collins has translated the text for Bobbs-Merrill (Indianapolis, 1957).

Chapter 4

Understanding Modern Rhetoric

Some Misconceptions and Pseudoconcepts

What empowers us to speak so forcefully about the superiority of the modern rhetorical perspective? What has it to offer beyond its mere modernity? Hasn't classical theory withstood a twenty-century test of time that supports its value and prestige? Let's start with the obvious. The fact that ancient rhetoric contains much profound good sense and humanity, for writing teachers as well as others, hardly depends on endorsement from us. And if writing teachers were actively reading the texts of antiquity, and those of later ages as well, our book would be superfluous. The argument we've posed is philosophical, not aesthetic: we *encourage* reading Aristotle, Cicero, and Quintilian, just as we would encourage reading Chaucer and John Milton — for the magnitude of their vision and the vigor of their imagination, though not necessarily to adopt their theology or their assumptions about the world-order. We speak of the "superiority" of modern rhetoric only with reference to its improved theoretical integration of evidence and insight regarding the processes of mind, the operations of discourse, and the nature of knowledge. It offers plausible explanations of the hitherto less-well explained: how the mind acts on experience to create meaningfulness; how new thought and learning are possible; how people use language to conceive and organize experience; how children can acquire language without being taught its grammatical principles; how people can make metaphor without knowing lists of tropes and figures; how they can discover things to say without having heard of the *topoi*; how they can make sense even outside the constraints of favored genres, formal structures, or preferred rules of performance. Modern rhetoric offers better answers to important questions — indeed, it raises better questions. Its frame of reference is a richer starting-point for thinking about discourse.

That frame of reference is also richer for the teaching of writing, providing a subtler awareness of why people compose as well as how. It can energize teaching by revealing the power of language and therefore the significance of efforts to develop that power. It clarifies the process of composing so that teachers can find imaginative ways to initiate student writing, ways of responding supportively to texts, and ways to encourage still more writing as the best means of nurturing growth in writing ability. But before teachers can make effective use of modern discourse theory they must appreciate its substantive differences from, indeed its fundamental reconstituting of, ancient rhetorical thought. The shift from ancient to modern perspective has not been a matter of gradual and slight conceptual adjustment, modern rhetoric growing naturally, imperceptibly, out of its ancient antecedents, so that its concepts bear familial resemblance to precursors in the earlier tradition. Instead, the two traditions are essentially opposed, representing a *disjunction* in intellectual history because they derive from two different and incompatible epistemologies, two irreconcilable views of the nature of knowledge and the functions of discourse.[1] Teachers will not see a slow modification of familiar ideas when they look at the history of rhetoric after the seventeenth, and especially after the nineteenth, century. Rather, they will see a displacement of one system of concepts by another, unrelated system, and they will have to struggle somewhat to comprehend the new system without reference to the old. Modern physics poses a similar challenge. One difficulty in coming to understand Einstein's concepts of space and matter is the still powerful classical assumption that space is an absolute emptiness in which objects relate to each other on the basis of mysterious actions between them rather than on the basis of properties inherent in space itself. To comprehend Einsteinian space one must forget the classical definition and think about a field of force rather than an emptiness: one must acknowledge the altered perspective of modern physics, which has fundamentally reconceived the world of Ptolemy and even the world of Galileo. Trying to imagine the new perspective in terms of the old is a hindrance, not a help.

The altering of perspective which has occurred in rhetoric is in some ways even more difficult to understand, not because the concepts are more difficult, but because of popular differences in attitude about philosophical as opposed to scientific thought. Since science deals in statements whose truth or falsity depends on their success in accounting for the empirical information they are designed to organize, people are accustomed to the idea of inadequacy in scientific theory: they believe that Einstein's statements about the world are preferable to Ptolemy's whether they understand the statements or not. They understand the principle that one statement can repudiate another. By contrast, however, the general view of philosophical discourse is that every argument has its measure of validity, that nothing becomes outmoded, that philosophical statements, like those of literature, endlessly reiterate classic themes and problems. The fact is otherwise. Philosophic statement is discursive, not literary, and it is therefore subject to rules of validation that do not affect literary statement.[2] The statement that words name "things" in "reality" is not a matter of opinion: it is false.[3] The statement that mind is a passive receiver of impressions from an intrinsically organized world outside the mind is also false, and demonstrably so.[4] Not only are these assertions untrue, but they occur within a "discourse," a philosophical perspective, which is itself outmoded, so that all of its statements, even those appearing superficially to be true, are compromised together by the faulty assumptions which have given rise to them.[5] Similarly, ancient rhetoric is a flawed perspective, its statements either false or misleading. The assertion in classical theory that writers compose for particular reasons (intentions) and to particular audiences is superficially "true" but also misleading because of the perspective in which it resides — where "intention" and "audience" are highly limited concepts and the behaviors associated with writing on different occasions largely prescribed by ceremonial rubric. At the same time, Aristotle's assertion that linguistic representation is only a concession to the sorry nature of audiences is simply false. Modern rhetoric offers not just a different but a better frame of reference.

The trouble is, ancient texts — the *Rhetorica*, the *Institutio* — appear to be as accessible as ever, seem to make more or less valid statements that are at least adaptable for modern use, if not precisely suited to it. Hence the recent effort to get an extra theoretical mile or two out of the *topoi*.[6] More seriously, ancient ideas still condition the thinking of writing teachers despite a lack of conscious awareness — much as people continue to speak of the sun rising in the east and setting in the west: if they thought about it they might see the limitation of their viewpoint, but for practical purposes they are comfortable with the misconception. If the similar misconceptions of ancient rhetoric were not so dramatically affecting instruction, if they were harmless figurative expressions like "the sun rises," we would leave them deeply embedded in the minds of teachers, confident they would do no damage even if they also did no good. But they do affect instruction, and therefore they must be frontally assaulted. And the texts that include them must be shown somehow to be *foreign* to the modern mind, even if their language appears to be intelligible. The fact is, those texts only seem to speak cogently: the perspective that gave rise to them is gone; the ideas taken for granted behind their statements — ideas about the organization of the world, the nature of human beings and their place in the world, the nature of society and mind and language, the magical forces in the world — all are gone.[7] People read ancient texts through the lenses of twentieth-century glasses, and what they see is not what readers would have seen centuries ago. Sometimes, the difference is insignificant: when Aristotle speaks of a timeless value such as integrity or courage, we can respond to it even from across the centuries. But the difference is important when matters of functional knowledge are at stake: as when we seek to understand the character of figurative expression with recourse to the cumbersome differentiation of tropes and figures. The difference is important when a failure to perceive the limitations of the classical perspective gives rise to teaching practices of the sort we outlined in Chapter 2.

Unfortunately, the continuing presence of ill-suited ancient assumptions and concepts in the teaching of writing is not even the whole problem. Because the ancient texts appear to be as serviceable as more recent arguments about discourse, they are typically seen as part of an intellectual continuum, so that there is a persistent tendency, sometimes conscious but more often not, to blend ancient and modern ideas together without regard for their incompatability. This is mainly a problem in teaching, where different parts of a syllabus are indebted to different intellectual perspectives. But it can sometimes be a difficulty in theory as well — for instance, in connection with stage-models of composing, where an essentially modern regard for the process of writing is compromised by a classical mechanistic view of its supposed "parts." In either case, when assumptions and concepts from one tradition are mixed with those of the other, the result is pseudoconcepts, half-truths which may represent partial advances on classical thinking but which fail to appreciate the fundamental epistemological opposition at stake. At the very least, pseudoconcepts are troublesome because they clutter the intellectual landscape, making orderly progress in the understanding of discourse that much harder to achieve. Imagine the difficulty of understanding mental illness if the aberrant behaviors which are sometimes its clinical symptoms were simultaneously accounted for in terms of chemical imbalances and diabolical possession. Imagine the retarding effect on astronomy of mixing Ptolemaic and contemporary beliefs, so that astronomers would seek black holes in one or another of the heavenly spheres. In rhetoric, unlike astronomy, such peculiar conceptual crossbreeding still occurs, partly because the discipline has not yet adequately appreciated the epistemological gulf separating Aristotle from Kenneth Burke or Cicero from Roland Barthes. But pseudoconcepts are even more damaging, from our point of view, when they find their way into classrooms, creating confused impressions among teachers and students alike about what should be going on, what activities are relevant and purposeful, and what the point of the whole enterprise of teaching and learning is supposed to be. Writing instruction includes a number of pseudoconcepts because of widespread ignorance of the history of rhetoric and uncertainty about how composition research can be adapted to the classroom.

Pseudoconcepts tend to arise from a confused understanding of one or more of three oppositions in terms of which classical rhetoric is distinguished from modern rhetoric. The first opposition is between process and its outcomes, the operations that make up composing versus the shapes of completed texts. The second opposition is between organism and mechanism, whole entities (such as plants) which may be viewed as parts — but only with the understanding that the parts do not equal the whole — versus collections of parts which are joined together to make wholes, such as automobile engines, where parts in the correct arrangement are equivalent to the whole. The third opposition is between competence and skill, intrinsic, natural capacities (such as the making of meaning through symbols) versus learned abilities (such as using a pencil or following the conventions of punctuation). In general, classical rhetoric tended to define a mechanistic, skill-based model of composition, using preconceptions about the shapes of completed texts as the basis for describing writers' activities. For instance, texts were supposed to have introductions and conclusions; therefore, introducing and concluding were regarded as skills to be learned separately and then combined to produce acceptable writing. Modern rhetoric, by contrast, tries to define the process of composing, not the shapes of texts, assuming that the process is organic, not a series of discrete parts, although it can be analyzed as complementary operations, and assuming that it is in essence a competence, which develops through use, though it also depends on certain skills which are best taught in the framework of developing competence. Pseudoconcepts result when these oppositions are not consistently maintained while representing or employing the ideas of modern rhetoric.

Consider, first, the range of pseudoconcepts which presently derives from an effort to salvage ancient prescriptions about the shape of discourse within the changed context of a modern emphasis on the process of composing. Some teachers argue, for example, that they teach "writing as a process" when they tell students to proceed mechanically from narrowing a topic to finding a thesis to stating a specified number of supporting arguments to locating examples for each argument and finally to organizing a "theme" complete with introduction and conclusion. This is not a process but a recipe: these activities are not fundamental to composing but only represent a teacher's instructions for making a particular text in a particular way. "Stating a thesis" assumes that finished writing is supposed to contain a "thesis statement" — indeed, the belief that writing should contain such a feature precedes the depiction of an activity for creating it. Numerous favored characteristics of completed writing are translated in just this way into "operations" for producing them. But there is a difference between true operations of discourse — which comprise the process of making meaning through language — and mere tasks within some contrived sequence of school activities. Writers can produce thesis statements when they wish (or must), but that production only manifests a composing ability which may equally yield other statements — it does not represent an operation essential to writing. The process of composing belongs to writers; production recipes belong to teachers. Whenever a teacher's own notion of some orderly procedure for writing usurps writers' personal choices in determining how writing "ought" to be undertaken, the teacher is working from a pseudoconcept of "process." When he or she insists that students write according to this procedure, the pseudoconcept is passed on to the students, who imagine that composing means following teacher's orders — and very little else.

A popular textbook perfectly exemplifies our contention that many teachers work from a pseudoconcept of "process."[8] The headline on its inside back cover reads: "Writing: The Process at a Glance." Beneath the headline are listed the following "operations":

> Pick a topic and explore it for possible things you might say about it. With your reader in mind, determine your purpose and phrase it in a "thesis" statement.
>
> Gather material, from personal experience, observation, interviews, or reading.
>
> Organize your material, generally by one of several patterns: illustration, comparison-contrast, classification, process, or causal analysis. For long papers, prepare an outline.
>
> Write your first draft, concentrating on getting it all down. Don't worry (yet) about details of grammar, usage, punctuation, and the like. Concen-

trate on saying everything clearly, in the best order, in enough detail, and in the style best suited to your reader.

Let it cool, at least twenty-four hours if you can. Then go back over it to check for *everything* — from the largest concerns of topic and purpose to the last comma. This means a number of readings, never less than four or five, at least one of which *must* be aloud.

Finally, copy into a final draft and proofread for errors and oversights.

This is a fairly typical performance recipe, having little to do with how writers actually search for meaning but much to do with the superficial classroom behaviors that are so often dignified these days with reference to the notion of "process." It implies something natural and inevitable about its pronouncements, as though all good writers performed exactly these activities and in just this sequence. Some of its advice reflects the naive classical assumption that statements like "concentrate on saying everything clearly, in the best order" actually mean something to unpracticed writers because the references of "clarity" and "best order" are self-evident. It confuses some classical ideas, as contemporary textbooks regularly do — for instance, when it suggests that *topoi* such as comparison and illustration are "organizational patterns." It offers arbitrary formulas, such as never rereading fewer than four or five times, at least once aloud, with an insistence far disproportionate to their usefulness. Above all, it creates "operations" of composing derived from *a priori* assumptions about what completed texts should look like. A thesis statement must come first — hence making one is an early operation. A text should manifest some familiar structural abstraction like comparison or causal analysis — hence, connecting causes and effects is an operation. A text should be synthetically ordered — that is, generalities always preceding more specific details — just as the traditional outline predicts. Hence, making an outline is the operation that insures synthetic arrangement in a first draft. Finally, a text should be somewhat confused and technically flawed in its first draft but perfect in its second: proofreading is the operation that creates perfection.

More than anything else, the various organizational schemes that teachers rely on, from generic constraints to the structures of different "kinds" of paragraphs, typify the pseudoconcept of process as a recipe for manufacturing prescribed textual shapes. People often speak of the "process" of writing a business letter or the "process" of making a topic-restriction-illustration paragraph, as though there were as many different processes as there are kinds of writing or formal alternatives, each with its own range of operations for achieving the desired product. Like the ancient rhetoricians, they continue to analyze completed writing in order to retrieve formal characteristics and then project those characteristics as requirements for new writing. The error lies in supposing the primacy of these forms — supposing that they are fixed, eternal, and necessary for the coherence of discourse — so that the process of writing is regarded chiefly as a matter of realizing in particular texts the formal absolutes that they are required to possess if they are to be meaningful. The fact is, composing — in essence — has surprisingly little to do with shaping the sorts of macrostructures — that is, broad segments of a discourse such as "introduction" and "paragraph" or superficial forms such as the standard business letter or term paper — which the ancient tradition emphasized and which many teachers still depend on when they teach "the process" of writing. Understanding the difference between classical and modern rhetorical views of organization is important, therefore, to eliminating the pseudoconcept of process that results from preoccupation with idealized shapes and forms.

Take, first, the matter of generic constraints, which might be said to represent the broadest organizational features of discourse. To be sure, these constraints are real enough in the minds of writers and readers: everyone knows in a general way how a business letter will differ from a poem, how a lab report will differ from a legal brief. But they are not rigid rules, they are not eternal, and they neither insure coherence merely by being followed nor deny coherence merely by being ignored. Genres come into existence (as the periodical essay did in the later seventeenth century), pass away (as the ancient epic form has done), and undergo transformation (as the novel has done between Defoe and, say, John Hawkes). Generic rules tend to be only the loosest of guidelines, endlessly shifting public conventions adapted for particular purposes by every writer who invokes them (hence, people can readily group various texts as "business letters" even though the texts differ in both content and shape). What begins as a violation of some generic rule may itself readily become a rule if the "violation" proves successful (for instance, Joyce's failure to observe the logical and temporal conventions of earlier novels in his stream-of-consciousness narratives). Moreover, following generic rules does not insure coherence — as student efforts to produce term papers and lab reports amply testify — nor does failure to follow them necessarily cause incoherence — as the ability to read Doctorow's *Ragtime* or the poems of e. e. cummings demonstrates. Our point here is that form at this macro level has less to do with the essential business of making meaning and creating order than many teachers suppose. It can set conditions for meaning, inviting readers to adopt certain expectations about what is said and how it is said. It can establish a social connection between writer and audience: hence, a writer behaves most like a scientist when using the genres of scientific communication; physicists don't use sonnets to communicate experimental results. But the capacity to structure assertions as meaningful patterns, that is, to discover form, lies deeper than the ability to manipulate the public conventions which genres represent. Teachers who exaggerate the relevance of generic constraints — for instance, by practicing every detail of the business letter — are mainly addressing a socio-political rather than a literacy issue. This emphasis need not be impertinent — especially if students have good reason, and hence motivation, to learn a particular genre for practical purposes. But it is problematic in the absence of that explicit motivation, and it is, in any case, wrongheaded if it derives from the belief that the technical (and often quite arbitrary) restrictions of a genre are elemental to the composing process.

What is true of generic constraints is true also of other presumed organizational structures which are not as broad but are no less inessential and historically relative. Perhaps all teachers would concede, for instance, that the six parts of the Ciceronian oration are neither fixed nor eternal nor essential to coherence (after all, no one writes orations anymore). But they are sometimes less willing to agree that more contemporary structures are equally contingent to the making of meaning. The paragraph is often regarded as a basic organizational feature of prose discourse, and many textbooks labor the presumed types of paragraph, the supposedly vital features of each type, and the "operations" necessary for achieving each. Some teachers even argue that there is a special value in requiring a set number of paragraphs in writing assignments, with particular functions ascribed to those at the beginning and those at the end, as though composing, say, five-paragraph themes, with introductions and conclusions, will somehow make students more organized or make them organized faster than some other constraint would do. In fact, however, the paragraph frame is no more crucial to the making of verbal meaning than are the technical details of some genre. As discourse conventions, paragraphs are far more arbitrary than textbooks imply. There are as many differences among paragraphs, and as many motives for making them one way or another, as there are differences among writers and among individual discourses — long ones and short ones, complex and simple ones, ones with topic sentences and others without, ones that emphasize a single point and others that introduce many, ones that appear orderly and complete in themselves but others that do not. Writing doesn't have to come in paragraphs at all — indeed, for many centuries it didn't.[9] And when it does come in such a form, the reason is as likely to be ease of reading as the pursuit of some organizational objective. Our point here is not that paragraphs are evil and to be avoided; actually, the paragraph has long been an especially convenient way to cluster assertions and facilitate reading. The point is only that making paragraphs is not an "operation" of the composing process, nor is it equivalent to being organized. It is a useful but inessential convention of modern writing. If writers "improve" from writing lots of paragraphs in composition classes, the reason is that they are *writing* — making assertions and coherent patterns of assertions which accomplish their purposes — not because they have been taught thirteen variations on paragraph structure. What organizes writing is not the shape or size of the segments into which the writer divides it, but rather an impression the writer's choices convey of intellectual/imaginative proximity and directedness among its interrelated assertions.

Organization in writing has essentially to do with this ability to discover relationships and convey them as sequences of assertions. The "composing process," as modern rhetoric conceives it, is the process of organizing experience through symbolic action — in this case specifically through writing as a mode of symbolic action. The process includes those elemental verbal activities which are common to all writing situations, the making and connecting of assertions within a context of evolving purposes and intended readers. Out of the effort to compose assertions and to join them on the basis of their perceived entailments, form emerges — the sense of a whole with integrated parts or aspects. By "form," however, we mean a fabric of argument, a texture of connection, a continuity and directedness of statement, not some conventional shape like the term paper or some conventional part of the whole like the paragraph (or section or chapter or book). These conventions exist, and they have value — chiefly as ways of making organization visible to readers. They enhance coherence, but they are not equivalent to it. Emphasizing such conventions in the classroom, as though manipulating them constituted the process of writing and the essence of organization, risks misleading teacher and students alike about what organization really involves: as an act of mind, not a technical procedure of putting the right things into the right boxes. The teacher is misled into supposing that introducing, say, the topic-restriction paragraph will make students organized, soon afterwards experiencing bewilderment and frustration when students continue to be disorganized despite the new pattern they've received. And students too have been misled — into supposing that their teacher can give them organizational facility by recourse to artificial forms, when in fact they must acquire it themselves through experiment and practice. Organization does not mean writing introductions and then "bodies" (whatever they are); it does not mean making general statements and then particular ones; it does not mean restricting a topic and then giving examples to support it. All these activities are possible manifestations of organizing ability — the process of composing — but they are not equivalent to it nor do they define its boundaries. When student writers are allowed to make their own choices and pursue their own connections — haltingly, imperfectly — teachers find that they already introduce and conclude, restrict and exemplify, generalize and concretize, as all human beings necessarily do when they verbalize their experience. Of course, students often do so ineffectively. But if they are not yet sophisticated, it is largely because they have not yet fully developed the intellectual power to perceive and articulate relationships, or because they lack the experience to estimate the needs of readers, not because they have failed to practice the general-to-specific paragraph frame long enough.

One range of pseudoconcepts results, then, from confusing the process of composing with the shapes of texts. Out of the confusion come recipes of performance, mock operations of discourse, and false notions about "form" and "organization." A second range of pseudoconcepts derives from another kind of confusion — between the organic perspective of modern rhetoric and the mechanistic perspective that predominated in classical theory. An organism is more than the sum of its parts, continuous or plastic in nature and therefore only artificially separated into components; a mechanism is precisely the sum of its parts correctly arranged, indeed a consequence of that arrangement. Both classical and modern rhetorical perspectives analyze composition into "parts"— operations, modes, and so forth — in order to learn about it. If ancient theory distinguished parts of speech, modern theory distinguishes phonemes, morphemes, and syntactic units. If classical rhetoricians separated the making of introductions from the making of conclusions, modern rhetoricians contrast making assertions with connecting them in sequences. Analysis goes on in each tradition. What differs, however, is the perspective that each tradition applies to the object of analysis, and therefore their opposed attitudes toward the status of distinctions derived from that analysis. When discourse is conceived in mechanistic terms, the parts are primary and focus is on the ways in which the parts work together to create a whole. When discourse is conceived in organic terms, its plasticity or continuity is emphasized, its integrity as a whole, while the differentiation of parts is regarded as the product of analytical investigation, not as an *a priori* condition. The parts of an automobile engine precede the engine viewed as a whole; but the parts of a plant, stem, leaves, roots, do not precede the plant as a whole.

Consider the opposed perspectives of ancient and modern grammatical theory as an example of mechanistic and organic views. The two prevailing metaphors used to characterize grammatical relations in classical theory, even as late as the seventeenth century, were the stringing of beads one after another to make ever lengthening chains and the placing of stones one upon another to make edifices. Ancient European grammar tended to regard language "atomically," that is, as comprised of discrete elements which speakers consciously join to make progressively larger units.[10] "Letters" were the building blocks of words and were studied in orthography, the first part of classical grammar. Words could be combined in strings to make phrases and clauses; they were studied in etymology, the second part of grammar. The third part of grammatical theory, syntax, described the laws of concord and government by which words, phrases, and clauses could be joined in sentences. Not accidentally, logic followed the identical mechanistic progression, first considering individual "terms" and their references in nature, then studying the combinations of terms to make propositions, and finally examining how propositions could be related in syllogistic lines of reasoning. In the classical view, a knowledge of the components of language or argument preceded and enabled the knowledge of how to join them. The educational implication is clear: parts must be learned first, "letters" before words, words before their combinations, and simpler combinations like the phrase before more complex ones like the clause or the multiple-clause sentence. Students, the ancient grammarians supposed, could hardly be expected to produce complex sentences before they had acquired conscious understanding of the building blocks of sentences and the techniques for combining them.

By contrast, the organic view of language, which has been evolving since the mid-eighteenth century as Chapter 3 suggested, emphasizes plasticity in verbal action, its essentially continuous rather than discrete character. Certainly it can be analyzed into elements, just as, for instance walking can be broken into stages or moments of physical effort. But in each case the "parts" are achievements of analysis, not prior components out of which more intricate structures or activities are contrived. Indeed, different modes of analysis can yield different components: language can be broken into parts of speech, or into phonemes and morphemes, or into subjects and predicates, or into paradigmatic and syntagmatic aspects. The different sorts of components are yielded from the application of different points of view: each enables the making of certain kinds of statements about language — that is the value of analysis — and each will be more or less useful as it serves to account for linguistic phenomena and the actions of language users. But the "parts" do not precede the whole, nor is the full complexity of the whole — the workings of language — adequately characterized by any single model of its components. The concept of "assertion" introduced earlier reflects an organic view of language, and it is also part of an analytical scheme which offers a particular kind of theoretical understanding. When we spoke about making and relating assertions, we were talking about an organic grammatical activity, though we didn't refer to it in grammatical terms. We were talking about the shape symbolic action takes when it is manifested as verbal expression. By definition, verbal assertions have grammatical structure, but human beings don't produce them by applying an overt knowledge of gramatical components to a series of decisions about what ought to go where. People "know" how to use language in the same sense that they "know" how to think; and they "know" how to make assertions because of their tacit thinking, symbol-making abilities. It would be possible to break "assertions" into their components, and to differentiate the operations of making and relating assertions, according to our analytical scheme. But assertions are nonetheless organic in essence, and the operations associated with them, which are also organic, are far subtler than our simple distinctions — or even more elaborate distinctions — could indicate. The whole is richer than the sum of its parts.

There are educational implications in an organic view of language, just as there were in the classical view. The ancient mechanistic perspective creates three false impressions at once. First, of course, it assumes that simpler elements, such as sounds and words, precede the larger patterns comprised of them — just as the parts of a watch or an automobile engine precede their interconnection as a watch or an engine. Second, it assumes that language users employ conscious technical procedures for joining linguistic elements together as discourse — much as a watch or engine maker employs techniques for putting different pieces together. Third, it assumes that a period of deliberate skill-learning must precede efforts to make real statements in real situations. Modern theory repudiates all three assumptions, arguing that grammaticality is implicit, organic, and con-textualized, not a matter of bolting one linguistic unit to another but a process of applying the structural potentialities of language unself-consciously in the context of a search for meaning. That is, a speaker or writer does not build sentences from left to right, one word after another, thinking along the way that it is high time here to embed a clause or there to insert an adjective or a metaphor, any more than a person walking thinks about manipulating leg and other body muscles. Instead, tacit structuring capacities enable the forming of assertions — meaningful wholes, not collections of parts — which possess grammatical structure because human beings are grammatical creatures who respond to their environments in grammatical ways. Since no technical virtuosity is required in order to put the "pieces" of language together, it follows that no deliberate learning is required before people are able to respond grammatically to the world, a fact borne out by simple observation of the complexly fluent verbal performances of young children. The ability to use language can — and does — grow, but it is not consciously learned; it can be nurtured but it isn't taught. One enables a plant to grow by watering its soil, not by paying elaborate attention to each of its leaves. And teachers can nurture language ability by stimulating its exercise in speaking and writing, thereby creating conditions favorable to its growth. They will not influence its maturation if their practice is merely to dismember it for students in order to examine relationships among parts of the carcass.[11]

Now, pseudoconcepts result when the distinction between organic and mechanistic perspectives is unacknowledged or forgotten while considering the nature of language and discourse, whether for research or teaching purposes. Many textbook writers and many teachers react to modern rhetorical theory with a still classical understanding of the status of analytical information, presuming that the whole of verbal activity is no more than the sum of its parts. As a consequence, they reify analytical concepts, turning them into classroom activities or into rigid rules of writing when they are not designed to these ends. Even competent researchers, when they turn to the classroom, are not always free of the tendency to reify their own distinctions, thereby mechanizing instruction. Hence, one well-known researcher offers a textbook, based on her investigations, which stipulates a series of steps or stages which writers are to move through in producing texts — steps ranging from defining a problem, purpose, and reader to planning to exploring the topic to organizing by various heuristic devices to reviewing and editing.[12] As in the case of "find a topic — state a thesis — etc.," this is a production recipe, one person's notion of the right way for writers to behave. But unlike the production recipe that results from a failure to distinguish between the process of composing and a certain desired shape for completed writing, the recipe in this case results from a mechanistic interpretation of analytical distinctions which may well have real value for characterizing the process of writing — as long as no one forgets that they are strategic oversimplifications of an organic activity which is more than the sum of its analytically derived parts.[13] In general, those who mistake the value of analytical information wrongly assume, not only that the distinctions some model supplies are meaningful as isolated elements, but also that the model is automatically transferable to the classroom merely because of its theoretical plausibility. In other words, they assume that the bits and pieces of the composing process which the model has yielded can become the parts of a syllabus or curriculum. Ultimately, these false assumptions reinforce a mechanistic view of writing as a network of separate operations or modes introduced serially on consecutive class days and followed religiously in the making of texts.

The various contemporary "stage theories" of composition are pseudocon-cepts — both as theory and as classroom procedures — for precisely this reason: they suggest that the operations writers habitually perform can be isolated and ordered as a temporal sequence, or that students can learn the operations by practicing them in isolation and in sequence. One such theory describes a progression from "prewriting" to writing to revision, implying that writers not only engage in these activities one-at-a-time but also, in some sense, do different things at each consecutive stage. In this theory, organic process gives way to mechanical plan; integrated performance is artificially regimented in a recipe. A little reflection should be sufficient to discover the limitations of the model. When is a writer clearly, restrictively "prewriting" and not writing? While taking notes or making an outline? Mustn't one write to create a note or plan? When thinking about a subject prior to writing something down? Perhaps, but what are the boundaries of this thinking? Suppose the thinking goes nowhere so that no writing follows, or suppose the writer just doesn't feel like writing afterwards: was it then not prewriting after all? Does thinking casually about the subject while brushing one's teeth constitute prewriting? Is Life prewriting? And when is a writer evidently revising but not writing? Isn't change a natural part of writing? Is composing the second edition of a book "writing" or "revising"? Is adding a new sentence to a text (thereby changing it) without altering any of the previously existing sentences "writing" or "revising"? Is changing a "prewritten" plan revis-ing? Even supposing some value to these distinctions, can anyone really argue from experience or common sense that planning occurs only prior to writing and never during writing or revising? Do writers make no changes while "writing" but only after a draft has been produced? Process is a pseudoconcept in this stage-theory, just as in the more traditional outline-to-conclusion recipe, because it is portrayed in mechanistic terms as a series of discrete, temporal phases of activity — with a strong implication (which too many teachers have been quick to seize upon) that the sequence is prescribed for all writers. Moreover, to the extent that the stage-model is intended to characterize outcomes (a plan, a first draft, a "polished" later draft), it also emphasizes product-centered distinctions rather than the process of composing.

Some teachers have taken the stage-model an additional step by arguing that each stage has its own distinctive strategies, which are best learned sys-tematically and practiced one by one, with or without actual writing. Exercises in the use of so-called "prewriting heuristics," such as Who, What, Where, Why, When, or Burke's "pentad,"[14] or Particle, Wave, Field, [15] in order to improve students' inventive capabilities are instances of this further mechanization. Of course, writers do think about their experience from the vantage points suggested in these invention schemes, and cataloguing them can have descriptive value. But within the context of a stage-view of composing, the strategies become part of an artificial temporal sequence predicting the "appropriate" moments for their use, which has the effect of mechanizing them along with the other features of composing in a stage-model. Moreover, as such catalogues are employed in the classroom, they imply the desirability, not to say the naturalness, of systematic search through each of the several strategies of a particular catalogue as a prelude to writing — which is in itself mechanistic. Such heuristic exercises reflect a partial awareness of the modern rhetorical view that writing involves intellectual search and experimentation, a "discovery" of ideas from exploration of some subject. But they also reflect the ancient exaggeration of an artificial, schematized review of "places" of argument at the start of writing, where ritual observance of a formula supplants writers' personal engagement with a subject and their own purposeful but not necessarily systematic searches for meaning. Students' confused impressions from such instruction can be that appealing to latter day *topoi* is a necessary step prior to writing or — worse — that it guarantees something useful to say, that mature thinking is just the technical trick of manipulating heuristics. Pointing out to students in the course of their writing that other vantage points on a subject can provide useful new directions to their thought is obviously valuable. But enforcing a rubric for "invention" amounts to yet another recipe, an exercise that can distract from useful thinking as readily as it might enhance thought, becoming so intrusive (or, as in the case of particle-wave-field, so intrinsically complex) that it draws more attention to itself than to the purposes it is supposed to serve.

Naturally, the writing and revising "stages" can yield their own ranges of pseudoconcepts, any time a teacher imagines that they *are* stages, or that either of them includes sub-stages, or that either is characterized by some restrictive sequence of operations or suboperations. All manner of fantastic instructional schemes can arise from the practice of abstracting principles and rules from complex organic processes, then making classroom constraints out of them so that learners spend their time validating the abstractions rather than saying things that matter. If — heaven forbid — someone were to adapt the ideas discussed in Chapter 3 to a school curriculum in which students practiced "finding information," "making assertions," and "combining assertions," mechanical pseudoconcepts would be the result. These ideas don't become useful classroom activities merely because they enjoy some measure of explanatory validity as abstractions within a modern theory of composing. They aren't intended for the classroom but only for the teacher who seeks a perspective on composing that can lead to positive instruction. They don't represent isolated operations which are combined in practice; they are only constructs that enable reference to an organic, undifferentiated process. If someone were to manufacture a procedure for revising, perhaps distinguishing such "operations" as adding, deleting, reordering, rephrasing, and editing, that too would be a pseudoconcept, and for the same reasons. If students don't revise, the reason isn't their ignorance of principles of addition and deletion but their undeveloped ability to perceive where changes might be desirable and their low motivation to make them. Good writers revise, not because they have learned the correct "operations," but because experience has enabled them to notice the dissonances in their writing which make change a necessary decision. Like other pseudoconcepts, mechanistic revision strategies create illusions about the nature of writers' performance and therefore misunderstanding about how maturity is achieved. They draw attention to themselves as principles to be learned, but their artificiality leads students to an awkward, uncommitted imitation of what writers do, thereby making frustration and disinterest more likely than growth.

Just as the confusion between process and product creates one range of pseudoconcepts, and that between organism and mechanism another, so the confusion between competence and skill creates a third. Skills are extrinsic to learners and mastered by choice; they are acquired abilities which do not presuppose any innate disposition to develop them. Competences, however, are intrinsic and develop inevitably with use, though the development may take extended periods of time. Classical rhetoric tended to regard composition as though it were a system of skills which apprentices needed to study and practice in order to attain proficiency. By contrast, modern rhetoric views *composing* as a competence, although "writing" is a skill to the extent that it is a technology for making and manipulating signs on a page.[16] Composing is natural to human beings, while writing is conventional. Handling a fountain pen or a typewriter is a skill; forming the signs (letters) of written language, spelling words, punctuating, and proofreading are skills. Making paragraphs involves skill, though the thinking and forming processes that make paragraphs worth reading are not skills. Making a business letter or a lab report involves skill because these are conventional shapes which must be recognized and learned before they can be used. But the ability to make meaning through language is a human competence. Grammar and organization are essentially competences, though representational skills attend them. Writing matters to human beings — just as mathematics, painting, or music matters — because it is composing, not because it is inherently interesting as a system of skills. People write because it enables the making of meaning, the discovery of coherence, the communicating of valued ideas, not merely because they enjoy technical accomplishment. When teachers regard the composing process as an elaborate multiplication of skills, they are working from a pseudoconcept. They are not just overlooking the motivations that make writing worthwhile by emphasizing control of a technology; they are treating the thinking and forming processes as though they themselves were technologies, when they are not.

Once native speakers of English have learned to use writing implements and to make the letters of the written language, they need practice and encouragement far more than additional technological training in order to attain the fluency, the clarity, and even the correctness associated with good writing. Consider the writing of sentences, for example, where correctness is a particular concern among teachers. Those who suppose that technical errors in written language demonstrate a lack of grammatical competence mistake inexperience for incapacity — a serious mistake because it leads them to believe that "learning" grammar is necessary rather than exercising grammatical ability in the process of making meaning. In light of the extensive competence a native speaker possesses, overdramatizing agreement errors or sentence fragments or dangling modifiers in writing amounts to repudiating a remarkable symbolic facility out of pique at finding it merely human and therefore occasionally flawed in performance. Recall the virtuosity involved in producing just the simplest English noun phrase, a structure which regularly includes an article, one or more adjectives, and one or more singular or plural nouns (some noun phrases can be even more complex). Native speakers at five years of age compose dozens of noun phrases every day, despite the fact that they have almost certainly never been taught that adjectives typically precede nouns, that some classes of adjectives tend to precede others, and that articles always precede nouns and adjectives. Their experience of the language, even at age five, has been sufficient to make them experts at creating such complicated structures. The transfer of this competence to writing certainly demands a mastery of the physical act of using a writing instrument and a knowledge of the written shapes of sounds. But this second-order symbolism builds on a writer's already extensive, if largely tacit, "knowledge" of spoken language;[17] and its effective use, like effective oral expression, depends mainly on experience, not analytical understanding.

Assuming native English speakers, what teacher has seen even a basic writer compose, in place, say, of the noun phrase, "the large stone house," a deviant construction such as "house stone large the" — or even the construction "the stone large house"? To be sure, many basic writers lack experience of the written medium, causing at once a limitation in the amount of writing they can produce and an uncertainty about the appropriate conventions to employ. They also frequently speak nonstandard dialects, a fact which adds to their disorientation in a medium which insists on both technical proficiency and standard usage. But neither the lack of technical familiarity nor the absence of standard dialect implies a deficiency of competence: basic writers will readily speak volumes on a subject that interests them, and in doing so they will follow the grammatical constraints of their own dialects. Starting from this competence, they can acquire new linguistic habits by using unfamiliar conventions within language situations that seem to require them or make them useful. They can also learn gradually to control the technology of writing, if only they can discover a satisfying reason for doing so. But the acquisition is not dependent on an analytical understanding of grammar or writing conventions outside the context of actual use. In fact, uncontextualized drill on the desired conventions is more likely to hinder development by implying a lack of competence rather than inexperience with technical alternatives. New habits are acquired as an adjustment of performance to circumstances which the speaker or writer perceives to be different from usual and where there is a powerful enough emotional reward for accommodating the difference. There can be little incentive in the belief that one is so deeply stupid as to be unable to use language effectively. And teachers can create such a belief when they fail to begin from what students already have in the way of competence to make meaning, concentrating instead on everything students presently lack as technicians. Like the rest of us, basic writers need to write — and in circumstances where it can matter to them; they don't need tape cassettes on subject-verb agreement.

The essential ability to organize experience by means of language is also, like grammar, a human competence, not a skill. The thinking that enables writers to discover relationships and convey them as sequences of assertions is not a technology and is not profitably taught as though it were (recall the limitations we suggested in connection with "invention heuristics," which might be represented as a technological view of thinking). In speech, people naturally and habitually put assertions together in order to explore lines of reasoning. They also naturally define, illustrate, compare, classify, and distinguish causes from effects (among other things), not because they have read logic or rhetoric textbooks, but because they are human beings and respond in these characteristic ways to the world around them. Students may not be practiced at such behavior in writing, and they may not have developed their intellectual powers sufficiently to make the tightest, most plausible connections or to sustain a complex system of connections. But, just as with the making of sentences, inexperience does not mean incapacity. Writers develop their abilities to make more satisfying or "creative" relationships among ideas through extended use of those abilities, somewhat as muscles develop through use. Teachers cannot provide students with "skills" of thinking or "skills" of forming assertions and connecting them as discourse. But they can create incentives and contexts for thinking and writing, so that the process of developing and strengthening composing ability may proceed. They can also offer some important development support, especially by responding to students' writing in ways that will enable the writers to recognize intellectual or organizational insufficiency as well as opportunities for further thought and alternative means of expression. To be sure, this support is indirect, dependent on students' own efforts and unsystematized in its concern for individualized reactions to particular texts rather than for generalized introductions to "all the ways" of thinking in writing. Since composing isn't a technology, it doesn't develop in a mechanically ordered way. Students need to do it — in the presence of discerning readers who are comfortable amidst the untidy creative immediacy of writers at work.

Unfortunately, however, many teachers continue to reify analytical abstractions about composing and distribute them through curricula as "skills" — indeed, even "subskills" — a practice that depends on a pseudoconcept of composing. Linguistic models are the most popular suppliers of skills: hence, in the context of traditional school grammar, subject-verb agreement becomes a skill; forming adverbial clauses becomes another; using gerunds is still another; and each might well constitute one chapter in a workbook. More recent grammatical models are equally susceptible to abuse in skill-centered curricula: hence, embedding phrases and clauses could be designated a skill (presumably acquired through sentence-combining exercises[18]); making "two-level narrative sentences"[19] might become a skill. Rhetorical theory also offers skills: given the classical perspective, "introducing" can become a skill, or "narrowing a topic"; given more contemporary stage models of composing, "prewriting" and "revising" could be characterized as skills; "making assertions" could become a skill. "Basic skills" can be (and regularly are) differentiated from the more "advanced," the differentiation then serving to justify curricula directed at more and less able students. The trouble is, this whole enterprise of skill designation is built upon illusion. Potentially, hundreds of skills could be distinguished, depending on how many grammatical, rhetorical, and logical perspectives one might wish to investigate, or on how thorough an analysis one wished to make. Is "using nouns" a skill (or a subskill)? Is putting adjectives next to nouns a skill? Why should subject-verb agreement be a skill but not "putting adverbs in the right place" or "choosing the correct preposition"? In practice, as if by magic, the number of skills an instructor identifies tends more or less to equal the number of available class hours in a term. That seems to be the only basis for limiting such a conspicuously arbitrary procedure. The question arises, therefore: how could an activity which seems rather silly on the face of it continue to loom so large in the teaching of writing?

Just clearing away the intellectual confusion surrounding an opposition between competences and skills is unlikely to eliminate skill-based curricula in writing programs. There is a strong motive among teachers for sustaining the pseudoconcept — the understandable desire to give something to students that they don't initially possess and that they depend on a teacher to provide. The idea of "compositional skills" puts teachers near the center of learning; the idea of composing as a competence puts them on the periphery. "But my students need to learn X" is a common teacher's objection to writing classes that are not centered on rules and the "right" or best ways of doing things. "My students need to know the six strategies of introducing an argument"; "they need to know how to juxtapose one syntactic pattern with another for stylistic effect"; "they need to know about metaphor and simile." Interestingly, we've never heard a teacher say that students needed to know about asyndeton and litotes, which were classical figures along with metaphor and simile. Students only "need" to know whatever the *teacher* happens to know: it's the teacher's need to tell, more than the students' need to know, that motivates skill-based instruction. Putting students in a dependent position is emotionally gratifying. Conceiving instruction in terms of "giving them what they need" is a powerfully satisfying justification of a teacher's existence. To view composing as a system of skills is to view the teaching of writing as a process of offering concrete means for accomplishing a succession of limited tasks, assuming that students will put everything together at some later point as "composing." The teacher is a controlling figure in this process of acquisition, identifying and describing the skills, directing the practice of skills, and finally evaluating students' "progress" in performing the tasks set for them. It is the rare instructor who correctly perceives that what is measured in this context is mainly a student's ability (and willingness) to follow directions, not necessarily a real improvement of writing ability.

By contrast, to view composing as a competence is to subordinate the teacher's role in the learning process — not to trivialize it but only to reduce its visibility and somewhat change its character. Teachers can facilitate maturation of a natural capacity, but they cannot control growth by means of their pedagogy, certainly not to the extent of predicting when it will occur or measuring its progress in different individuals. They can create contexts for exercising the capacity and thereby developing it. They can respond to students' efforts in ways that will keep them thinking and writing. They can even offer some of the technical skills that do attend the writing process — once students have achieved the fluency and purposefulness that will make the attaining of those skills seem worthwhile. But they can't create thinkers and writers after their own image. This limitation is unsettling to many teachers, and altogether unacceptable to some, who would rather invent intellectual "skills" to give students, even conceding the arbitrariness of their designation, than accept the peripheral role of nurturing a competence that students already possess and will develop in their own idiosyncratic ways as well as on timetables of their own choosing. The next chapter will suggest some means by which teachers can serve as nurturers of writing ability rather than as providers of fictional skills. But the pseudoconcept of "composing skills," and most of the other pseudoconcepts we have discussed, are, for many people, deeply embedded beliefs beyond the force of argument. We can offer lines of reasoning, but only individual teachers can change their beliefs. Pseudoconcepts will continue to influence instruction — mainly for the worse — until teachers accept the necessity of examining the real, irreconcilable differences, both in intellectual attitude and in concept, that separate classical and modern views of discourse — and then make up their minds to teach differently because of what they know.

Notes

[1] Michel Foucault writes in connection with the "progress" of intellectual history: "the problem is no longer of tradition, of tracing a line, but one of division, of limits; it is no longer one of lasting foundations, but one of transformations that serve as new foundations, the rebuilding of foundations." *The Archaeology of Knowledge* (New York: Harper & Row, 1972), p. 5. Earlier he speaks of "the phenomena of rupture, of discontinuity," and of the "incidence of interruptions" including "epistemological acts and thresholds," and of "displacements and transformations of concepts," p. 4. These usages all suggest Foucault's disjunctive view of intellectual history, a view that we regard as productive for the understanding of rhetorical theory.

[2] See Susanne K. Langer's distinction between discursive and presentational symbols in *Philosophy in a New Key* (Cambridge: Harvard University Press, 1957), Chapters 3 and 4. Naturally, many philosophical statements can be simply arguable or implausible, but in principle they are answerable to standards of truth and falsity.

[3] The ancient theory of direct reference, expressed for example in the Biblical account of Adam's naming of the animals, is attacked vigorously in the seven-

teenth century, particularly in Antoine Arnauld's *Art of Thinking*, trans., James Dickoff and Patricia James (New York: Bobbs-Merrill, 1964), especially Part I "Conception." See also Locke's *Essay Concerning Human Understanding*, especially Book III. Since the seventeenth century, numerous philosophical movements, supported by recent research in cognitive psychology and psycholinguistics, have demonstrated the insufficiency of a narrowly denotative view of meaning. See, for instance, C.K. Ogden and I.A. Richards, *The Meaning of Meaning* (New York: Harcourt, Brace and World, 1923); Ludwig Wittgenstein, *Philosophical Investigations*, trans., G. E. M. Anscombe (New York: Macmillan, 1953); and L.S. Vygotsky, *Thought and Language* (Cambridge: MIT Press, 1962).

[4]The "active" character of mind is suggested in British empiricist thought, emphasized in Western philosophy after Kant, and taken as axiomatic in psychology from associational theory onward. For representative insights into the relations between mind and "world," especially the nature of concept formation, see Vygotsky, *Thought and Language*; Jean Piaget, *The Child's Conception of the World* (New York: Humanities Press, 1951); and Piaget, *The Construction of Reality in the Child* (New York: Basic Books, 1954).

[5]We have in mind specifically the ontological and epistemological assumptions most "scientifically" elaborated in Aristotle's *Physics, Metaphysics, Psychology, Categories,* and *On Interpretation*, where views of mind, nature, and language, generally opposed to contemporary thought, are set out and serve as backdrop for ancient rhetorical theory.

[6]See, for example, Frank D'Angelo's efforts to transform the *topoi* into cognitive activities in *A Conceptual Theory of Rhetoric* (Cambridge: Winthrop, 1975), Chapter 4.

[7]Foucault paints a richly evocative picture of the inaccessibility of lost intellectual worlds in *The Order of Things: An Archaeology of the Human Sciences* (New York: Vintage, 1970).

[8]James McCrimmon, *Writing with a Purpose*, fifth edition (Boston: Houghton Mifflin, 1974).

[9]For interesting historical perspective on the paragraph, see Paul Rodgers Jr., "Alexander Bain and the Rise of the Organic Paragraph," *Quarterly Journal of Speech*, 51 (December 1965), 399-408; see also Ned A. Shearer, "Alexander Bain and the Genesis of Paragraph Theory," *QJS*, 58 (December 1972), 408-17.

[10]A good review of classical grammatical theory is R.H. Robins, *A Short History of Linguistics* (Bloomington: Indiana University Press, 1967).

[11]Organic and mechanistic metaphors have long influenced philosophical discussion. Samuel Taylor Coleridge's *Biographia Literaria* is a good example of how their contrast can help to clarify issues related to language and mind. In rhetorical theory, taxonomic or "grammatical" models of discourse represent the mechanistic perspective, while "phenomenological" models represent the organic. In linguistics, ancient European grammatical theory depends on a mechanistic view while Noam Chomsky's theories of linguistic structure — see for instance, *Language and Mind* (New York: Harcourt, Brace and World, 1968) — suggest an

organic view. In psychology, associational theory tended to be mechanistic, while the growth models of mind developed by George Kelly, *A Theory of Personality* (New York: Norton, 1963) and Jerome Bruner *et al.*, *A Study of Thinking* (New York: Wiley, 1956), among others, are organic. In general, we believe, the "human sciences" are better served by the organic perspective: an important article arguing the appropriateness of phenomenological research in the human sciences and the limitations of positivistic empirical research is Elliot G. Mishler, "Meaning in Context: Is There Any Other Kind?" *Harvard Educational Review*, 49 (February 1979), pp. 1-19.

[12] See Linda Flower, *Problem-Solving Strategies for Writing* (New York: Harcourt Brace Jovanovich, 1981).

[13] In an important review of Flower's textbook, Anthony R. Petrosky makes precisely these points. See *College Composition and Communication*, 34 (May 1983), 233-35.

[14] See Kenneth Burke, "The Five Key Terms of Dramatism," in *Contemporary Rhetoric: A Conceptual Background with Readings*, ed., W. Ross Winterowd (New York: Harcourt Brace Jovanovich, 1975), pp. 155-62.

[15] See Richard E. Young, Alton L. Becker, and Kenneth L. Pike, *Rhetoric: Discovery and Change* (New York: Harcourt, Brace and World, 1970), especially Chapter 6.

[16] For a good recent overview of the competences and skills associated with writing as a composing activity, see John Mellon, "Language Competence," in *The Nature and Measurement of Competency in English*, ed., Charles R. Cooper (Urbana, IL: NCTE, 1981), pp. 21-64. See also Frank Smith, *Writing and the Writer* (New York: Holt, Rinehart and Winston, 1982).

[17] See Mellon, "Language Competence," pp. 23-24; 28-29. We do not imply that writing is merely recorded speech, but only that, as Mellon suggests, a child's competence as a native speaker serves as fertile ground for developing the skills of writing. On differences between speech and writing, see Vygotsky, *Thought and Language*, and Janet Emig, "Writing as a Mode of Learning," *College Composition and Communication*, 28 (May 1977).

[18] We view sentence-combining as another aspect of the technology of intellect that currently opposes the phenomenological perspective which we regard as a more productive basis for writing instruction. Perhaps the best (impartial) review of the benefits and limitations of the procedure is John C. Mellon, *Transformational Sentence-Combining*, NCTE Research Report No. 10 (Urbana, IL: NCTE, 1969).

[19] See Francis Christensen, "A Generative Rhetoric of the Sentence," in *Contemporary Rhetoric*, ed., W. Ross Winterowd, pp. 337-51.

Chapter 5

Modern Rhetoric in the Classroom:

Making Meaning Matter

At last we ascend to the classroom — where all the abstractions and the philosophizing can begin to pay dividends in more reflective instruction. We have not wished to imply that the classroom is last in importance. On the contrary, its preeminent importance sustains our argument that students deserve intellectually sophisticated teachers who make reasoned instructional choices within contexts provided by a modern philosophical perspective. Since, historically, more than one perspective has evolved, and since the alternatives are profoundly opposed, teachers must make some theoretical commitments if they wish their work to be coherent and purposeful. The activities which are most relevant to a writing class predicated on modern assumptions about discourse and knowledge are quite different from those typical of a class in which traditional rhetorical principles are upheld or in which the teacher has tried to merge opposed perspectives. Therefore, the insistent request of new teachers — "just give us the methods, the exercises, the class activities, the textbooks, and not all that theory" — must be deferred, as we have deferred it, until a basis for differentiating alternative possibilities has been established. Too often, apprentice teachers clamor for training programs which are myopically pragmatic, as though all possible class activities assumed the same theoretical underpinnings and were therefore inter-changeable, a matter of personal taste.[1] But unreflective instruction, proceeding from unarticulated, perhaps even unconscious, and therefore unexamined, as-sumptions and values, insures that teachers and students alike will wander in an educational wilderness, lacking not only a compass but even a clear destination. Under these conditions, the "methods trading post" might support rudimentary classroom survival, but it will not enable a flourishing environment for writing.

Having now established our philosophical bearings among the concepts of ancient and modern rhetoric, we can review the methods available to writing instruction, not as a random scattering of unrelated possibilities chosen according to casual preference, but as integrated, mutually supportive activities, various to be sure, but also consistent within an intellectual perspective. Unfortunately, the greater part of writing instruction today remains characterized by inconsistency, theoretical confusion masquerading as pragmatic (and therefore presumably desirable) eclecticism.[2] The inconsistency can take several forms. It's not unusual, for example, to find classrooms in which plausible ideas about composing, consistent with insights from modern rhetoric, fail to have instructional value because of inappropriate teaching practices, as when teachers lecture about the composing process instead of encouraging students to write. Conversely, naive notions about writing are regularly promulgated through teaching methods that are sounder than the ideas they are conveying, as when teachers invite students to write more than one draft of an essay, not because they value the writers' evolving meanings, but because they want to insure technical correctness. Two other forms of inconsistency are also possible and occur with some frequency. Plausible ideas about writing can be mixed with less useful ones, as in the case of pseudoconcepts such as stage models of composition. And good teaching strategies can be mixed with less helpful ones, for instance, when teachers make assignments that encourage students to think for themselves on some issue but then imply by the way they "correct" the writing that, in fact, their own ideas and rhetorical choices are superior to those of their students. All of these inconsistencies are undesirable because, reflecting contradictory assumptions and values, they convey mixed messages to students about what they do and ought to do as learners and writers.

Of course, more than one brand of consistency is available to teachers. It's possible, for instance, to accept the premises of classical rhetoric, teach in accordance with them, and thereby preserve intellectual congruence in the narrowest sense. Following ancient practice, a teacher can set students to ceremonial writing tasks (such as "the similarities and differences between city and country life") in order to illustrate a particular "mode" (here comparison/contrast), with full knowledge of the classical heritage supporting the exercise and with full approval of its philosophical presuppositions. The professed and contented classicist will proceed in an orderly fashion, teaching by design, not by accident, and students will recognize what's expected of them. This teacher's problem, in our opinion, is not confusion about what he or she wants to have happen in the classroom but rather the insufficiency of the conceptual premises behind it. An astronomer who is thoroughly versed in Ptolemy and who accepts his model of the solar system may be consistent in applying Ptolemaic principles, but the consistency is not enough to commend belief in Ptolemy when better models, embracing more scientific evidence, are available. It's an open question whether this astronomer is to be more highly regarded than another who believes, out of intellectual confusion, that Ptolemy and Copernicus were saying more or less the same thing. Conceptual and methodological consistency is important, indeed essential, in the classroom, but only assuming that the consistency derives from a viable theoretical framework. Since the modern rhetorical perspective represents a substantial advance on ancient theory, the pedagogical consistency we advocate ought to grow out of an appreciation of that advance.

The traditional writing classroom is familiar enough to most teachers, but let's recall what it looks like before suggesting how it ought to change. The teacher, first of all, occupies center-stage, typically behind a desk that is larger than any other desk in the room, an emblem of authority and power. Students are arranged by rank and file, the personification of obedience, a tidy organizational unit more conspicuous for its corporate image than for the identities of its members. In general, the teacher talks and the students listen; or the teacher gives directions and students follow them. Only occasionally, an illusion of mutual intellectual inquiry is cautiously introduced through "discussion" sessions. But the "inquiry" is often superficial because students are expected to come ultimately to the "right" conclusions — those the teacher prefers — ideally on their own, but if necessary by means of as much insistence as the occasion requires. The normal sequence of class activities is from lecture to "discussion" to practice to testing. First, some rule or structure or formula for composing is introduced by lecture, then an example, often taken from a professional writer, serves as the basis for discussing the new constraint, then students practice conforming to it, often in isolation from other rules and forms considered on other class days. After a token practice period, a few minutes of class time or perhaps a homework assignment, the constraint presumably becomes a "skill" in each student's repertory, and at some point a test is administered to insure that students can name the constraint and use it on demand. Throughout the sequence of activities, classroom talk is both limited and artificial: the teacher does most of it, but to no one in particular, concentrating on an "average student" who doesn't exist. Some restricted one-to-one teacher/student conversation is tolerated but only at the teacher's discretion and only after permission has been duly sought by hand-raising. Almost no student-to-student conversation is encouraged because such talk is regarded as disruptive and impertinent, coming from people who are, as yet, ignorant of the subject the teacher has mastered. The paramount objective of the traditional writing class is to cover the course material by substantially completing each day's lesson plan; anything else that might take class time — answering student questions, working with slower learners, clarifying concepts, even the activities of writing and reading — are potential threats to the timetable and therefore subordinate to the teacher's preemptive syllabus.

Lying behind these conventional practices are attitudes about writing and learning to write, rooted in the ancient epistemology, which limit teachers' flexibility to employ methods that could enhance the development of writers by placing responsibility for that development where it mainly belongs — on writers themselves. Teachers often believe that the specialized knowledge they possess about composing — a conscious grasp of grammar rules, as well as logical and grammatical structures — must be conveyed to novice writers, who obviously don't possess it, before maturation can take place. Teachers readily accept the burden such a belief places on them to give students "what they need," realizing at the same time that the way to offer people complicated information they don't yet understand is to transmit it in as clear and orderly a fashion as possible. Hence, they design syllabi which "cover" all the relevant principles of writing in a logical way, progressing systematically from "the basics" — grammar, word usage, punctuation — to advanced skills — paragraph patterns, rhetorical modes, professional genres. They control class business because they know the principles, emphasizing lecture, drilling, and testing to insure that students come to know precisely what they know.[3]

Of course, what we've described is the perfect image of a traditional classroom, the kind many teachers remember sitting in themselves as students.[4] These teachers may never have created such a setting in their own instruction; they may feel that they are quite modern, in fact, because they have a much more open style — students gathering in groups from time to time, more free discussion than the old-fashioned school room tolerated, not *quite* as much lecturing and drilling as in bygone days (and with much of the drilling handled by means of computers and tape cassettes), maybe even some "personal writing" to make students feel comfortable and enthusiastic before taking on the "persuasive essay" and the "term paper" later. But we're talking about attitudes more than methods. It isn't the existence of a peer group or an occasional "free writing" exercise, or the fact that the old mahogany desk has disappeared, that makes for modern teaching. It's an attitude about the enterprise — sustained by modern conceptual premises about the nature of language as symbolic action, about the competence of all human beings to make meaning, about the nature of intellectual development, and about the role of teachers as nurturers of writing ability. The old mahogany desk abides in the hearts and minds of many teachers, who remain closet classicists whatever the superficial shape of their classrooms. Such teachers might assemble peer groups to discuss students' writing but also offer checklists of "good points" and "bad points" to look for — which is simply to turn students into accomplices of traditional instruction. Or they might have "prewriting" exercises one day, then more "organized" first drafts the next day, followed by a revision that includes inserting all the topic sentences left out before and also a proper conclusion paragraph — which is to offer an ancient performance recipe (invention, arrangement) in the new clothing of modern terminology. Closet classicists know about peer groups, personal writing, and revision, like everyone else. But they think like Cicero just the same.

Modern rhetoric offers a philosophical perspective on knowledge and learning, as well as the nature of discourse, which makes traditional assumptions and attitudes obsolete. The classical pedagogy related to those assumptions and attitudes is therefore obsolete as well,[5] but any pedagogy, however superficially "modern," that continues to proceed from them is flawed for the same reasons. Modern rhetoric leads to a fundamentally altered view of teaching. Discourse — the ability to make and convey meanings through language — is conceived to be a natural human competence, not a system of basic and advanced skills to be acquired. As a competence, it can grow but it can't be instilled; teachers can facilitate writing development but it isn't something that can be transmitted.[6] To be sure, modern rhetoric generates its share of abstractions about composing in the interest of scientific understanding. However, it also acknowledges the difference between knowing *about* discourse and knowing (or learning) *how* to write.

Teachers familiar with the abstractions can better understand the nature of composing and therefore the processes their students are striving to control. As a result, they can more surely devise classroom activities to promote growth and can more readily define their roles as facilitators of growth. But what they know about modern rhetoric only informs their teaching; it doesn't constitute class business. The lecturing characteristic of a traditional classroom has no relevance because there's nothing to lecture about — only writing and reading to be done. For the same reason, the majority of composition textbooks, those focused on modes of discourse, essay patterns, paragraph and sentence structures, are equally irrelevant. First, these books emphasize and overrestrict the shape of completed writing when what matters should be the personal search for form in the process of making meaning. Second, they see writing as bits and pieces, when it is organic and contextual. Third, they create sequences of concerns — small bits of discourse to large bits, or the reverse, when composing happens — and ought to happen in classrooms — all at once. Finally, the stifled discussion, repetitive drilling, and mechanical testing that so often accompany a traditional format are also irrelevant because their major effect has always been chiefly to validate the abstractions conveyed in books or lectures, not to develop writing competence.

The teacher's role in a classroom informed by modern rhetoric — let's call it a writing workshop to distinguish it from classical instruction — is vastly different from the traditional role. The teacher is an authority only in the sense of being a more fully matured writer and reader, not in the sense of being able to articulate more principles. Indeed, the teacher's greater experience is supposed to have demonstrated the fact that rules and formulas, ultimately, are distracting, debilitating, and false. The teacher is a guide, a coach, a stimulator, a listener, an informed responder, who knows too much about the potential and diversity in compositional choices, too much about the complexities of writing and the talents of writers, to assume a more ambitious — and less informed — role of Arbiter or Judge.[7] The teacher does not supply the ingredients for improved performance; cannot present failsafe, all-purpose guidelines for good writing; cannot anticipate with absolute assurance what a writer "ought" to say or where or how it should be said; and ultimately cannot predict or regulate the growth of individual writers. Teaching in the context of modern rhetoric involves fewer absolutes, less teacher control, and more student involvement. It's collaborative, rather than authoritarian, so that the signs of authority — the large desk, the ranks and files, the dominant teacherly voice, the dutiful hand-raising — pass from view (from the heart and mind as well as the room), while the signs of collaboration take their place — students working in orderly but unregimented ways among themselves, groups of people struggling jointly with issues and problems, writing to each other, reading each other's writing, describing reactions, offering opinions, doing more writing. The teacher's experience is valuable, indeed essential, for sustaining class dialogue. But the teacher's voice is joined by student voices in an environment where right thinking is not the possession of one and merely the aspiration of others but rather, as in the rest of life, a collective achievement, born out of negotiation and continuously evolving.

If the circumstances and activities of a writing workshop differ from those of a traditional class, so too do the learning priorities. The classical perspective valued correctness first, making the teaching of grammar the starting-point of a literacy curriculum. Once students had mastered the structures and usage rules of the language, they proceeded to work on the clarity of what they said, its intellectual cogency and argumentative effectiveness, which were the business of logic and rhetoric. Only much later, after correctness and clarity had been achieved, did students earn the right to pursue fluency as writers — the authority to discover valuable meanings of their own through the power of individual, unprescribed expression.[8] Many conventional writing classrooms today still accept this sequence of learning priorities. Indeed, the typical composition curriculum, proceeding from remedial to advanced courses, institutionalizes the priorities in many schools. But, ironically, from elementary grades onward, year after year, students return to the *same* starting point — "the basics": textbooks and workbooks remain essentially the same; lectures, drills, and exercises remain essentially the same. Correctness is perpetually re-introduced — and with the same results. Yet, instead of asking themselves why "the basics" never seem to get learned, teachers blame colleagues working in earlier grades for not doing their jobs. And then these teachers resolutely begin again — "This time *my* students are going to get it right!"

Modern rhetoric argues precisely the opposite view of learning priorities. Since making meaning is regarded as a competence, with clarity and correctness among the more mature manifestations of that competence, the classical priorities are inverted in the writing workshop.[9] Teachers can assume that clarity and correctness will, in many cases, not yet have been achieved. But they can also assume that students already possess sufficient linguistic resources to make valuable, personal meanings right at the start. Hence, they can work from this essential competence, regardless of surface inadequacies, dialect problems, grammatical and technical lapses, flawed lines of reasoning, awkwardness of expression, in order to nurture fluency and plant the motivational seeds for technical sophistication. Even — indeed especially — in the case of "basic" or "remedial" writers, the teacher's first concern ought to be to encourage writing, and the more of it the better, intentionally overlooking correctness in the interest of fluency as the higher priority. Rhetorical, logical, and stylistic maturity comes through the steady exercise of verbal competence over an extended period of time, in any circumstances where the writer is motivated to seek improved facility because his or her meanings, and efforts to make meaning, are valued by readers and therefore personally valuable as well. The most important activity in the workshop therefore, is writing in the company of interested readers. The most important attendant activities are reading and talking about that writing (that is, individual texts, not "writing-in-general") with a view toward stimulating additional writing. To the extent that clarity and correctness become issues at all, they are items in the conversation regarding a particular text, elements of a specific dialogue between its writer and an engaged reader who is primarily concerned with the meanings the writer is striving to create.

To summarize, then, the basic features of a classroom predicated on assumptions of modern rhetoric are the following: (1) It's student centered rather than teacher centered; that is, its agenda is students' own writing and their development as writers, not a teacher's prescriptions about writing or a contrived time-table for that development. (2) It assumes that composing is a competence which develops through use, not a system of skills to be serially introduced through lecture/discussion and then practiced one-at-a-time in drills and exercises. (3) It is facilitative, not directive, and collaborative, not authoritarian; that is, teachers join in the process of making and responding to discourse in order to sustain students' composing by implicating themselves in the guesswork, exploration, and reformulating in which all writers engage. Rules and other absolutes disappear in favor of repeated acts of writing and a continuous, collegial responding which assumes, in part, that other students' reactions can be as relevant as the teacher's, and that *all* responses are valuable, useful, individual impressions to be weighed in rewriting, while *none* are ultimatums for revision. (4) It reverses the ancient priorities of correctness, clarity, and fluency out of conviction that writers who have not learned to value their meanings by seeing how others value them have no reason to develop, indeed lack the basis for developing, any special expertise in their transmission. In light of these four basic features, the writing workshop is attitudinally distinct from the traditional classroom, and therefore irreconcilable with a traditional approach. It's an environment in which everyone, beginning with the teacher, is a writer and also a reader. The governing spirit of the writing workshop is the modern rhetorical perspective, where writing has heuristic value, where writers search for ways to organize their experience as coherent assertions and patterns of assertions, where authentic purposes and intended readers guide the choices about what to say, as well as where and how to say it, where revising is perpetual in the search for meaning, and where individual creativity, the energy of personal statement within a community of interested readers, is more valuable than timid or enforced capitulation to hackneyed thought.

Noble sentiments! But how are they actualized in the classroom? The main concern of the writing workshop is to start and keep students writing, since no other activity is more important to their growth. In the traditional classroom — and also that of the closet classicist — "getting students writing" refers to something rather different from what we have in mind in connection with a workshop. Traditionally, it suggests inventing tasks, sometimes quite restrictive (such as an exercise on avoiding fragments), other times broader (such as five paragraphs on "the problems of inflation"), all designed for practicing patterns, forms, and strategies in order to achieve proficiency. Hence, the writing is actually subordinate to concepts about writing: its production is in the service of learning those concepts (whether they include the "topic-sentence paragraph" of a true

Ciceronian or the "prewriting exercise" of a closet classicist). In the workshop, however, writing is not conceived as a series of exercises, each intended to demonstrate a pattern, form, or strategy. The proximate goal is to experiment with the making and sharing of meanings that matter to the writers. The ultimate goal is to develop competence through this experimentation under the influence of multiple reader responses. Writing is not a matter of five or eight or ten "assignments" in a semester, each accompanied by some arbitrary ritual governing stages of production. It's a continuous process, in class and out, of using language to examine ranges of experience, personal and public, intellectual, emotional, and imaginative, testing ways of rendering the experiences coherent, then reformulating the tentative coherences to reflect new perceptions of the experience. Focus, in other words, is on the individual writer's verbal confrontation with the world, not on mastering concepts and skills. And because the writing matters to the writer, he or she has a more sustaining motivation to develop competence than the austere insistence of a school demand for exercising.[10]

The problem of demand in a school setting, the fact that writing is more often required by teachers than initiated by students, is significant, because demand affects motivation and leads to different strategies among teachers, depending on their philosophical perspectives, for engaging students in writing courses.[11] In most composition instruction, the recognition that school writing is a forced activity leads teachers to search for "assignments" that will interest their students as much as possible in order to make the mastery of principles both more efficient and more palatable. The concern for interest and engagement is worthy, but in the conventional setting it's accompanied by some misconceptions about where incentive to write comes from and how teachers can encourage it. Many teachers assume, for instance, that, if only they are sufficiently inspired or work hard enough at design, they will discover the Ideal Assignment, one which will deeply involve every student and insure vibrant, responsible writing. The Ideal Assignment, to the extent that it has to do with motivation, means, of course, the Ideal Topic chiefly, since other elements of design, such as the mode and procedure of writing, are fixed by the curricular allegiance to concept and principle (that is, comparison/contrast or "personal narrative" is a set requirement, so the burden to motivate students to do the comparing or to write "personally" falls largely on the topic). Teachers realize, of course, that the ideal is unachievable, but they think they can approach it at least, and they value it as an incentive to discover ever better assignments, meaning more interesting topics and more inventive treatments, which will then result in higher quality performance. Unfortunately, the concept of Ideal Topic is deeply problematic, because it implies that topics are somehow intrinsically engaging whether or not writers see any value in what they're doing.

What causes a person to write? Rarely, outside the traditional classroom, does the mere declaring of a topic represent a signal to begin the process of making assertions and discovering connections. People write for many reasons — to make sense of something that matters to them, to share ideas or experiences with others, to transact business. In each of these circumstances, the writing goes on in a context of some internal need to explore and convey personally important meanings. The need consists of feelings that a task must be accomplished, or a concern raised, or a dissonance reconciled, or a question examined, or a confusion sorted out, or an understanding reached, or a position asserted. It assumes a belief that the writing is to be taken seriously because it can have a useful consequence. An assigned topic is the most artificial of possible stimuli, having no motivational value in itself unless, as in the case of some professional writing, it brings back to mind a context of personal need associated with previous efforts to address issues related to the topic. In the traditional classroom, assigning topics almost invariably yields ceremonial writing because of the nature of the academic environment. Lacking a broader context of personal investment, students' only motive to write is the obligation to respond to a school demand. No topic is more or less engaging than another when writers perceive that the demand for performance has greater significance than their degree of investment in the subject. In fact, the topic appears quite arbitrary, satisfying the necessity for writing to be about something, but inessential to the traditional school concern for instilling principles of correct expression. Whether the topic is "summer vacation," "abortion," "women's rights," "violence on tv," or "premarital sex," it's equally inert and undynamic, even if it names a potentially significant range of student experience, as long as it's unaccompanied by incentives to personal engagement beyond the requirement to produce a certain number of pages for a teacher's scrutiny. Students may well be involved in the areas of life and thought designated by topics, but they need not for that reason be moved to confess or explore those involvements earnestly in ceremonial composition. Teachers must go beyond the designation of a topic, beyond the unprofitable search for an intrinsically interesting assignment, if they hope to create richer motivations to write in the classroom.

Some teachers, aware of the prescribed nature of school writing, attempt to compensate by allowing students to choose their own topics. This creates the appearance of freedom, of course, an impression that students have control of what they will write about and therefore, presumably, more incentive to invest in the effort. But it doesn't change the nature of the traditional classroom situation, nor does it alter the essentially abstract and artificial character of topics as stimuli for writing. A topic is no less assigned, no less a teacher's idea, just because the student is charged with selecting it. If anything, allowing students to come up with topics is only an additional sign that what they write about is irrelevant because only the proficiency of the writing will finally be at issue. In any case, they will be searching for their topics in what remains a school setting, where demand for performance is the major motivation, not the desire to communicate something that matters. A sure indication that students recognize the artificiality of their circumstances is the frequency with which they come up with topics identical to the ones teachers have given them in the past — abortion, and the rest. If any writing will do for purposes of school critique, why strain after novelty?

The intrinsic difficulty of writing on a topic, regardless of who chooses it, also should be recognized as a negative influence on motivation. Topics are abstract and neutral, mere labels for ranges of experience and as such not very helpful as catalysts of personal involvement. Teachers sometimes attempt to make them into catalysts by exhorting students first to "narrow" their topics, in order to find what is pertinent, interesting, or concrete in them. But "narrowing" is an illusion: it makes a relatively more abstract topic into a relatively less abstract one, but the result is *still* an abstraction, no more evocative than the first one. "Baseball pitchers" is a narrowing of the topic "baseball"; and "Sandy Koufax" is narrower still. But all are abstractions, none easier or harder to write about, none more or less engaging, than another. Nor does it help to take the next step teachers recommend, which is to assume a position on the topic and state a thesis: "Sandy Koufax was the greatest left-handed National League pitcher of the 1960s." It remains distant from experience and it remains a school exercise: designations of topic, narrowed topic, position, and thesis are mere rubrics of performance dictated by the classroom, not incentives to write.

But perhaps only the most traditional teachers believe that the bare designating of a topic, with instructions regarding the mode and manner of treatment, will be sufficient to interest students in their writing. A subtler approach to assignment design is the attempt to contrive "more realistic" circumstances for composing by offering "cases" in which intentions and audiences are built into stories reminiscent of actual life. The argument here is that students are learning principles of composition in order to write effectively in the world outside the classroom; so, a good way to make the mastery of principle more enjoyable is by simulating real-world writing. In case assignments, students are expected to imagine themselves in writer-roles — school principal, sales customer, oppressed taxpayer — with a message to communicate to some imagined reader — parents of an uncooperative student, the manager of a department store, or a local congressional representative. An added advantage of the case, supposedly, is the possibility of employing a particular genre as part of the response to given rhetorical circumstances — a business letter or "position statement." One trouble with a case approach, however, is that teachers, disinclined to join in the make-believe, tend to renege on the rhetorical contract. Students know perfectly well that teachers will not read as though they actually were congressional representatives, department store managers, or parents. They will read like teachers, red-pencilling comma splices that few parents would notice, commenting on paragraph development when a department store manager would not, and noting a lack of "persuasive detail" where a politician would find the simple existence of a constituent's letter persuasive enough. Another problem: cases presume that students who have not truly performed in the roles they are asked to play will be able to estimate acceptable performance in the absence of personal experience. Finally, perhaps worst of all since it involves teachers' self-deception, cases assume that teachers can make realistic judgments about effective writing in some concrete, actual world situation on the basis of nothing more than a few generalizations in a story. And they assume, further, that teachers would *wish* to be so pragmatic in their judgments, so understanding of the broad tolerance and technical disinterest of most real readers, given their commitments to valued rhetorical and grammatical conventions.

How, then, can teachers hope to encourage engaged writing, particularly given the fact that classroom composing is, to a degree, inevitably artificial since the impulse to write comes from outside the writers? A good beginning is to concede what must be conceded. Even in a writing workshop, teachers ask for the writing. To the extent that student incentives develop, they develop in the context of required performance. Any school writing alters the normal circumstance in which a writer takes initiative to communicate to some reader, and in which the reader is interested in the substance of that particular text but not especially interested in the writer's overall ability or continuing maturation. Not only is the writing unavoidably a response to directive, but one of its significant values, beyond what it attempts to say, is its effect on the growing competence of the writer. The writing workshop, however, creates a different kind of demand situation than the conventional classroom does, by taking advantage of the strengths of the school setting as, itself, a legitimate rhetorical environment, influencing writers' performance just as powerfully as any other setting does. Many teachers overlook or fail to make the most of the fact that classrooms can present authentic and positive contexts for writing when they are shaped to support positive impressions of the purposes and reader expectations implicit in them. The case approach often fails, for example, because it presupposes that intentions and readers in the stories will be more influential presences for students than the looming school purposes and teacher-reader behind them. The workshop, by contrast, relies on authentic academic purposes and a real but nonauthoritarian teacher-reader whose readiness to take school writers' meanings seriously creates incentives to write which include, certainly, but are also richer than the school demand for it. Given the circumstances of an academic setting, it strives to instill in students a motive to *learn* by writing and an attitude toward the teacher-reader (as well as the peer-reader) which will lead them to take personal responsibility for the learning they acquire.

What are the strengths of the school setting as an environment for writing? The most productive answer to the question assumes that we enfranchise students, even the youngest and least experienced, in the same intellectual community in which teachers and scholars include themselves. School is a place in which learning is encouraged through repeated opportunities to confront new experience, new information, and to test ways of ordering it, making it comprehensible through talk, through argument and negotiation, through mathematical reasoning, through artistic expression — and through writing. School supports intellectual and imaginative investigation for its own sake, recognizing that the chance to explore and experiment, to confront experience in different ways and from different perspectives, leads to conceptual, emotional, and moral maturity, the highest goals of education. Students already know, or at least are ready to accept, their roles in school as learners, explorers, and experimenters: they assume, or are willing to assume, these roles in any classroom in which the teacher is equally willing to allow them the freedom to do so. In school, as in other environments, people talk to each other, exchanging views as one means of testing and developing their conclusions about the world. And in the school setting particularly, numbers of people with similar exploratory and experimental commitments come together to engage in the process of collaborative inquiry. Students are accustomed, or willing to become accustomed, to talking to each other as a means of learning, and also to talking with teachers (which is importantly different from merely listening to them) in order to profit from their greater intellectual maturity.

The school setting, then, is a particularly rich, if not the richest, context for writing. Given the recognition of modern rhetoric that discourse is implicitly heuristic, that it enables and articulates new knowledge, composing, written and otherwise, is the most important activity going on in schools. Certainly, therefore, the fact that writing is demanded need not preclude the possibility that deeper motives might be simultaneously encouraged for producing it. But teachers need to recognize the pivotal role they play in determining whether or not these more profitable incentives are allowed to evolve.[12] A teacher influences motivation by the stance he or she takes toward student writing, a stance which can either encourage students to value what they are doing or not. In the rhetorical environment of the classroom, writers' perceptions of their intended reader determine in large part the degree of their commitment. In the writing workshop, the instructor is a responsive collaborator in students' efforts to discover insights, positions, commitments, and new knowledge for themselves, a reader whose posture as engaged collaborator also influences the ways in which students respond to each other. Students in a workshop read each other's writing, not as critics or judges, but as participants in the inquiry after understanding. The teacher is also such a reader, also an interested participant, who responds to the writing by listening to the writer's own views of it, and by raising questions or offering observations that can lead to new insight and therefore to renewed composing. Together, these readers sustain incentive by reacting in the writer's presence to the meanings he or she is striving to convey, demonstrating their appreciation of the effort involved in discovering coherence by the specificity and energy with which they both support and challenge the writer's thinking. Through talk the subjects of writing emerge; through writing the subjects gradually take on a pertinence for individual writers; through reading, more talk, more writing, tentative lines of reasoning or ways of representing experience grow and change and suggest additional lines of inquiry. In short, the writing workshop becomes a microcosm of the intellectual community that "school" is supposed to represent. The writing goes on "for its own sake" in the same sense that thinking in an academic environment proceeds for its own sake — because the thinking leads to learning (and coincidentally to an improved ability to think), both individually and collectively, and therefore to the growth of the mind. A mature mind can grapple on its own with the pragmatic contingencies of life outside of school — by virtue of its development through the activities that school uniquely affords.

The problem of what to write about is less serious in the workshop than in conventional classrooms because "assignments" have given way to repeated challenges of active inquiry. The absence of a range of fixed principles and concepts to be "covered" liberates the writing from any inhibiting necessity to embody formal abstractions that were artificial or random to begin with. Students can write about what matters to them and in ways of their own choosing — though prompted all the while by the responses of readers who are considering their own intellectual as well as rhetorical experience, and offering observations in light of it. The teacher (or any student) can introduce some initial stimulus to begin the process of collaborative talk, thinking, and writing. It can be a class reading, or a conversation about personal experiences; it can be a public issue or problem; it can reside in concrete observation or a sensory appeal of some sort. Unlike "topics," however, it represents a challenge to probe, investigate, draw conclusions. As we suggested earlier, people write to answer questions, state positions, discover values, explore the world. The stimulus, therefore, ought to suggest something problematic, something that will give rise to questions, a dilemma or polarity, a clash of competing values, a paradox, puzzle, or anomaly, a confusion or mystery, anything that excites wonder or speculation or reflection or curiosity, anything that stimulates the deep, natural, human need to order things by means of symbolic action.[13] Starting from reading can be especially effective because the nature of reading is to generate multiple responses varying with the individual, whether the work is a poem or story, a news article or familiar essay, a piece of dialogue or an advertisement. Students can be encouraged to locate their own dissonances, issues, ambiguities, in the reading and to explore them through writing. A teacher can assist the process by offering additional perceptions of conflict or complication, though resisting the inclination to control reading just as he or she resists controlling writing — out of conviction that absolutes are inappropriately imposed on both of these complex, creative activities. Aside from reading, teachers can also help students move toward a sense of the problematic by reflecting with them on personal experiences, incidents from past or present, interactions with family and friends, instances of change or growth, expectations for the future, connections to public issues of all sorts. But teachers know these resources already. It's not the stimulus that matters but the context of talk, writing, and learning, the atmosphere of intellectual attentiveness that sustains motivation to explore.[14]

It's this atmosphere of intellectual attentiveness that mainly differentiates workshop activities from those designed by the closet classicist. Writing from personal experience is a case in point, because it's quite different from the official "personal" or "expressive" writing so often introduced in classrooms professedly modern but secretly allied to Cicero. The difference is between an opportunity for writing in certain areas and a procedure for writing in certain ways. "Personal narrative" is just another school genre, in concept precisely the same as "expository writing" or "persuasive writing," a ritual exercise nearly always resulting in formulaic writing. Most students know exactly when the personal narrative is going to be assigned — early in the course before the more "serious" writing that comes later; and they also know what's expected of them — they're to be "sincere and honest," to be somewhat more "emotional" than "rational," to write "in their own voices," to give a lot of "concrete detail" and "vivid description." In short, they're supposed to follow the Rules of expressive writing, which are just as fictional, mechanical, and unrelated to performance as the Rules of exposition — "academic" voice, generalization supported by examples, and the like. In workshops, writing from and about personal experiences represents an opportunity to articulate one's own responses to persons, events, and situations, to probe, to create significance, to discover coherence. It assumes disciplined intellectual and imginative effort, not self-indulgence, a pose of authenticity, or an adaptation to somebody's Rules.

Crucial to sustaining the atmosphere of intellectual responsibility in a workshop is the teacher's willingness to trust students' abilities to discover their own stances on important questions and willingness to give them time and flexibility for pursuing their own conclusions. Since, for example, most writers require periods of imaginative incubation, which may include conversing with others, reading and research, moments of contemplation, and unfocused or partly focused scribbling, it's reasonable to suppose that student writers can profit from these activities as well. Teachers should not regard it as wasteful to spend entire workshop sessions on small-group talk about the object, issue, or reading which serves as the initial stimulus, and also on exploratory sketching of ideas and positions, the reading of those plans to one another, and further discussion and exploratory writing. Useful thought takes time, and workshops make time available. There's no syllabus to cover, no next "mode" to practice, no compelling reason to deny the opportunity for getting closer to an issue than syllabus-centered classes are able to do. Besides making use of time, however, teachers also must recognize the importance of lowering their visibility in order to show that students do indeed have authority to make their own intellectual way, and that students are expected to be responsible for what they say — expected to contribute to the community of writers and readers. Lowering visibility means discarding the traditional image of master-of-ceremonies in favor of a new image of participant writer, participant reader, and participant learner. Students will believe that they possess intellectual authority in proportion as they see their teacher's readiness to take them seriously, to look for serious, enlightening discourse from them, and to join with them in probing issues through talk and writing.

Teachers show their relationship to students as more experienced members of the same community of learners through the kind of talk they encourage, which we will discuss more fully later, and — just as important — through the writing they do along with students. In workshops everybody writes. Teachers who compose along with their students have no choice but to implicate themselves in the same messy struggle toward meaning. Anyone who has tried to say something useful on demand with an hour or so time-limit, circumstances that students habitually face, knows the difficulty, indeed the unlikelihood, of achieving much initial success. We all need time, thought, and second chances, teachers no less than students. The process of making assertions about difficult, substantial questions takes effort and energy, requires an investment of personal resources and a search for outside sources as well. Teachers who write often themselves know this, but they also need to show it to students, who sometimes think that skilled writers can generate consistently publishable writing on first tries, with no anxieties and no mistakes, in isolation from critical readers, with help from no one but the Muses. Teachers who acknowledge the perspective of modern rhetoric, who understand the heuristic value of composing and its progressive, endlessly renovative character, resist the fiction that writing is formulaic, that ideas spring readily to mind and organize themselves like magic, given a prescribed structure in which to locate them, that tidy end-products matter more than the on-going effort to make sense of the world. They know that they do not, or could not, or at least would not want to, obey the formalist nonsense entombed in many textbooks as they pursue the meanings that matter to them. Their own writing in workshop is a constant reminder, to themselves and to their students, of how writing actually happens and what makes it worth all the trouble.

Of course, the teacher's concern for motivating students by giving them freedom to pursue their own questions, issues, and ideas does not imply a relaxation of intellectual rigor or a willingness to accept trivial efforts from those who would avoid careful, original reasoning and the solving of complex rhetorical problems. In fact, the case is precisely opposite. The writing workshop is not a place for pampering ineptitude by allowing writers to find easy refuge in vapid or aimless "self-expression." Encouraging students to take responsibility for their thinking carries with it an expectation that they will indeed *do so*, that they will struggle past truisms into insight, that they will challenge themselves to learn. Students are expected to experiment with narrating information, developing lines of reasoning, depicting personal attitudes and impressions, drawing conclusions, representing alternative points of view, even storytelling, play with language, and other forms of dramatization. These activities go hand in hand, varying in usefulness according to purpose and occasion. Students are not coerced into following any planned sequence of such activities, but are encouraged, individually and as occasions present themselves, to take the imaginative and intellectual risks implied in each, simply in order to see how the personal construing of experience changes when achieved in diverse ways. There's no need to introduce the possibilities abstractly, as though naming twenty alternatives were important for performing in twenty different ways. Students already know how to express themselves in both more concrete and more generalized, more personalized and more distant, more descriptive and more argumentative ways, not because they have learned how in school but because they are human beings. They may lack sophistication as writers, but they do not lack competence as composers. What they need is an opportunity to experiment, not a review of the rules. A workshop offers the opportunity, assuming that personal narrative and argument are equally valuable and worthy of equal attention, that honesty and application are as necessary — and as expected — in the use of one as in the use of another, and that facility in their use depends on chances to try them out in the presence of readers, exploring their advantages and limitations for articulating what one wishes to say.

Numerous books and articles are available to help teachers set up writing workshops.[15] But here, by way of summary, is a picture — only one of many possible — of workshop activities over several class days. First, however, a caution: the picture may superficially resemble what many more or less traditional teachers do every day. We've already pointed out, for instance, that it's not unusual to see a group format in classrooms that are not writing workshops. When groups are only doing the same correction chores that teachers used to do by themselves, they don't represent the collaborative learning we have in mind. When students are asked to discuss among themselves their perceptions of an assigned reading, only to have the teacher deliver, at the end of class, a tidy summation of what they should have seen or what they can now write about, they are not being encouraged to assume intellectual responsibility. When students are asked to revise earlier writing but only to clean up mistakes, they aren't working toward deeper insights regarding a subject. Attitudes shape methods, not the other way around. Our picture will be misconstrued if it's seen as a display of methods without reference to the philosophical perspective that gives them life. Moreover, the methods will *fail* if teachers are waiting to see if they "work" before changing their attitudes: it's the attitudes that cause the methods to work.

Imagine on a given day that the workshop teacher brings in a question for class deliberation — a stimulus for talk, reading, and writing. The question is, "Who knows you the best?" There's nothing magical about the question — it's simply a beginning. The teacher may elaborate it briefly, perhaps through anec-dote or questioning: "Would you be inclined to say that nobody knows you better than you know yourself? or have you ever found yourself thinking that someone, a member of your family or a friend, knows you better than anyone, perhaps even better than you know yourself?" Students are then invited to write for a few minutes about some personal experience of the question, an incident, perhaps, that may have led to the reflection, "No one knows me better than I know myself," or "That person really understands me." Naturally, the teacher joins in this writing, possibly trying intentionally to choose an incident that will contradict an anticipated "typical" response. After a brief period, ten or fifteen minutes, students form in their usual groups of four or five members each. Since many workshop activities assume this format, the groups are created early in the term so students can become accustomed to working together. Once in their groups, students read their anecdotes to each other, using them as part of an effort to understand the issue involved in the question. The teacher moves from group to group, listening to anecdotes, reading his or her own when occasion permits, but especially if a given group seems unanimous on a position that the anecdote would contradict. The teacher might also help students raise questions about their anecdotes: "Are you 'one person' or different people at different times? do even *you* know yourself all the time? when people know you, what do they know — your actions? your motives? facts about your life? your moods? your likes and dislikes? your innermost feelings?" At the conclusion of this class day, students might be asked to bring to the next class a tentative personal position — a page or two — on the question, "Who knows you best?" for further exploration.

At the start of the next day, students form again in their groups to read their position statements. After each reading, members of the group take some time to respond orally or in writing to the student's position, referring to their own experiences, commenting on the plausibility of the writer's opinion, adding more information, discussing their uncertainties about the issue or about the writer's statement of his position, considering the impact of the writer's rhetorical strategies. Again, the teacher moves from group to group, offering responses with everyone else but not dominating discussion or insisting on his or her own point of view. What matters is stimulating thought, not directing its outcome. After the readings are completed, including time for people to clarify their own beliefs or ask clarifications from others, the teacher introduces a problem into the discussion, a short essay from a psychologist, one or two pages in length, which argues that people do not have fixed centers of personality but rather multiple facets comprising identifiable patterns. Time permitting, students read the essay and talk about it with the teacher or in their groups. In preparation for the next session, they will analyze the essay and consider their reasons for agreeing or disagreeing with it. They may be encouraged to go to the library for additional information. Their writing this time will be more substantial than on the first exploratory occasion, perhaps three, four, or five pages (depending on the abilities of the class).

The next class might offer opportunity for a debate. The students, by now becoming more expert on the issues pertinent to the original question, can take sides and argue the matter by turns, perhaps to a panel of class members charged with deciding the more persuasive case. Students thereby gain a sense of the process of argument, even apart from their focus on a particular problem. Other activities are equally possible, the concern being mainly to provide time for examining a complex intellectual puzzle seriously and in detail, time for sampling perspectives and means of representing them, time for developing lines of thought and conclusions that might amount to something more than perfunctory opinion. The teacher, meanwhile, reads students' essays, responding to them in ways that cause the writers to reassess their statements, reconsider their positions, look for additional evidence, find new avenues of inquiry, probe related questions. The instructional concern is to offer reasons for more thought and writing, deeper penetration of the subject. After returning the essays with written responses, the teacher asks students to write a final essay on the question "Who knows me best?" perhaps twice as long as the preceding, reflecting all the thought and talk, all the response and negotiation of the last several classes. In some schools, that final essay would eventually be evaluated according to how well it satisfies the writer's intention to communicate his or her point of view. In any case, the goal of the several workshop sessions devoted to examining personality and self-knowledge has been to help writers develop expressive competence through their sustained effort to investigate a genuine, provocative issue, on which they have the authority to take personally meaningful positions and about which they have full responsibility for articulating conclusions.

The activities we have described are familiar enough to many teachers and do not require elaborate specification. But once again, the assumptions and attitudes behind them make all the difference. These activities, viewed as mere technique, are accessible to any teacher, regardless of what he or she believes. It's the sense of purpose and value suffused through a workshop, far more than what transpires in it, that makes it different from a traditional classroom. Apart from the educational philosophy we've been describing, groupwork can be as artificial as case writing, and as unproductive; exploratory writing becomes "prewriting," just one more classroom ritual; revision becomes shuffling and editing; "discussion" becomes just a subtler form of intellectual coercion; "Who knows me best?" becomes just another tedious classroom topic. Activities are important. But attitudes, and the philosophical perspective shaping them, are more important. Let's add that these attitudes and the activities they encourage aren't limited to writing courses, or even to English courses. What we've been talking about — teachers' views of students and the process of learning, the importance of collaboration to the advance of knowledge, the benefits of writing in order to explore serious intellectual questions — has, it seems to us, an evident relevance throughout the curriculum, anywhere active thinking and judging are going on. Both collaborative exploration of ideas and writing as a way of learning are integral to scholarly life. Why should they not be integral to student academic experiences as well? Student minds are very much like teacher minds, differentiated by unequal powers of discernment, certainly, but not by unequal capacities to learn and grow. The chance to talk and write, as well as read and hear lectures, is important to the maturation of scholar-teachers. It's important to students' growth too.

Notes

1 A recent *English Journal* article describes the prevalent demand among high school teachers for narrowly based in-service preparation emphasizing methods but not the attitudes and values that give them relevance. See Robert Perrin, "Teachers' Institutes: Are Teachers Getting What They Want?" *English Journal*, 72 (April 1983), 33-35.

2 Textbook sales are the best demonstration of the preference for smorgasbord instruction. The best-sellers, running through many editions, are those that combine chapters of grammatical drills, stylistic prescriptions, and discourse

modes with newer activities such as free writing, sentence-combining, and invention heuristics, adding the latest ideas, edition by edition, as they become popular. See, for instance, recent editions of McCrimmon's *Writing with a Purpose* (Boston: Houghton Mifflin, 1973) or Crews' *Random House Handbook* (New York: Random House, 1977), whose tables of contents speak for themselves.

[3] Paulo Freire has called this traditional theory of instruction the "banking concept" of education where students draw information from a teacher's storehouse. See *Pedagogy of the Oppressed* (New York: Herder and Herder, 1972). Freire goes on to describe an active pedagogy more consistent with a developmental theory of learning.

[4] The traditional classroom is, however, far from dead. Judging from Arthur Applebee's recent survey of how writing is taught and used in the schools (*Writing in the Secondary School: English and the Content Areas* [Urbana, IL: NCTE Research Report, No. 21, 1983]), little has changed in teachers' practice despite decades of research and thought which have proven it inadequate. See also the findings of James Britton, Tony Burgess, Nancy Martin, Alex McLeod, and Harold Rosen, *The Development of Writing Abilities (11-18)* (London: Macmillan Education, 1975).

[5] Jean Piaget traces the "developmental" educational theory that parallels modern rhetorical thought, both growing out of the same epistemological climate, both emphasizing the active nature of the mind, not only in its capacity to manifest itself in symbolic forms but also in its capacity to grow in response to educational nourishment. See *Science of Education and the Psychology of the Child* (New York: Viking, 1970).

[6] Janet Emig refers to the "magical thinking" of those who believe that "children learn *because* teachers teach" in "Non-Magical Thinking: Presenting Writing Developmentally in Schools," *Writing: The Nature, Development and Teaching of Written Communication* (Vol. II), (Hillsdale, NJ: Lawrence Erlbaum Associates, 1982). The essay is very useful for distinguishing, as we have done, between the basic tenets of traditional pedagogy and those of modern "developmental" instruction.

[7] Donald Murray has written wisely and well on the roles of a teacher in the writing class, particularly the teacher's concern for listening responsively. See his essay "Teaching the Other Self: The Writer's First Reader," *College Composition and Communication*, 33 (May 1982), 140-48. Murray's entire teaching philosophy is relevant here. See his *Learning by Teaching* (Montclair, NJ: Boynton/Cook, 1982) and *A Writer Teaches Writing* (Boston: Houghton Mifflin, 1968).

[8] Donald L. Clark has described these priorities in his work on education in the ancient world: *Rhetoric in Greco-Roman Education* (New York: Columbia University Press, 1957). See also Quintilian, *Institutio Oratoria*, especially Books I and II.

[9] For a parallel argument about the inversion of classical learning priorities, see John Mayher, Nancy Lester, and Gordon Pradl, *Learning to Write/Writing to Learn* (Upper Montclair, NJ: Boynton/Cook, 1983).

[10] This seems to include a greater willingness to seek assistance with grammatical and stylistic difficulties. Our experience in workshop classes has been that

students who have become involved in their writing (and learned to trust the teacher) frequently ask technical questions — how to make a description more vivid, how to manage dialogue, how to create suspense, how to vary and balance sentence rhythms. And when *they* do the asking, they also hear the answers. Once technical issues matter, students appear to develop technical expertise more readily.

[11] Britton *et al.* have described the difficulties of making assignments and coaxing students to find personal value in them, as well as the often perfunctory writing that results. See *The Development of Writing Abilities (11-18)*, pp. 7-8.

[12] The impact on writing of students' perceptions of the kind of teacher-reader they are addressing — say teacher as examiner versus teacher as partner in dialogue — is discussed in Nancy Martin, Pat D'Arcy, Bryan Newton, and Robert Parker, *Writing and Learning Across the Curriculum 11-16* (London: Ward Lock Educational, 1976), pp. 18-22. See also Britton *et al.*, pp. 63-73.

[13] For a discussion of writing assignments that engage students on intellectual issues, see William E. Coles, Jr., *The Plural I* (New York: Holt, Rinehart and Winston, 1978) and *Teaching Composing: A Guide to Teaching Writing as a Self-Creating Process* (Rochelle Park, NJ: Hayden, 1974).

[14] For discussion of this classroom environment see M. Torbe and R. Protherough, *Classroom Encounters: Language and English Teaching* (London: Ward Lock Educational, 1976).

[15] Helpful guides to creating writing workshops include the following: Stephen N. Judy and Susan J. Judy, *An Introduction to the Teaching of Writing* (New York: Wiley, 1981); Peter Elbow, *Writing Without Teachers* (New York: Oxford University Press, 1973); Ken Macrorie, *Uptaught* (Rochelle Park, NJ: Hayden, 1970); Mary K. Healy, *Using Student Writing Response Groups in the Classroom* (Berkeley, CA: University of California, Bay Area Writing Project, 1980); Mary H. Beaven, "Individualized Goal Setting, Self Evaluation, and Peer Evaluation," in Charles R. Cooper and Lee Odell, eds., *Evaluating Writing: Describing, Measuring, Judging* (Urbana, IL; NCTE, 1977); Thom Hawkins, *Group Inquiry Techniques for Teaching Writing* (Urbana, IL: NCTE, 1976). Textbooks offering useful workshop activities include: Ann E. Berthoff, *Forming/Thinking/Writing* (Montclair: NJ Boynton/Cook, 1978); Ken Macrorie, *Telling Writing* (Rochelle Park, NJ: Hayden, 1980); and Lil Brannon, Melinda Knight, and Vara Neverow-Turk, *Writers Writing* (Montclair, NJ: Boynton/Cook, 1982).

Chapter 6

Responding to Texts:
Facilitating Revision
in the Writing Workshop

There is a stock comic situation in which two people go through the motions of communicating but finally fail because each assumes that an idiosyncratic perspective is shared by the other when in fact it is not. A classic instance is the abortive conversation between Walter Shandy and Uncle Toby running through Sterne's marvelously madcap *Tristram Shandy*. Toby is preoccupied with his hobby-horse: he constructs models of famous battles as a means of making order out of the experiences that matter to him (the tentacles of modern rhetoric have a long reach). He employs a language, rich in military allusions and similes, that reflects his priorities, and he hears the remarks of others largely in terms of his own military interests. Walter, meanwhile, has a hobby-horse of his own, a fascination with the austere intellectual world of ancient logic, where presumably dispassionate rational analysis can get at the truth of things and inject coherence into human affairs. Since neither of these peculiar characters is prepared to take into account the viewpoint of the other, talk between them is hilariously oblique and unproductive. Walter's reference to a "train of ideas," for example, suggests to Uncle Toby a "train of artillery": on another occasion, mention of the "bridge" of Tristram's nose is misunderstood as a reference to the Marquis d'Hôpital's drawbridge; and elsewhere, Walter's elegant dissertation on the logical value of auxiliary verbs suggests nothing more to Toby and Corporal Trim than the auxiliary troops at the siege of Limerick. Each time these individuals attempt to converse, their hobby-horses interfere, extinguishing the hope that any constructive meeting of minds can result from acts of language.

The rhetorical principle violated in these abortive conversational efforts is one we have discussed often before now: people cannot communicate unless they first strive to accommodate each other's points of view and decide on a shared basis for talk. Human beings put the principle into practice many times every day in order to accomplish their purposes in both speaking and writing. Probably, the majority of writing teachers are sufficiently persuaded of the importance of audience expectation that they include lectures and exercises on the subject, or even "cases" that require students to anticipate different readers on different occasions. Presumably, these teachers understand quite clearly that communication entails a projecting from the self, a struggle to see things as others might see them, so that, by making connections between someone else's understanding and one's own, a strategy can evolve for making and sharing new meanings. What is peculiar, however, about the commitment of writing teachers to "audience" is the extent to which anticipating the perspectives of others is for them a one-way obligation. There's a curious disjunction between what these teachers tell students about projecting outward as the starting point of communication and what they do themselves as aspiring communicators. For in their ways of talking to students, and especially in their habits of responding to student writing, they tend, every bit as much as Uncle Toby does, to ride their own hobby-horses — sometimes to the extent that their students fail utterly to conceive what they might be talking about.

Too often, if not typically, when reading student writing, teachers ignore writers' intentions and meanings in favor of their own agendas, so that what students are attempting to say has remarkably little to do with what teachers are looking for, and therefore little bearing on what they say in comments on student texts. In the least subtle instances, while students are engaged in — let's say — describing personal experiences, their teacher is concentrating on the effective use of comparison or example; while they struggle dutifully to find significance in *King Lear*, the teacher is defending the imperiled constraints of a term paper or the canons of some, not necessarily announced, critical predisposition; while students are writing to understand the workings of a nuclear reactor, the teacher is enforcing detailed instructions of the assignment on "process analysis"; while they are locating personal meanings in public issues, the teacher is insuring that only the most orthodox opinions are appropriately paraded in all the tiresome pros and cons that arrange themselves repeatedly in school writing. Generally speaking, the hobby-horse of writing teachers is prose decorum, the propriety of discourse extending from its technical features to its formal appearances and even to its intellectual content as a display of approved ideas in conventional relationships to each other.[1] Their point of view largely determines what they talk about, even though it's a point of view that students barely comprehend or see the value of. To an extent, of course, by sheer power of position teachers can demand that students begin to pay attention to their pronouncements about structure and convention, enjoying the modest benefits of one-way conversation. But the question of *quid pro quo* seldom arises, that is, the value, for communication's sake, of paying attention to what matters most to writers by starting with their meanings instead of teacherly priorities when responding to their writing. And what is jeopardized as a consequence is the possibility of real communication, the chance to make intellectual progress through purposeful dialogue.[2]

Given the environment surrounding traditional instruction, it's perhaps not so surprising that teachers have missed the fact that responding to student writing is a species of communication, subject, therefore, to the same rhetorical principles that govern other situations. For communication, or dialogue, is a democratic act: both sides get to score points. Yet, the classic teacher-student relationship is defined, as we have suggested, in authoritarian terms, master and apprentice, knower and learner, talker and listener. In typical writing courses, students produce discourse not in order to be listened to but in order to give teachers something to talk about. Since the authority for judging pertinence, propriety, and effectiveness in writing rests with the teacher, then, paradoxically, the control of compositional choices ultimately belongs with the teacher as well. Could a more peculiar rhetorical situation possibly exist than one in which the person supposedly creating a text must yield control of its character and shape to the ostensible audience? Such is often the case in classrooms: the teacher's agenda is the one that matters, so the responsibility for anticipating expectations lies wholly with students. To the extent that the teacher's expectations are not satisfied, authority over the writing is stolen from the writer by means of comments, oral or written, that represent the teacher's agenda, whatever the writer's intentions may initially have been. A student's task is to match an Ideal Text in the teacher's imagination which is insinuated through the teacher's commentary, not to pursue personal intentions according to the writer's own developing sense of what he or she wishes to say.[3] The student writer, in other words, is obliged to work diligently at locating a teacher's hobby-horse, experiencing some predictable frustration in the process, while the teacher is under no requirement to anticipate the writer's purposes before making comments on a text. The teacher's reading strategy is simply to apply his or her own inevitably reductive Ideal Text to students' actual writing, and to remark on discrepancies between the two, which the students are then called upon to reduce as the measure of their competences as writers.[4] It's the rare composition teacher who reads student writing with the assumption that composers legitimately control their own discourses, who accepts the possibility that student intentions matter more than teacher expectations as a starting-point for reading, and who recognizes that writers' choices are supposed to make sense mainly in terms of those intentions, not in proportion as they gratify a reader's view of what should have been said.

An experiment we have conducted suggests the pervasiveness of the concept of Ideal Text among writing teachers and the strength of their resistance to honoring writers' intentions when responding to their writing. We asked forty teachers to comment as they normally would on a particular student essay. The writer had studied the Lindbergh kidnapping trial and had produced a text simulating the closing argument of the prosecuting attorney. His text was heavily laden with emotional appeals to the jury because, he had told us, his intent was to create sympathy for the injured Lindberghs and revulsion against the accused. He believed that emotional language would be suited to this intent. Here is a portion of his writing:

> Ladies and gentlemen of the jury, I whole-heartedly believe that the evidence which has been presented before you has clearly shown that the man who is on trial here today is beyond a doubt guilty of murder of the darling, little, innocent Lindbergh baby.
>
> Sure, the defendant has stated his innocence. But who are we to

believe? Do we believe the testimony of a man who has been previously convicted; in fact convicted to holding up innocent women wheeling baby carriages? Or do we believe the testimony of one of our nation's greatest heroes, Charles A. Lindbergh. Mr. Lindbergh believes the defendant is guilty. So do I.

All I ask, ladies and gentlemen of the jury, is that you look at the evidence. . . .

When we asked teachers to read this text, but without benefit of the writer's explanation of intent (a disadvantage which did not, however, appear to bother them), they divided into two groups. One group felt that the emotional language showed the writer's immaturity and undeveloped rhetorical sense: their comments betrayed an Ideal Text featuring detached logical rigor and care for the details of evidence as the essential characteristics of a trial prosecutor's summation. The student's writing failed to anticipate these characteristics and therefore failed, in the eyes of one group of teachers, to demonstrate proficiency. The second group's conclusion was more interesting. Its members upheld the same Ideal Text, showed the same concern for logic and explanatory detail; but they reasoned that, since the writer could not possibly have been serious in resorting to blatant emotional appeals, the discourse must represent a wonderful spoof of the genre of "trial summation." Therefore, the writer must be unusually mature and the writing a clever demonstration of exceptional competence (though containing some technical flaws that could be corrected readily enough). The significant point here is that neither group stopped to consider the possibility that the student might have had a serious intent to use emotional appeal or that its use might constitute a plausible strategy in this situation. Instead, secure in their shared concept of an Ideal Text, both groups advanced without hesitation to precisely opposite conclusions about the merits of the writer's text and the ability of the writer himself.

Later, we showed these teachers both the student's description of intent and a transcript of portions of the actual summation delivered during the Lindbergh trial, which revealed the very emotional appeals to which the student writer had resorted, thereby suggesting the arbitrariness of the teachers' assumed Ideal Text:

Why, men and women, if that little baby, if that little, curly-haired youngster were out in the grass in the jungle, breathing, just so long as it was breathing, any tiger, any lion, the most venomous snake would have passed that child without hurting a hair of its head.

Of course, the fact that the original attorney used such appeals does not imply that only one strategy exists for preparing trial summations. It only suggests that emotional appeals are no less legitimate than other strategies, so that the teachers' refusal to take the student writer's choices seriously, acknowledging the authority of that writer to choose in accordance with his own intentions, indicated the inappropriate tyranny of an Ideal Text over their commenting practices. The fact that their judgments were polarized, yet derived from a common prejudice, helps to make our point about Ideal Texts. But it would not be surprising if the student writer found either response puzzling since, in each case, the teachers were attending to their own predispositions and not to the student's effort to make meanings. The likelihood of serious, purposeful communication with that student would have to have been severely reduced.

The writing workshop depends on a style of response which differs altogether from that of traditional instruction because its concern is not merely to elicit writing in order to judge it, but to sustain writing through successive revisions in pursuit of richer insights and concurrently the maturation of competence. The workshop style assumes, above all, that, if teachers seriously aim to communicate with students about their writing and thereby affect students' performance, they must begin with what matters most to those writers, namely, the making of meaningful statements consistent with the writers' own purposes and their own estimations of how best to achieve them. In nearly every circumstance except the classical composition course, reading entails accepting a writer's authority to make precisely the choices that have been made in order to say precisely what the writer wishes to say. Readers seek gradually to understand and appreciate a writer's purposes by assessing the effects of textual choices on their way of seeing the subject. They suspend their own preconceptions, to a degree, in order to understand the writer's position, taking for granted the writer's capacity to make a position clear unless there is substantial reason to believe otherwise.[5] This seems a fair starting-point in responding to student writing as well, no matter how skeptical a teacher may be about a particular writer's ability to control choices. Instead of beginning with the supposition that the teacher-reader is rightfully in control rather than the writers, so that their discourses are valued only to the extent that they meet the teacher's preconceptions, the workshop reader begins — as most readers do — with an implicit trust in the writer's choice-making and with a concern to discover the writer's intentions rather than automatically preempting them with personal concerns. The main reason for returning to this normal reading habit is that the responders imply by doing so that they value writers' efforts to make meaning, thereby creating a powerful incentive to write. Conversely, the traditional tendency to preempt intentions diminishes incentive because it shows students that readers fail to value what they have to say.

What every teacher knows, of course, is that student writing does not always succeed in conveying or achieving its intentions. The workshop teacher knows this as well as anyone, but knows also that motivation to write depends crucially on the belief that the writing will be taken seriously — in other words, that the writer's authority to make statements in his or her own way will be respected. We are not recommending a suspension of the critical faculty in responding to student writing, but only an essentially receptive rather than essentially evaluative reading posture.[6] Rather than taking for granted a writer's proven or unproven ineptitude, which encourages the usurping of the writer's text as frequently as the teacher prefers, we suggest the normal posture of taking the writer's competence *generally* for granted, which encourages respecting the writer's choices as plausible alternatives as long as they appear to support his or her own purposes. When teachers begin reading student texts with the calculated (as opposed to naive) expectation that the writing is purposeful and suited to its own ends, their style of responding to it necessarily changes. Comments begin to register, not the discrepancy between a discourse and some teacher's personal Ideal Text, but rather the discrepancy between a writer's projected intentions and the effects of actual choices on an experienced reader's awareness of what the writer wishes to say. Any response will be designed to reveal the reader's uncertainties about the substance of the writer's communication, depending on a knowledge of the writer's purposes as the touchstone for recommending revisions. This reading posture is specially suited to the writing workshop because of its emphasis on revision as a natural feature of composing. The idea of response is to offer perceptions of uncertainty, incompleteness, unfulfilled promises, unrealized opportunities, as motivation for more writing and therefore more learning about a subject as well as more successful communication of whatever has been learned.

The relationship between response and revision is important. In traditional practice, commenting on student writing is essentially a product-centered, evaluative activity resembling literary criticism. Students write "papers" so that teachers can describe their strengths and weaknesses, grading them accordingly. The papers are then, often, simply retired and new ones composed, presumably under the influence of recollected judgments of the previous ones. The assumption has been that evaluating products of composing is equivalent to intervening in the process. Teachers have concentrated, therefore, on retrospective appraisals of "finished" discourses, where students either do no rewriting at all or perform superficial copy-editing exercises to make their discourses conform to a teacher's Ideal Text. This emphasis on product encourages a directive style of commentary, the function of which is either simply to label the errors in writing or to define restrictively what a student would (or will) have to do in order to perfect it in the teacher's eyes. The following response to a sample of student writing suggests the character of a directive commenting style. It may seem an exaggerated instance, and perhaps it is. But both the essay and the comments are genuine, coming from an actual first-year college writing class.

> A lot of factors can contribute to the
> rejection of a student by a college. It   *This is obvious—*
> could be the student is not the type   *cut it out!*
> of youngster that the college wants,
> perhaps he/she did not do well on the
>   ^ or
> SATs or did not have a good high school
> recommendation.
> No matter what the reason is, a

rejected student should never feel sad

about it because being rejected is not
as ~~that~~ awful as people image. *Proofread! ¶ Start new paragraph with this idea* First of all,
avoid this — use many
all colleges are basically the same, but

once you made a choice of a few, you have
don't use you in a formal essay — you started with "student"
~~kind of~~ idealize it to be the kind of

college which is perfect for you, however

Whew! This should be 2 or 3 sentences.

it is not true! There are thousands of

colleges throughout the country, a lot

of them could be ~~very~~ suitable for you.

Therefore, do not intend to restrict
unnecessary — this weakens what you want to say.
yourself, go reach out to more colleges

and find a better one for yourself.
"a more suitable one" Maybe?

If the college of your choice is a

Use a dictionary!

highly-reputated and you get rejected
Do you really mean "Do not worry?"
by it, do not worry. Find yourself a
second choice college
rephrase —
~~lower-ranked one~~ and work hard in it,
often *a*
because it is easier to get high

RUN ON SENTENCE BREAK IT UP!

average in those schools, then you can

~~always~~ transfer back to ~~some really~~ *your first choice*
or perhaps
~~famous school, maybe you~~ can go to ~~their~~ *one of its*

graduate schools ~~later.~~

anymore, it is not totally a bad idea, *What?*

Unclear!

society is a wonderful college itself and

once you come out to work, you acquire

knowledge from it. You can also go back

like
to evening school if you ~~prefer to do so~~ */simplify!*

~~after working for a while.~~
everybody has
Finally, we all have disappointments
life
in our lives. Getting rejected by the

college of your choice is only a minor

one, most people, including ⟨me⟩ have — *keep yourself out*
of the essay.
and should survive it and ⟨take it   *This is a formal*
essay.

Is this
what you
mean?   easy.⟩

Your last ¶ should also restate that, as you have shown, there are
good reasons not to despair about rejection. Use the last ¶ to
tidy up the essay.

You're on the right track here, and your overall structure
of developing new ideas in each paragraph is pretty good.
But your writing becomes unhinged a bit within each ¶.
You need to work on expressing your ideas as simply as
possible – avoid unnecessary wording. (see my comments on
your second sentence for example.)

Also, watch your tendency to write run-on sentences.
For example, the second sentence of your second ¶ is
quite a mouthful and goes zig-zag all over the place.
Again, simplify!

Be sure you mean what you say. Don't use "it" if you
can avoid it. Be more definite with your words.

Finally, proofread and use a dictionary if you are
unsure of a spelling or word meaning. Errors in these
areas are annoying and teachers will mark you down
because of them.

Rewrite – be more careful, and good luck!

In the worst case, this essay with attached corrections would simply be put
away and the student would be expected to move on to the next assignment with
some memory of the mistakes committed earlier. But even if revision were
required, the writer would mainly be obeying the teacher's prescriptions about
structural and technical deficiencies, as though the text in its present form were a
fixed entity and the revising only a matter of making the product as respectable as
possible. Notice the authoritarian character of the teacher-critic's responses,
aiming in effect to take control of the writer's discourse: "This is obvious — cut it
out"; "don't use 'you' in a formal essay"; "start a new paragraph with this idea";
"simplify!" We could reconstruct this teacher's Ideal Text rather easily, but it's
more important to note how uncommunicative and how unresponsive to the
writer's perspective the teacher's comments are. Formal constraints, the teacher's
hobby-horse, are far more important than the writer's concern to make a state-

ment about being rejected by a college. Indeed, the first sentence of the teacher's end comment suggests that the "ideas" in the essay are adequate enough (which is really a way of dismissing them), and that the important matter is prose decorum. The teacher's confidence that this student somehow secretly understands the operative Ideal Text allows for comments such as "avoid unnecessary wording," "be sure you mean what you say," and "be more definite with your words," which are surely as incomprehensible to the student as Walter Shandy's discussion of auxiliary verbs was to Uncle Toby. An interesting question is, how much "better" would this writing be if all the local problems that bothered the teacher were removed? It seems to us that it would still be intellectually shallow and rhetorically immature, even if its newly polished surface covered the shallowness and immaturity with a somewhat more pleasing veneer. But the teacher's concern for a salvageable product rather than the writer's evolving meaning accounts for the directive preoccupation with veneer.

An alternative to directive commentary, a style that is valued in the writing workshop, is facilitative response, the purpose of which is to create motivation for immediate and substantive revision by describing a careful reader's uncertainties about what a writer intends to say. Here's the same student text with responses that are facilitative rather than directive.

How important are these factors? Do you imply that they are relative or that they don't always matter? Is your essay going to be about these factors?

A lot of factors can contribute to the rejection of a student by a college. It could be the student is not the type of youngster that the college wants, perhaps he/she did not do well on the SATs or did not have a good high school recommendation.

No matter what the reason is, a rejected student should never feel sad about it because being rejected is not that awful as people image. First of all, [all colleges are basically the same,] but once you made a choice of a few, you have kind of idealize it to the kind of college which is perfect

What criteria lead you to decide this? Size? Location? Program offerings? the kind of student body?

for you however it is not true! [There are thousands of colleges throughout the country, a lot of them could be very suitable for you.] Therefore, do not intend to restrict yourself, go reach out to [more colleges] and find a better one for yourself.

But if all colleges are the same, then aren't all of them equally suitable? why only "a lot"? Do you really believe they are all suitable? What might determine suitability?

← any old college?

If the college of your choice is a highly-reputated and you get rejected by it, do not worry, Find yourself a [lower-ranked one] and work hard in it, because it is easier to get high average in those schools, then you can always transfer back to some [really famous school], maybe you can go to their graduate schools later.

If some are "lower ranked" then in what sense are they all "the same."

Is this a difference between colleges?

If you feel as bad after being rejected that you do not feel like going to college anymore, it is not totally a bad idea, society is a wonderful college itself and once you come out to work, you acquire knowledge from it. You can also go back to evening school if you prefer to do so after working for a while.

Are you saying that it doesn't really matter? Do you believe that?

Finally, we all have disappointments in our lives. Getting rejected by the college of your choice is [only a minor one,] most people, including me, have and should survive it and take it easy.

For everyone? Would it be for you?

This sounds interesting – have you been rejected? Would it be worth talking about?

127

I can't tell whether your purpose here is just to make someone feel better or really to argue that all colleges are alike and that going or not going is an unimportant decision: in either case, do you really believe your statement? That is, would it make no difference if, for instance, you were forced to leave [the student's present school]? If so, why are you here now? Would you be just as happy at East Altuna Junior College in North Dakota? If you don't think you would, then do you think your reader would be consoled by what you say?

The comments of a facilitative reader are designed to preserve the writer's control of the discourse, while also registering uncertainty about what the writer wishes to communicate. The questions posed suggest the possibility of negotiation between writer and reader, leading to richer insights and more meaningful communication. [7] Negotiation assumes that the writer knows better than the reader the purposes involved, while the reader knows better than the writer the actual effects of authorial choices. The dialogue initiated by the comments (which may also be sustained by oral conversation) enables the writer to reflect on the connection between what was meant and what a reader has understood, using any difference between intent and effect as an incentive to test new choices. But importantly, the reader's engagement with the text is on a level similar to that of the writer's, namely, the level of meaning, line of reasoning, intellectual potentiality, thereby enabling dialogue and negotiation as opposed to editorial prescriptions. Emphasis is on the writer's developing understanding of the subject — in other words, the process of composing rather than the absolute quality of an achieved text. The comment on the writer's last sentence, for instance, concerning the somewhat veiled reference to a personal experience of rejection, suggests the possibility of a radically new focus to the writing, which the composer is free to consider though not constrained to adopt. Meanwhile, the end comment, which confesses the reader's uncertainty about the writer's purposes, suggests some of the problems of stance and intent which can lead to additional writing while avoiding the temptation to take control of choice-making from the writer by supplying a formula or direction for solving the problems. The writer and reader may, of course, discuss possibilities together, but the quality of a negotiated agreement to revise in one way as opposed to another depends on the teacher's skill at supporting the writer's exploration of alternatives while not directing its outcome.

Let's be clear about the difference between directive and facilitative commentary: it's not a difference between "form" response and "content" response, nor is it a difference between making statements about a text and just asking questions, nor is it a difference between being negative and being positive, that is, criticizing writers versus praising them. Responses to content can be as directive as responses to form: for instance, given the paper on college rejection, a teacher could say, "you need to give us an example of a college of high repute" or "colleges don't care about SATs, so omit the reference" — both plainly directive comments. Alternatively, facilitative responses can pertain to formal problems at times: for instance, "I can't tell what the 'it' in the second sentence of your second paragraph refers to, given the previous references to 'all colleges' and 'a few' colleges — are you thinking now of a single college?" Similarly, directive comments can take the shape of questions: "Is this a complete sentence?" means essentially "Change this into a complete sentence"; and facilitative comments can take the shape of assertions: "I don't see why you think being rejected by a college can be a beneficial experience." The distinction lies deeper than superficial comment form. Finally, criticism of what doesn't seem effective and support of what does can be found in both directive and facilitative commentary; they are equal parts of any healthy interaction between teachers and students, by no means parallel to the methodological distinction between giving directions in one style of commentary and characterizing a reader's uncertainties in the other. The essential difference between the two commenting styles is the degree of control over choices that the writer or the teacher retains. In directive commentary, the teacher says or implies, "Don't do it your way; do it *this* way." In facilitative commentary, the teacher says or implies, "Here's what your choices have caused me to think you're saying — if my response differs from your intent, how can you help me to see what you mean?" The essential difference — as is so often the case in the teaching alternatives we have been discussing — lies more in attitude and outlook than in perceivable changes of technique.

Of course, the majority of facilitative responses on the college rejection essay do take a question form and all of them happen to be "content" oriented. The tendency of a facilitative comment to take the form of a question is natural enough, since the reader's posture is probing and provocative, aimed at making a writer more reflective about the sufficiency of choices, rather than prescriptive about changes that must be made. But it's important to emphasize the posture beneath the surface appearance of a comment: attitude shapes practice, not the other way around. The content orientation is also natural, given the primitive, exploratory nature of the writing and given the priorities of the writing workshop — fluency, then clarity, then correctness. Doubtless, this writing has numerous formal and technical deficiencies: but it's also so far away from the copy-editing stage suggested by the comments of the teacher-critic that pointing out the deficiencies is superfluous. If the writer's ideas are not further developed, then none of the technical recommendations will make the writing any better than it is. On the other hand, if a next draft does substantially alter the writing in this earlier text, then many of the choices here will have been eliminated in the revision. We're not saying that form and technique are irrelevant and never to be responded to; we're only arguing that first things should come first, that a writer's on-going pursuit of meanings should be a teacher-reader's first consideration. As meanings emerge, as the relationship between intention and effect stabilizes, as successive revisions develop, narrower and more local concerns about structure and technical subtlety may well become appropriate. But the maturity of the writer and the intellectual/imaginative quality of his or her writing determine the usefulness of a more technical response: in general, the less real control of technique a writer possesses, the less intrusive should be the commentary on technical matters and the more conspicuous should be the response pertinent to emerging meanings.

The purpose, then, of facilitative commentary is to induce the reformulation of texts, the pursuit of new connections and the discovery of richer or more comprehensive meanings. By contrast, the main function of directive commentary is to make a given text look as good as it can. We would not suggest, however, that the mere presence of facilitative comments automatically leads to the substantive revision we have in mind. Without additional support, students will tend to make only the limited textual changes that directive responses elicit, even when the facilitative responses offer a fuller potential for new discovery. An inexperienced writer's natural tendency is to restrict revising to changes that minimally affect the plan and order of ideas with which she or he began, readily making only those adjustments that involve least pressure to reconceive or significantly extend the writing already done. This is not a matter simply of laziness. The resistance is normal, arising out of the anxiety that even experienced writers feel at having to reduce an achieved coherence, however inadequate, to the chaos of fragments and undeveloped insights from which they started. Practiced writers overcome their anxiety through habitual success in rewriting, but no such comforting pattern of successes exists to steady the resolve of the apprentice. Nor is this natural psychological resistance the only barrier to self-initiated revising. Another is the sheer difficulty of perceiving alternatives to the choices that have already been made, choices that lie reified as a document. The temptation is strong, even among experienced writers, to forget the arbitrariness of so many initial decisions about what to say, imagining in retrospect an inevitability about the patterns and connections that make up the existing discourse. Seeing through that apparent inevitability in order to recover additional options requires an intellectual discipline and a rhetorical awareness that unpracticed writers frequently have not acquired — indeed that they come to writing courses to develop.[8]

Perhaps the most concentrated effort in a writing workshop, therefore, is devoted to supporting substantive revision, for it is during revision that new learning is most likely to occur and competence most likely to develop. The first concern is to reveal to students, through the expectations implicit in facilitative responses, that "revision" does not mean copy-editing or, in general, making a given text more presentable. Nor does it mean superficial additions — "give more details," or subtractions — "this isn't relevant to your thesis," or redecorating — "move this paragraph to page 4." It means deeper intellectual penetration of a subject through additional composing, even to the point of repudiating earlier formulations altogether because subtler or more powerful insights have inspired new organizing principles and lines of reasoning. In-class writing to which students have not as yet committed major effort offers a good initial context for nurturing this view of revising. Making substantive changes is likely to entail less intimidation, less psychological resistance, when investment in a given text is still relatively small, as in the case of fifteen or twenty minutes of exploratory writing in class to be revised following comments from peers and the teacher-reader. Repeated short experiments in revision, with attentive teacher and peer support, can help create a willingness to try again, a strength of mind for reconceiving texts, which will carry over into larger-scale efforts. But encouragement remains equally necessary later, once students have become more willing to take chances. Writers need opportunities in workshop for discussing their rewriting plans with each other and with the teacher-reader. They need time to ask questions about responses and to test new choices on their readers. Less adventuresome or self-reliant students may need particular coaching — perhaps being encouraged to rewrite short statements with the instructor looking on and explaining his or her uncertainties about evolving meanings. Such activities are time-consuming, but there's no better way to spend the time. The revisions will be halting and inconsistently successful, especially at the start, but there's no more productive kind of failure, provided that what is emphasized is not the kinds and degree of failure but the glimmerings of communicative success.

Two awkward questions arise about the connection between facilitative commentary and the process of revision. Teachers naturally feel that their obligation in responding to writing is to locate the "major" problems or the most promising opportunities for change — hence, the first question: are there optimal responses that will help writers make the best possible revisions? At the same time, teachers often believe that the whole point of revision is to make texts better than they were in earlier versions — hence, the second question: shouldn't improvement from one draft to the next be expected as a sign both of commenting effectiveness and of writers' "progress" toward maturity? The insights of contemporary reader-response theory suggest some answers that will trouble teachers who expect the significant features of student writing and the degree of textual improvement to be readily and objectively verifiable. Louise Rosenblatt, first, and later Wolfgang Iser, David Bleich, and others,[9] have argued that all reading experiences entail transactions between reader and text, not a passive retrieval of meanings residing in the text and equally accessible to all careful observers, but an active creation of personal significances and impressions of quality based on individual responses. Readings are always, to a degree, idiosyncratic, dependent on the life-experiences, attitudes, feelings, beliefs, prejudices, which cause individuals to value different things and to construe in different ways. For reader-response theorists, therefore, the idea of a single "correct" or authoritative reading is problematic. Even highly experienced readers will view the same text differently, with dissimilar focuses of attention, various expectations, opposed notions about which textual cues are important or how they are important. The result is alternative but equally plausible transactions. Is there any reason to assume that responding to student writing entails more objectivity, less eccentricity, than responding to other texts? We think not.

So, our answer to the first question, in light of reader-response theory, is that there are no optimal responses, only more and less honest ones. Different readers find more or less meaning in different cues, and one teacher will view the potential in a student text differently from the way another does. Genuine personal reactions to a student's writing — for instance, the teacher's interest in the writer's own brush with disappointment in the college rejection essay — may not find duplication from reader to reader, but they are no less honest or potentially provocative for the writer's further efforts because of their individuality. Indeed, they are preferable to more formulaic, directive responses — for instance, to strike the reference to personal rejection as unsuited to the text's "main point" — which may well be dishonest in their overrestriction of valid lines of inquiry or development. Our answer to the second question is equally dependent on reader-response research: if different readers have alternative views of what is meaningful, valuable, interesting, or flawed in a text, then they will also have different notions about what would constitute "improvement" of that text. Teachers are sometimes tempted to correlate improvement with their personal preferences, to associate a student's willingness to follow directions with "better writing" on subsequent drafts. The chances are good, however, that no two teacher-readers will have the same opinion about how or why or the extent to which one draft of an essay is better than another. The perception of improvement in revised writing will always involve subjective, idiosyncratic judgments, even when the criteria for improvement include nothing subtler than avoiding surface errors and following teacher's directions about where or how to say things. Once richer criteria are also included, such as intellectual penetration of the subject, or quality of imaginative insight, or even closer proximity between intention and effect, the teacher's own consistency of judgment from student to student, essay to essay, is likely to deteriorate, let alone the consistency among different readers which would be required to assert an objective basis for evaluation. Since such a basis would be hard, if not impossible, to establish, teachers might be well-advised not to place such store in their powers of discernment as to expect that they can readily distinguish flawed from improved drafts. And if improvement is so difficult to perceive reliably, it seems pointless to depend on such a concept as the measure of commenting effectiveness. We would argue, instead, that once student writers have pursued worthwhile meanings through successive drafts, assisted by readers' personal reactions to the coherence, value, and communicative effectiveness of their developing discourses, their efforts have been successful by definition, because they serve the long-range goal of intellectual growth and the maturation of composing ability. Whether or not a second draft represents improvement over a first draft in some objective sense is not only extremely difficult to determine but is also irrelevant to the value of the process itself.

What follows is a student writer's revision of an earlier text in response to the facilitative commentary of a teacher-reader, illustrating our principal point that a writer's control of personal choices and opportunity to discover personal meanings are more important for growth than local textual "improvement," superficial or otherwise. Notice that the writer's basic strategy in her first attempt is to relate a particular, personal irritation — a roommate's smoking — to the general decline of morality in the world. It is this connection which the reader of her text will find not altogether plausible or rhetorically successful and which she will take greatest pains to reconceive in subsequent rewriting.

There are no morals left in this world. People smoke, drink, abuse courtesy, cheat, marry and have sex as freely as they like. What happened to being ashamed of misdeeds? It has become a world of excuses. If a person knows or feels he/she has done something immoral then they will excuse it with some sweeping statement.

This is not a revolutionary idea but it has been brought to my mind most severely by a recent example. Unfortunately I live with this example everyday. It is my roommate and she smokes.

Of all things dear to me on this earth, the air I breathe is one and I simply can't tolerate cigarette smoke. It is one of the most offensive circumstances I could be amongst.

When I first found out she was a smoker I was aghast. I could not believe I was to live with such a monster when I had made it clear on my roommate questionnaire that I could not and would not live with a smoker. No way, absolutely not. What I had not accounted for was the trouble involved in switching rooms. Of course I didn't find out until a few days after I was well situated. By that time I was assured of the terrific personality of this girl and not thrilled with any of my other choices. In other words I didn't think I could find a nicer roommate and therefore relegated myself to living with the smoke.

The reason I find it immoral is because my roommate is a pre-med student. She studies nothing but chemistry and biology all day long. If anyone would be aware of smoking's hazards, she would. Yet time and time again she lights up in response to some nervous habit. In total disregard of herself and others. Her friends are the same and often congregate in her tiny room filling it with a sickening haze of smoke. How can they live like this? They weren't born smoking. It's such an unnatural behavior — to inhale fumes and fire — that I don't see how it is even adopted. The mere thought of it, to me, is revolting. In fact I've never been confronted with it more in my life than since I moved to New York City. I had thought smoking was dying out. You carried a stigma if you smoked or at least I could say you were probably uncomfortable with your habit.

That is not the case in New York City. Here everyone smokes. No wonder you can't see the stars from the city. There's too much smog. And who creates that smog? the exact same people who smoke because it's chic and to calm themselves down. . . .

These people anger me that they are so selfish, but in this melting pot of immorality they find the word go. Someone even set fire accidently to a trash can in my dorm! It is absurd. . . . If someone as aware of life systems as a medical student is, smokes, then I think the morals of everything are deteriorating because it goes much deeper than that. Smoking is just another example that's indicative of the deterioration.

Perhaps the rules and standards become more lax as life itself toughens. That is not due cause though. Why doesn't everyone straighten up and try to be strong and individualistic about personal matters instead of throwing care to the wind? We have allowed ourselves to become a mass of contradictions.

Here's the teacher-reader's response, a single comment at the end of the writer's text. Notice that it probes the sufficiency of the writer's conclusions, her possibly overzealous connection of smoking to a general moral decline and her seeming self-righteousness in condemning the weaknesses of others. Naturally, the reader could have commented on any number of issues in the text: the response he chose to make is neither better nor worse than another in its focus, though it's a strategic response in its facilitative character, designed to keep the writer writing by drawing attention to something perceived as problematic in her argument.

You seem to me to be saying that there's no more morality left in the world. You exemplify your belief with reference to your roommate's smoking. You seem to be puzzled about why anyone would pick up this immoral habit and thrust it upon innocent victims like yourself. You wonder why knowledgeable and bright people would even consider smoking.

My central question is why do you link smoking with morality? Is smoking really a misdeed equivalent to illicit sex and cheating? Is smoking as terrible as stealing? If so, would you explain why? I have known some kind and generous people who happened to smoke. Should I consider them to be as terrible as rapists and wife-beaters?

I can understand how your roommate mistreated you by smoking and allowing her friends to smoke in your room. But does this mean that the world is as bad as you say it is, that everything has gone to the dogs? I agree that smoking is unhealthy, but do you think your roommate is intentionally trying to poison herself and you? Have you considered the issue from her point of view, considering that it may not be a simple matter to quit? Would it be helpful to try to understand her motivation before abruptly condemning her behavior?

Since the writer had been encouraged to respond to the teacher's commentary if she wanted to, she offered the following statements along with her revision (the Pamela she refers to was a member of her class). Notice its tone: clearly, the writer believes that she remains in control of her own discourse and asserts responsibility for her authorial choices. She even feels free to fault the reader for defensiveness (presumably at the implied condemnation of his own smoking friends)!

Thank you for your comments on my draft. Your comments combined with my group's were helpful. Pamela's reaction to my paper was unexpected. She thought that my emotions were overriding the theme of the work. She suggested that I remove the flaming comments directed towards my anti-smoking theme. So I put aside my personal feelings and concentrated on the event.

But your reactions to my paper, defensive as they were, proved to me that it is impossible to divorce emotion from content. Now that I have finished the paper I believe it has lost some of the brimstone that I originally intended. So, Pamela's point of view does seem valid in lessening potential reader alienation.

Otherwise, any issue as to whether it is morally right or not, is beyond the intent of my paper and not within my grasp at this point. I would still appreciate your comments on my revised draft especially on those points which do not concern my views on smoking.

Here, finally, is the new text, in which the problematic connection between smoking and morality has given way before a new concern, which may or may not have arisen directly from the reader's response, for the writer's efforts to accommodate herself to a roommate whose smoking habit she finds distateful.

Moving away to school in a new city can involve many dramatic and new situations. I expected to be confronted by quite a few when I went away to college in New York City. Having always had trouble getting along with other people, I was told by many that I'd have to learn to bend and not be upset so easily. So I spent the months prior to moving away trying to prepare myself for the idiosyncrasies of a roommate or roommates that would greatly annoy me. I considered the roommate who would leave the room unlocked, the roommate who charged exorbitant long distance phone calls and the roommate who outright didn't like me. For all of these I had a solution, except, the roommate who smoked. For that, I was to learn, there is no resolve.

I first found out she was a smoker on moving-in-day, where I saw, amongst her possessions, an ashtray. I was aghast. I could not believe I was to live with such a monster when I had thought I made it absolutely clear on my roommate questionnaire that I could not and would not live with a smoker. Of all things dear to me on this earth, the air I breathe is one, and I simply can't tolerate cigarette smoke. I find it to be one of the most offensive mannerisms anyone can have and am immediately incensed by the presence of it.

Yet even though I hold a strong opinion against smoking, I am also too cowardly to tell most people. I am more likely to remain uncomfortable than complain to someone. But never in my wildest dreams, did I think I would actually have to live with a smoker every day for a year. Maybe if I had found out sooner, I could have made it my first opportunity to publicly voice my stand. As it happened though, I didn't find out she smoked until two hours after I had found a place for everything I had ever owned and given it a name too. That really threw water on my anti-smoking fire because if I wanted to change roommates, I would have to switch rooms entirely. According to the Housing Office, this was impossible. So I gritted my teeth and decided to stick it out.

Being stuck there didn't stop me from contriving plans to get my roommate to stop. I thought of everything from making her feel bad to threatening to tell her mother she smoked. I even considered a curfew pro-rated by half hours where I thought I might at least make some money from my suffering.

Eventually though, my roommate and I became very good friends, and I became concerned I would offend her by complaining. The smoking seemed trivial to her wonderful personality, and I was sure I couldn't have been placed with a better, more compatible roommate. As the semester progressed and the workload toughened, I noticed a dramatic increase in her smoking, especially when she was in large groups of people or friends. This was very upsetting for two reasons: (1) I didn't think I could tolerate it anymore and (2) because she rarely smoked when alone. Not only that, but she and her friends are all pre-med students. Of all people to smoke, why would those who study life and the body allow themselves to smoke? I found it very sad that they, in particular, smoke, because if they don't care, then why should anyone else care? It began to sadden me as well as anger me that she disregarded her own health and mine.

Smoking is more than just harmful; it's a selfish and filthy habit. Her friends often congregate in her tiny room, filling it with a sickening haze of smoke. Finding cigarette butts and ashes hidden among the dirt of your ficus tree can be infuriating. Watch smokers invent things to use as an ashtray, even themselves. Watch smokers try to carry something, get dressed, or eat with a cigarette in hand. They look absolutely foolish and act as if the cigarette is dearer than life itself. They'll even go so far as to hold hot ashes in their hands or burn holes in their clothes. For this, I say it is a selfish habit because it is self-satisfying that they allow the cigarettes to make fools of them.

Unfortunately, I can't change the world by myself. I can't stop everyone from smoking and a lot of people in New York smoke, so this isn't the place to start anyway. I also don't have the right to force my opinion upon another, only to present it.

Consequently, my schemes have been to no avail. My roommate still smokes at least a pack a day. Several days ago, I confided in an old friend who has a mother who smokes. I told him of my desire to end her vile habit. It seems I must continue to be upset by it because he bluntly told me to forget about trying. He spent eighteen years trying to convince his mother to stop and speaks from experience. So I too will end this crusade and hope that my roommate will at least exercise some courtesy in the future. But next year on moving day, I will ask before I unpack my bags.

In this instance, then, a writer has substantially altered a text in response to facilitative comments from a teacher-reader and fellow student. She has not followed directive instructions for "making her writing better" but has used a reader's reactions as the stimulus to look more deeply into issues she wishes to address. How confident could any teacher be, however, that the second text represents an "improvement" on the first? We asked a group of teachers to offer their impressions of the quality of the two essays and then give reasons for finding one better than the other. Here are some opinions. One reader said, "I like the first essay better — I'd give the student an A — it's entertaining and it makes the point from a very personal perspective about how a non-smoker feels about smoking. Essay 2 I'd give an A-. It's more factual and 'correct' in style and also gets the point across — but it lacks sparkle. I like pieces that entertain me as well as inform me." A second reader said, "The first essay contains fragmented ideas. In one part it speaks of immorality and in the next of the inability to tolerate cigarette smoke. The second essay systematically describes the writer's experience of leaving home and tolerating the idiosyncracies of a roommate. The first essay jumps around. The second flows nicely. Its theme develops consistently and the writer uses more complex sentences in a more coherent manner. Essay one — D, essay two — A." And a third reader said: "Essay one — C, essay two — B-. As a reader I am offended by the assumptions and assertions that create the context in the first essay. I feel insulted by the writer because she is asking me to take seriously totally unsubstantiated premises. Essay two has problems, particularly as far as sequencing goes, but the framework is legitimate. The writer is clearly engaged in this issue and I respect that effort." We could multiply these responses to show even more disagreement about grades (essay one: from D to A-; essay two: from C + to A), and about perceptions of superiority (from one is better than two, to one and two are about the same, to two is better than one), and about reasons for viewing each text one way as opposed to another. But the point seems clear already, and will become clearer in Chapter 7 when we discuss evaluation: readers' interactions with texts are complex and multifaceted, based on too many variables to allow any easy definition of the criteria on which "improvement" should be based. What matters, however, is not one person's estimate of improvement or degeneration, but the process of writing, responding, and writing again.

If the inescapable limitation of reader subjectivity serves to qualify the value of teacher's responses, it serves also to enhance the value of peer responses. In the writing workshop, the responsibility for facilitative response does not lie solely with the teacher. Peer response is fully as important, a crucial class activity. The concern in a workshop is to give writers access to the reactions of as many readers as possible, multiplying perspectives, introducing legitimate differences of opinion, and portraying the broadest possible range of effects that a given discourse can have on diverse readers. Writers confronted with these diverse reactions learn over time to gauge and anticipate the impact of their choices, forming in their own minds a Questioning Reader, comprised of recollections of all the actual responses they have experienced, which sharpens their critical sense and guides future composing. The style of facilitative commentary which a teacher-reader brings to student texts in the workshop serves also as a model for students' conversations among themselves about their writing. That is, peer groups discuss writing as an effort to make and communicate meanings. Members of a group identify and, when possible, explain for the writer's benefit the impact that a text has on their view of a subject and on their awareness of the writer's stance toward it. They discuss both the issues that a text raises and also the choices in the text that cause those issues to appear the way they do or to affect a reader in the way they do. Student-readers offer their opinions along with the teacher, collaborating to present the writer with a provocative range of responses from which to infer what else to say, what more to do, in order to convey personal intentions in satisfying ways.[10]

But two complaints frequently arise in connection with peer responses. The first is that, just as students lack the expertise to write effectively, so too they lack the expertise to comment on the writing of others. The second complaint, an extension of the first, is that not all the responses of group members have equal use or even equal validity and that the confusion sabotages instruction. To an extent, of course, students are inexpert at examining and communicating the impact a text has had on them. But the inexperience does not mean that students have no reactions to what they read or have the wrong reactions. Rather, students have typically had few opportunities to articulate their reactions or to discover that what they have to say might be valuable and pertinent. One reason for the denial of opportunity has been the assumption of teachers that "expertise" means knowledge of formal and technical conventions, rather than the more common sort of reader reaction focused on what a writer wishes to communicate and how the communication is affecting a particular individual. All readers, educated or not, technically conscious or not, respond to what they read and can, with opportunity and practice, articulate their response. Since facilitative commentary in the classroom parallels this common variety of reader interaction with a text, there's no more reason to assume students' inability to react usefully to each other's work than there is to assume that they do not have legitimate and meaningful experiences of literature or other kinds of reading. Granted, they require practice at conveying what a text has done to them, and a workshop strives to provide that experience. But with practice students become quite adept at characterizing their responses, though naturally the quality of response varies in proportion to their degrees of intellectual maturity. Not all students react subtly or richly, but their reactions are not for that reason false or unhelpful. Indeed, they may at times have more pertinence to the writer, who is after all another student, than the teacher's observations will have, being perhaps more sophisticated but also, often, less comprehensible.

The second objection — that students' responses disagree and are sometimes opposed to the teacher's — derives from the dubious assumption that teachers' judgments of texts are inevitably correct and may therefore serve as the measure of what else can legitimately be said. And this assumption derives in turn from teachers' experiences in traditional classrooms, where no one present has sufficient authority to challenge the master's pronouncements. If a group of teachers were to sit together in a peer discussion of the features and merits of a discourse, the likelihood of even rough agreement of views would be minimal, as we have shown in connection with the "smoking" essay. There would be argument, differing perspectives, even inaccuracy, personal prejudice, and obstinate refusals to hear alternative possibilities. Which of these peers has the "right" opinion? To answer "the most experienced one" is to invite more argument and more insistence on personal opinions. The fact is, no one has access to the Absolute Reading of a text, and everyone will occasionally err in voicing opinions even about technical matters, let alone the validity of a line of reasoning or the sufficiency of a manner of presentation. Students should learn to be as wary of teachers' comments as they are about those of other students, as willing to sort the useful from the frivolous, just as one experienced writer is invariably cautious about the opinions of another. Error surrounds all of us and all of us blunder into it. So, the first reason to tolerate student disagreement and even apparent mistakes of judgment is the humble realization that our own hobby-horses can interfere with clear perception too, that we are neither invariably right in what we say nor invariably right about whether our students are right. A second reason to tolerate it is the additional recognition that diversity is healthy and provocative, that the truth lies in negotiation, in compromise, in the mutual challenging of opinions, and in a willingness to concede that others will occasionally have insights superior to our own — even perhaps others with less experience.

Again, however, students require practice at articulating their own views because they are not, as a rule, accustomed to this degree of intellectual responsibility, or familiar with the possible varieties of response, or with the value that feedback can have for writers. At the start, therefore, peer reactions will often be formulaic ("I liked this"), traditional ("You need more details" or "This word is misspelled"), and rather stifled. A teacher who wishes to have students respond productively begins by dramatizing the style in her own talk while also encouraging students to trust that their reactions will be as valuable, as pertinent, as listened to, as her own. By modeling facilitative commentary in the workshop, she can lead students to adopt a similar style. Given an environment of mutual intellectual respect and encouragement, students will gradually overcome the reticence built up over years of enforced classroom silence. Here's an example of student interaction in a workshop where that supportive environment has been developed. The transcript below offers part of an extended conversation that members of a peer group in a college-level writing class carried on with the writer of the following short text. In the transcript, "W" refers to the writer, while "A," "B," and "C" refer to other participants in the conversation.[11]

> Just a minute ago, I was in Gristede's buying a Coke when I saw a man taking a 7-Up from the refrigerator and putting it in his pocket. Then he was in front of me in line at the register and he paid for one 7-Up but the other was snuggled away. I could see into his jacket and the top of a little vodka bottle was peeking out. Those tariff labels are all the same. Then I saw him in the elevator and he was obviously very inebriated. He began to shout GOING UP! and he stood in the middle of the elevator with his feet in second position parallel trying to stabilize himself. I felt strange. Should I have said something at the store? I just winced when I saw him stick the soda in his pocket and I felt a flash flood of remorse, compassion, and anger. I fought the urge to be righteous. Am I a coward? Or am I just tired?

> A: Was there only one incident like that? The first one you've ever had like that?
> W: Yeah.
> B: But did it occur to you that . . .
> W: Yeah, right before class . . .
> B: that the guy might be really poor?
> W: Oh! Yeah, I thought about that too, but . . .
> A: If you were revising that, would it be as spontaneous?
> W: Well, I know what I'd do — I'd elaborate a lot. I'd describe what the man looked like; I'd change the tone and . . .
> B: But what about the frantic thoughts, the moment, what was going through your head while it was happening. You weren't *thinking* about what he was wearing, were you?
> W: No, that's true, but I . . .
> A: Then, uh, your only impression was that he was being a thief?
> B: What bothered you was that he stole it?
> W: Not just that.
> B: Didn't it bother you that he was an alcoholic?
> W: Well, my concentration was on how I dealt with the man. My choices. I could have said something to the man at the cash register. But I didn't.

A: Would it have scared you to do that?

W: No, I've dealt with it before — people who've stolen. Like when I was in high school, these guys I knew, they were vandalizing and stealing stuff and I went and told them that I thought that was really crass and they were going "Oh, Maria, you think you're so righteous" and like that and so I talked to my teacher and he said he'd done something like that once — telling someone to stop ripping stuff off and the next day he got his tires slashed. But this thing — well, I could go at it a few ways...

B: You could dwell on the feeling.

C: What about the thing with the vandals in your school? Does that fit in somewhere? I thought that was interesting. But would it change the focus?

W: It would get back to — an open letter to myself about guilt and being cowardly and choice. That would be a fine approach except I don't like the idea that writing is self-referential. Do you know what I'm saying? All those papers that are just "I this" and "I that" and so on. It's so boring to read that sort of stuff.

B: The reader could learn a lot from your feelings. He can see how it is for others.

A: Yes. Everyone asks themselves the same question in that situation — should I? shouldn't I?

W: Yeah, I guess. Well, I have to think about it. I'm not real sure about how I want to do it yet.

These oral student responses are distinctive for their serious intellectual tone, suggesting the students' recognition that they have both the ability and the authority to help a writer discover ways to explore a subject further. The "rightness" or comprehensiveness or maturity of the responses is at most a subordinate issue: the writer must come to personal conclusions about what is helpful and what is not. From a teaching point of view, what matters is that the writer is privy to authentic and legitimate reactions of interested readers, which helps to clarify the sense of purpose and presentation with reference to questions and uncertainties those readers have seen fit to raise. Through dialogue, the writer can begin to develop an internal Questioning Reader, regardless of whether the responses of eighteen-year-olds are more or less expert than those of the teacher-reader (who will, in any case, have been responding also). Of course, student reactions can be written as well as oral, and can take place outside of classes as well as during the workshop. Here's an instance of written response, where students have broken into pairs in order to take turns in writer and reader roles. The student whose writing appears below appended to her complete first draft some personal estimates of what the choices in the text, paragraph by paragraph, were designed to achieve. What follows is, first, the entire draft, and then, the student's appraisal of her choices:[12]

As I started toward Beauty Therapy's door, the receptionist, Joan saw me and buzzed the door so I could open it. I pushed it open and as I walked in, I felt all eyes look up at me and all the girls left what they were doing to focus their attention on me.

I had just come from playing tennis so I was dressed in my white Tacchini warm-up suit with its navy and red stripes down the sides and my new Puma sneakers. My hair was up in a ponytail with a bandana tied under my bangs; I hate to sweat in my bangs.

I was wearing the usual thick mascara and lipstick. It was an ordinary Friday and everybody around was on display for each other as usual.

I hung up my Flatbush jacket and found an empty chair to sit in until Luda was ready to give me my manicure. I said hello to most of the girls who happened to be my friends or at least my acquaintances. After all, everybody in the community knows each other or at least who belongs to the community.

The women and younger girls were gossiping about the most important things in life; how many carats Mary's diamond ring is; Sally lost five pounds; Rochelle's outfit was seen in Bonwit Teller for $500; Denise and Robert were seen together three times which means that they must be getting engaged soon; and of course 134 is the prettiest nailpolish color for this time of year.

I thought the whole scene was amusing this Friday, while I had never before realized how trivial and silly the conversation really was. Luda called me to sit down and she began filing my nails.

My mind drifted for a while and I found myself wondering what it would be like living outside the community. I wouldn't be on display anywhere I went and I would have more privacy.

I would probably be close to my family like I am now, and we would probably live the same exact way. The difference would be that our lives wouldn't be open to all for discussion. We would still have a few select friends. The difference would be that everybody around wouldn't know what jewelry my mother owned or who I went out with.

But then who would I marry? My whole way of thinking is geared toward the family life available only in a close, tight-knit community. We are all similar to each other: religion-wise, financially, and most importantly, we want the same things out of life. Maybe that is why divorce is so uncommon in my community. No. I would never be able to live outside the community. I love it and need it too much; despite its faults. The farthest I'll ever get from the community will probably be living in the city my first year of marriage, and I'll probably come home to my mother's house for weekends then too.

I was unconsciously glancing at the various nailpolish colors deciding which to choose when I heard the door buzz. All eyes looked up to see who was entering the salon, what she was wearing, and waiting to hear what she had to say. Deep down inside, I was no different than the rest of the girls.

Paragraphs 1 and 2

I'm describing going to Beauty Therapy. The reader has no idea what it is except that there are girls there. They all looked up at me when I entered the place and I felt as if I was on display. I explain my routine tennis outfit to let the reader picture the scene and comment that although it was an ordinary Friday, I felt silly this week. The reader still doesn't know why I'm describing this, so they'll have to read on.

Paragraph 3

Beauty Therapy is apparently a manicure salon and I happened to know most of the girls there because they belong to my community. I am sarcastic about the fact that those in the community know who "belongs" in the community. I think the reader will wonder "What community"? But I hope that by reading on they'll find out.

Paragraphs 4 and 5

The girls were gossiping about other girls in the community and I was out of it. It all seemed so trivial to me and the reader can see why. The girls weren't talking about anything really significant. But the reader can see from these paragraphs that the girls know a lot about each other and it must be a tight-knit community. Who they are or where they come from, the reader still doesn't know.

Paragraph 6

I wondered what life would be like living outside the community and state that it would be much more private. I assume that I would still be close to my family. This is a normal assumption involving keeping some part of my present identity.

Paragraph 7

I'm finally asking the questions that a reader would ask. What is my community? Why do I live there? It sounds like a place where your life is an open book to all. I hope my reader will keep on and find out why I do live here.

Paragraph 8

I stop dreaming about life outside this (unknown) community. I claim that I will probably live there despite its disadvantages. The reader can easily see the disadvantages, but probably has no idea of what the community's assets are. What *is* the community? Who are these people? How many members? Where do they live? How did I become a part of the community? Why would I want to live there voluntarily? How long has the community been in this unknown place? What makes them a community? The reader doesn't know the answers to these questions. My advice to myself is to either get out of the community or come up with some good substantial reasons to stay there.

Paragraph 9

A girl walks into the place and all eyes look up to "check her out." I do the same. I realize that I am just like the rest of the girls in this community. A gossip! The community sounds really shallow in this paper and that's not what I intended.

The writer's text was then given to a student reader but without the writer's attached commentary. The reader was asked to estimate and characterize personal responses to the text, paragraph by paragraph, just as the writer had done. Here are the results:

Paragraph 1

Deborah walked into somewhere; place is not described. She is just starting her essay. I feel confused and must read on. I guess that's a normal feeling so far.

Paragraph 2

Deborah describes her outfit and appearance exactly and says that in this unknown place called Beauty Therapy, everyone is on display. Really, for all I know at this point, it could even be a house of prostitution. Why she explains her outfit in detail, I don't know.

Paragraph 3

Deborah now says that she's in a manicure place. Friends and acquaintances are there and now she hints that everyone knows each other in her community. This makes me think, are the friends the girls who are on display for each other? And what community? (even though I know). Still it's only the beginning of the essay, and it hasn't really gotten off the ground yet, so I'll wait and see what happens.

Paragraph 4

There's a hint of sarcasm here insinuating how shallow these friends and acquaintances are. I still am striving to understand what she's trying to say.

Paragraph 5

This is saying that the usual conversations that used to seem normal, now seem trivial. I am now starting to see the essay beginning to focus on something.

Paragraph 6

Deborah starts to think about what it would be like to live outside her community. It would mean having more privacy. All I know is that Deborah's community has no privacy and that people are on display, with their trivial conversations. This seems like a heck of a community. Poor Deborah — what a place to live. (Of course, I know she likes living there, so that means she's not letting her reader see the good side yet.)

Paragraph 7

Deborah assumes that her family life would stay the same. How does she know this? Also, she again says that lives wouldn't be open to all for discussion and everybody wouldn't know everything. All this community sounds like is a bunch of Rona Barretts gossiping all day long. What kind of horrible community is this, anyway?

Paragraph 8

Why is family available only in a tight-knit community? There is another assumption that's not backed up. Deborah says that the people/community are all similar and she loves it and could never live without it, despite its faults. Well, all I heard about this community in this essay so far is that they're close-knit and gossipers. What *are* the community's good points? How many people live there? Why are they called a community? The word community is used very often, but for all I know we could be talking about close-knit, gossipy werewolves.

Paragraph 9

Deborah uses a little example to show that she's just like the rest of the girls. Looking up and waiting to hear gossip in the manicure place.

Overall Response

Well, well. Deb — I think I know what you're trying to say and it's a great idea — but look what you make the community out to be! What is "community"? How can anyone *feel* anything for this when everything is so vague? If you were to build and zero in on your major ideas, not on what you're wearing, then the reader might catch on right away. What if you changed the beginning a little and said you walked into your usual manicure place and overheard two women gossiping about someone. If you really zero in on the trivial gossiping conversation you heard in detail, the reader could understand why you felt so annoyed. Then you could say something like how, even though the community is this and that (but you have to explain the community in detail so the reader can have something to hang on to), it's still a good place to live. You could explain that despite the pressure and the competition between people, we all help each other. You could tell how we built the center and the Hillel School — the good points. When you said you could never live without your community as a reader I had to say "why" because, based on what you'd said, I'd get out as fast as possible. But if you build up an impression of the community for the reader, then the whole thing will make more sense. I still don't see why you went to all the trouble to describe your outfit.

Notice how frequently the writer and reader raise similar questions about the text, suggesting points of agreement about where change might be desirable. Notice too where perceptions differ, creating the possibility of discussion and negotiation. Working together, the writer and reader compared their separate appraisals and talked over opportunities for revision. The writer then attempted a second draft in which she tried to make the purposes for writing more apparent in light of the student-reader's uncertainties. Here's that second draft.

As I started toward Beauty Therapy's door, the receptionist, Joan, saw me and buzzed the door so I could open it. I pushed it open and as I walked in, I felt all eyes look up at me and all the girls left what they were doing to focus their attention on me.

I had been too busy to get a manicure for weeks, but this week I managed to squeeze in the hour. I had just come from playing tennis, so I was dressed in my white Tacchini warm-up suit with its navy and red stripes down the sides and my new Puma sneakers. My hair was up in a ponytail with a white bandana tied under my bangs; I hate to sweat in my bangs. I was wearing the usual thick mascara and pink lipstick. It was an ordinary Friday and all the girls were on display for each other as usual. The difference was in me — I felt as if the whole scene was funny this week.

I hung up my Flatbush jacket and found an empty chair to sit in until Luda was ready to give me my manicure. I said hello to most of the girls who happened to be my friends or at least my acquaintances. After all, everybody in the community knows each other or at least who belongs to the community.

The women and younger girls were gossiping about the most important things in life: how many carats Mary's diamond ring is; Sally lost five pounds; Rochelle's outfit was seen in Bonwit Teller for $500. Denise and Robert were seen together three times which means that they must be getting engaged soon; and of course 134 is the prettiest nailpolish color for this time of year.

I thought the whole scene was amusing this Friday, while I had never before realized how trivial and silly the conversation really was. Luda called me to sit down and she began filing my nails.

My mind drifted for a while, and I found myself wondering what it would be like living outside the community. I wouldn't be on display anywhere I went and I would have more privacy. I would probably be close to my family like I am now, and we would probably live in the same lifestyle. The difference would be that our lives wouldn't be open to all for discussion. We would still have a few select friends. However, I strongly doubt that everybody around would know what jewelry my mother owned or who I went out with.

I began to fancy the idea of living outside the community and I started getting worried. Wait a minute! Why is the community so great? Why does my family choose to live here rather than anywhere else in the world? My mind wandered back to the beginning.

The "community" started about seventy years ago when my grandparents, along with many other Syrian Jews, left Syria and immigrated into the United States. They all came penniless, since conditions were terrible in Syria at that time and they could rarely sell their homes or furniture if they were leaving the country. Many owned nothing but the shirts on their backs — literally.

These Syrian immigrants started their new lives in the lower East Side in New York. They began as peddlers of the textile industry — they sold linens, tablecloths, towels. Since they were very poor, most of the Syrians worked six days a week (they didn't work on Sabbath — the day of rest), from early in the morning until late at night. Their ambition, along with G-d's help, caused them to build up their financial status gradually. Soon these Syrian Jews were able to move to a nicer neighborhood in Brooklyn. Those Syrians who became wealthy invested or loaned their money to other Syrians. After many years of hard work, the Syrian "community" became very wealthy.

These nouveau riche people changed in certain ways, as would be expected, but they never forgot the important elements that kept them together. The synagogue never ceased to play a major role in the Syrians' lives — the Chief Rabbi married their children and he would teach and lecture the community about some new topic every Saturday in synagogue. The synagogue would hold drives every so often in order to raise money to build a yeshivah exclusively for the Syrian children. After much effort and money donations, Magen David Yeshivah was established. It is this school that ensured the educating of the youth in the manner desired. Basic tenets of Judaism were taught as well as Syrian customs. The Syrian method of praying differs from that of other Jews — in melody and even in the pronunciation of many of the Hebrew letters. Magen David helped keep many traditions that without it would definitely have disappeared.

The community continued to live in Brooklyn, except by now, many families were able to renovate or redecorate their homes, thus enhancing the beauty of the area.

The most important factor that kept the Syrians together was the shunning of intermarriage. According to Jewish law, a Jew can marry any Jew. The Syrians tend to take this law one step further. They even frown upon a Syrian marrying a Jew from outside the community. This may sound snobbish or narrow-minded, but this key factor seems necessary to maintain the Syrian traditions and customs: the spicy food; the Syrian tradition of naming the first born son after the father's father and the first daughter after the father's mother; the phrases in Syrian that became part of their everyday conversations. All this sets the community apart from others.

Now, seventy years later, the community has grown tremendously. Approximately 35,000 people belong to the community. There are various new schools, synagogues, and Syrian stores to accommodate this quickly growing group. A recent addition is a Community Youth Sports Center — a new place for Syrian youth to congregate and meet.

The other day my sister Michele came running home from the center screaming, "Mom, I just met the most gorgeous hiloow (handsome; sweet) boy and he asked me out! His name is David Cohen. Can I go? Please?" At the mere mention of his name, my mother figured out who his family is. She teased my sister and said, "Is that the David Cohen who has two brothers, one sister, and he lives a couple of blocks away from us?" My mother knew more about the boy than Michele did herself. Of course, a Syrian girl must spend a great deal of time with a boy before she gets married, but a great advantage of the community is that it eliminates a lot of the preliminaries that other people must go through. There are usually no "deep dark secrets" that we find out about later. Maybe that is why divorce is so rare in the community.

I stopped myself and thought — how can I have ever doubted the community? This is the only place I know of where I would want to raise a family. We are protective of one another. I love the community and need it too much; despite its faults. My G-d! With so many women living so close to each other, who know so much about one another, how can there not be gossip? As of now, I think that the farthest I'll ever get from the community will probably be living in the City my first year of marriage, and I'll probably come home to my mother's house for weekends then too.

I was unconsciously glancing at the various nailpolish colors, deciding which to choose, when I heard the door buzz. I watched all eyes look up to see who was entering the salon, what she was wearing, and waiting to hear what she had to say. Deep down inside I was no different than the rest of the girls because I too looked up.

In response to the reader's observations, the writer has included a lengthy passage on the "community" mentioned rather mysteriously in draft one, feeling the necessity to elaborate on her desire to remain a member despite its faults. At the same time, however, she does not regard the reader's comments as instructions for change: she retains her description of the tennis outfit, for example, despite the reader's confusion about it. The point is, a student-reader has responded facilitatively and productively to a writer's effort, enhancing the writer's awareness of opportunities for deeper understanding and for sharpened clarity of intention. When this support is supplemented by the responses of a teacher-reader, still further possibilities for development are likely to emerge. There are certainly many other ways of enabling students to join with teachers in the process of responding to texts in order to promote additional writing. We are content to leave methodological variation to the imaginations of teachers who accept and wish to proceed from the philosophical premises we have introduced. Methods are important, but attitudes are more important. The teacher who devises a check-list of critical items — "is the introduction interesting?"; "does every paragraph have a single idea?" — and who distributes the list to peer groups so that students can mechanically evaluate each other's writing according to the teacher's Ideal Text has altogether missed our point. Making students accomplices in a traditional instructional activity is not equivalent to leading them toward intellectual freedom and responsibility. The philosophical attitude governing *any* method restricts that method within the limitations of that perspective.

Notes

[1] A recent study has shown that more than half of the teachers it surveyed restricted their commentary on student writing to narrowly technical corrections, while practically no teachers offered substantive responses intended to encourage revision. See Dennis Searle and David Dillon, "The Message of Marking: Teacher Written Responses to Student Writing at Intermediate Grade Levels," *Research in the Teaching of English*, 14 (October 1980), 233-42. On the limitations of technical correction, see W. U. McDonald, "The Revising Process and the Marking of Student Papers," *College Composition and Communication*, 24 (May 1978), 167-70.

[2] Nancy Sommers has pointed out the uncommunicative nature of typical responses to student writing in "Responding to Student Writing," *College Composition and Communication*, 33 (May 1982), 148-56.

[3] The concept of Ideal Text, and the argument related to the Lindbergh essay, are developed in Lil Brannon and C.H. Knoblauch, "On Students' Rights to Their Own Texts: A Model of Teacher Response," *College Composition and Communication*, 33 (May 1982), 157-66.

[4] Study after study has shown the futility of this method of responding to writing, students' subsequent efforts revealing little or no change as a result of the commentary. See, for instance, in addition to Searle and Dillon, R.J. Marzano and S. Arthur, "Teacher Comments on Student Essays: It Doesn't Matter What You Say," a study conducted at the University of Colorado, Denver, in 1977 (ERIC ED 147864). For a review of several studies, all reporting negative results, and an argument for the reasons, see C.H. Knoblauch and Lil Brannon, "Teacher Commentary on Student Writing: The State of the Art," *Freshman English News*, 10 (Fall 1981), 1-4.

[5] "Ethos" is, of course, an ancient concept — see Aristotle, *Rhetoric*, 1356a2. When readers accept writers' authority, and usually they do at least at the start of reading, they work at understanding what the writer intends to say. I.A. Richards has noted the power of authority in *Practical Criticism* (New York: Harcourt, Brace, 1929), p. 297. The mere name of a well-known poet is enough to insure attentive reading of a mediocre work, yet a perfectly fine example of student writing will be criticized and subordinated to an Ideal Text, whatever its merits.

[6] This reading posture is perhaps a version of Peter Elbow's "believing game." See *Writing Without Teachers* (New York: Oxford University Press, 1973), pp. 169 ff.

[7] Donald Murray has shown how oral facilitative response, not just written, can help students become wise questioners of their own texts by first hearing the supportive questions of teachers. See "Teaching the Other Self: The Writer's First Reader," *College Composition and Communication*, 33 (May 1982), 140-47.

[8] Several studies of the revision process of less experienced writers illustrate this point. See Nancy Sommers, "Revision Strategies of Student Writers and Experienced Adult Writers," *College Composition and Communication*, 31 (December 1980), 378-388; Lester Faigley and Stephen Witte, "Analyzing Revision," *College Composition and Communication*, 32 (December 1981), 400-414; Richard Beach,

"Self-Evaluation Strategies of Extensive Revisers and Non-Revisers," *College Composition and Communication*, 27 (1976), 160-164; Richard Beach, "The Effects of Between-Draft Teacher Evaluation Versus Student Self-Evaluation on High School Students' Revising of Rough Drafts," *Research in the Teaching of English*, 13 (1979), 111-119; and Lillian S. Bridwell, "Revising Strategies in Twelfth Grade Students' Transactional Writing," *Research in the Teaching of English)*, 14 (October 1980), 197-222.

[9]Louise Rosenblatt first explored the active behaviors of readers in *Literature as Exploration* (New York: Noble and Noble, 1938), and later in *The Reader, the Text, the Poem: The Transactional Theory of the Literary Work* (Carbondale: Southern Illinois University Press, 1978). For the work of various reader-response theorists, see Jane Tompkins, ed., *Reader Response Criticism: From Formalism to Post-Structuralism* (Baltimore: Johns Hopkins, 1980) and Susan R. Suleiman and Inge Crosman, eds., *The Reader in the Text: Essays on Audience and Interpretation* (Princeton: Princeton University Press, 1980).

[10]John Clifford in "Composing in Stages: The Effects of a Collaborative Pedagogy," *Research in the Teaching of English*, 15 (February 1981), 37-53 and Douglas Barnes and Frankie Todd in *Communication and Learning in Small Groups* (London: Routledge and Kegan Paul, 1977) demonstrate the effectiveness of peer group interaction in the writing workshop. Douglas Barnes in *From Communication to Curriculm* (Harmondsworth, England: Penguin, 1976); Nancy Martin, *et al.*, in *Understanding Children Talking* (Penguin, 1976); B.M. Kroll and R.J. Vann, eds., in *Exploring Speaking-Writing Relationships: Connections and Contrasts* (Urbana, IL: NCTE, 1981); and Douglas Barnes, James Britton, and Harold Rosen in *Language, the Learner and the School* (Penguin, 1971) all argue for the connections between talk and learning and between talk and writing.

[11]The student text and responses cited here are from a textbook by Lil Brannon, Melinda Knight, and Vara Neverow-Turk, *Writers Writing* (Montclair, NJ: Boynton/Cook, 1982), pp. 120-124. The book can be useful to teachers interested in setting up peer groups and encouraging peer response.

[12]*Writers Writing*, pp. 111-119.

Chapter 7

The Development of
Writing Ability:
Some Myths About Evaluation
and Improvement

After all the labor of a composition course, the repeated challenges to write, the responding to texts, the collaboration and revision, teachers and students alike understandably expect improvement to be the consequence. Understandably, too, they expect that evaluation procedures will reliably reflect student improvement and enable the distribution of appropriate rewards in the form of numerical or letter grades. School administrators join in supporting the need to evaluate students' improvement as a check on teaching and a guide to curricular change. And their concern is reflected elsewhere in society, among parents and school boards in particular, where evaluation serves to guarantee that classrooms are fulfilling their expected functions. Recent pressure, however, to *quantify* improvement in order to measure student growth has led to a misunderstanding about the nature of improvement and evaluation in a writing workshop. The growth of students as writers is not the same as the improvement of texts. And though writers can progress in a workshop, their performance as estimated from completed writing is not always the best indicator of development. Moreover, the difficulties of accurately assessing the quality of written texts makes the connection of performance to growth highly problematic. Everything research has suggested in recent years about the nature of writing development, and everything research has revealed about the complex reading activities that underlie evaluation, point to the limited relevance of both concepts, "improvement" as well as "evaluation," when they pertain to quantifiable, short-term "outcomes" of instruction. If more and more elaborate, not to mention costly, testing programs are being advocated these days, with ever-increasing reliance on the ability of tests to facilitate policy decisions about placement, competence, and instructional quality, the reason is not supportive research conclusions[1] but rather a strong public pressure that has so far subordinated what researchers know to what society feels compelled to require. Evidence is mounting, however, that poorly articulated concepts of "improvement" and "evaluation" have far more potential to hinder effective instruction than they have to assist it. For that reason, knowledgeable teachers and administrators must qualify these concepts with some rigor if an ill-considered craze for quantification is not to damage the teaching of composition more than it has already.

Everyone would agree that one ultimate concern of writing instruction is improved ability among student writers. The ideal of improvement lends energy and purpose to the enterprise. But the kind of improvement that matters most in writing workshops is also a kind that progresses at its own natural pace, not at the pace of instruction, and a kind that is extremely difficult to measure in its subtle manifestations over short periods of time. Workshops seek chiefly to promote growth of the rhetorical competences that enable disciplined intellectual inquiry, imaginative reach, and communicative effectiveness. Technical proficiency is also valued, but not for its own sake, not apart from the context of meaning, and not prior to other, more important achievements. The maturation that workshops assist does indeed occur over time, and it will often be accelerated by the directed practice that a classroom provides. It results from sustained performance, in school and elsewhere, just as it fails to proceed when people stop writing. But to assume that improvement *will* occur, and in some readily perceivable form, provided the teaching is "effective," is to misconceive the nature of intellectual development, which continues, as Piaget, Bruner, Perry, and others have shown,[2] in an organic fashion, to an extent independent of, even though nurtured by, outside support, and often through extended stages of evolution. It is also to misconceive the relationship between writers' growth and the objective condition of their texts. Writers are "improving" as long as they write, but their texts need not show it in the ways that evaluators expect. Errors, for example, can be indicators of growth, if they represent efforts to experiment with structures or stylistic possibilities that writers don't yet fully control.[3] Inadequate revision can signal growth just because a writer has willingly attempted to reformulate an idea.[4] The measurement of texts, therefore, doesn't tell the whole story. In fact, it doesn't tell the most important part.

We can argue confidently that providing multiple opportunities to write as well as diverse responses to the writing will create conditions conducive to growth. These activities encourage writers' willingness to take greater risks, to profit from the advise of readers, to revise more readily and extensively, to offer their own advice — all of which can serve as indications that growth is underway. But the character of intellectual growth insures that no one can predict the kind or degree of improvement in writing performance that might result in a four-month or nine-month period. Nor is it possible to measure infinitely subtle gradations of improvement in such short time spans by any evaluative instrument currently available. In fact, the procedures currently in use offer such gross indications of change in writing ability, susceptible to such wide disagreement among evaluators, that the very concept of improvement must be considered, for classroom purposes, as merely hypothetical. How, after all, can improvement be said to occur when no means exists for detecting it reliably even to the satisfaction of trained observers? In short, the value of writing instruction cannot depend on confident expectations about the improvement of writers' performances as measured by a sample of their completed work. Nor is it responsible to tie that value to the demonstrability of superficial or short-term classroom "outputs," as many competency tests tend to do.[5] Narrowly utilitarian defenses of writing courses, which mistake these "outputs" for real growth, will never be persuasive because the superficial demonstration of test mastery fails repeatedly to prove students fully competent once they leave the writing classroom. The workshop is best defended on the basis of what it encourages and what it creates in the way of incentive and attitude, not on the basis of what assorted pieces of student writing demonstrate at the conclusion of a semester's effort.

Let's review the cases against naive concepts of "improvement" and over-optimistic expectations of "evaluation" as they pertain to the writing classroom. In the most traditional settings, improvement is related to mastering various surface constraints and organizational structures: spelling, punctuation, usage, grammatical propriety, the forms of paragraphs, and so on. Some of those constraints are real, while others are artificial. In either case, students perceived to lack mastery are introduced to correct performance and then tested on their retention of principles and their ability to avoid performance errors. To an extent, evaluation in this setting is fairly reliable — in the sense that any number of examiners could locate the same features and mark errors with some agreement about what error looks like. An examiner looking for technical lapses can discern readily enough whether a word is misspelled, or a comma misplaced, or a modifier dangling, or a topic sentence missing. The problem here is not test reliability but the validity of a concept of "improved writing" which is too restrictively defined as mastering surface conventions. If evaluation is to make sense, both reliability *and* validity need to be as high as possible, for the worth or meaning of what an examination measures is at least as important as its accuracy. But in the instance of technical features, worth is rather low even if accuracy is quite high.

Suppose, for instance, that a teacher spends a week on the comma splice, showing students that the proper punctuation between two connected but independent clauses is a semicolon. The teacher corrects instances of comma splice wherever they occur and sets students to workbook exercises identifying correct and incorrect punctuation. Eventually, in measuring students' improvement, the teacher will note the presence or absence of comma splices as a criterion for grading. But how much does the avoidance of comma splices really tell about writing ability? Competent writers regularly violate technical rules, the comma splice included, while unpracticed writers often manage to avoid technical lapses without thereby much enhancing the quality of their texts. Student writers who discover that a teacher disapproves of a particular practice may learn to adopt an alternative that the teacher recommends. But they may also simply learn to avoid any situation in which the likelihood of infraction is increased: hence, out of fear of producing comma splices, some students will simply decrease the size and complexity of their sentences, hardly a desired outcome of writing instruction. So, the concept of improvement invoked in this setting tends to be trivial and misleading: trivial in the sense that the presence or absence of comma splices says little about writing ability; misleading in the sense that the mere absence of comma splices does not necessarily prove that something desirable has been learned (beyond the survival skill of avoiding risk). Worse, the quest for a narrow ideal of improvement as technical facility may actually retard real development by encouraging linguistic timidity or a preoccupation with formal tidiness over intellectual depth.

Our first point about evaluation, therefore, is that those features of discourse which are most accessible to reliable measurement — the surface conventions — tend also to be the features having least to do with writers' true competence — their ability to make and connect substantial assertions, to penetrate a subject, to discover plausible lines of reasoning, to articulate imaginative insights, to think well in language. Hence, organizing curricula around minimal technical expertise may make evaluation reassuringly possible, but it also makes it trivial. Meanwhile, centering curricula on artificial constraints, the management of which is also highly measurable, makes the enterprise of evaluating improvement not just trivial but downright false, because the constraints are fictitious to begin with. When students are asked to memorize and reproduce the five-paragraph-theme structure, for example, their performance is certainly measurable — either they reproduce that structure correctly or they don't. But what is measured here is mainly their ability to follow directions, to do things the teacher's way, not necessarily their ability to compose mature discourse. Training students to follow simple orders offers the alluring possibility of "instant improvement," since only obedience is directly at stake, not intellectual development. Multiplying the number of artificial constraints to include the making of an outline, the recollection of some set of prewriting heuristics, the declaring of a thesis statement, the making of topic sentences, the writing of a "conclusion paragraph," and so forth, testing them all in turn, will enhance the illusion that improvement is occurring, thereby making this style of curriculum irresistible to teachers and administrators under public pressure to deliver "results." But the deeper development of writing ability, to the extent that it occurs at all, is proceeding at best accidentally in the context of the technical skill activities which constitute the focus of measurement — just as swimming in handcuffs or swimming under orders to keep one's bathing cap from getting wet may accidentally improve the ability to swim, though the artificial constraint is not directly responsible. Determining whether or not the handcuffs are in place or the cap indeed dry poses no evaluative problems; but determining the quality of the swimmer's improvement is another matter.

Of course, not all readily measurable features are trivial or false. Syntactic patterns, for example, are accessible to fairly reliable evaluation. And a writer's ability to manage those patterns in appropriate rhetorical circumstances, with full control of such technical complexities as embeddings and subordinations, is a real and significant indicator of writing ability.[6] But the validity (as opposed to reliability) of any measurement of syntactic complexity is qualified by the fact that the control of syntax is only a single variable bearing on competence, the meaning of which can only be estimated in the context of other variables, including argumentative sophistication and rhetorical appropriateness, that cannot be as reliably measured. [7] It is possible to induce greater complexity by giving students extensive practice in sentence-combining exercises, and it is possible to measure the change afterwards. But how significant is the change? Is the writer who proliferates complex sentences because of extensive sentence-combining practice, but who does so without equivalently developed regard for the quality of meaning or the needs of an audience, an improved writer? Is the greater complexity accompanied by intellectual maturity or imaginative insight? [8] Our second point about evaluation is that even features of discourse that are relevant indicators of writing development, and measurable as such, must be viewed in relation to other features that are far more difficult to define and measure, so that validity of interpretation inevitably complicates judgments about maturity regardless of the accuracy of the measurement. These other features, meanwhile, can prove notoriously difficult to assess, since different readers of any text will draw at least subtly distinct inferences, and will sometimes come to strikingly different conclusions, about argumentative control, or quality of insight, or even the most significant meanings in that text. So, a third point about evaluation is that the characteristics that probably matter most in judgments about development or maturity are also those least susceptible to reliable measurement and most likely to involve interpretive dispute.

Suppose, however, that a variety of features, excluding artificial constraints but including real surface conventions such as punctuation and diction, deeper elements such as syntactic complexity, and also the subtlest rhetorical and intellectual characteristics, were all taken into consideration as criteria for measurement. Would not the reliability of evaluation and its validity as a depictor of writing competence increase as a result, thereby enabling at the same time a definition of "improvement" as something more sophisticated than simply the ability to follow superficial directions? The answer is yes, but only given certain conditions and only up to a point. Paul Diederich's book, *Measuring Growth in English*, offers a useful corrective to naive ideas about evaluating writing. [9] Diederich describes many of the problems of reliability and interpretation that we have introduced. He mentions, in particular, a 1961 study that bears importantly on our argument, an experiment in which 60 judges from different professions — lawyers, business executives, and writers, as well as teachers — evaluated 300 texts written by first-year college students during their first month at three different colleges. The judges were not brought together to discuss criteria but were free to grade the essays on their own and with reference to whatever values seemed relevant to them as standards of acceptability. They were to sort the essays into nine piles in order of general merit. Teachers may find Diederich's results startling: he writes that "out of the 300 essays graded, 101 received every grade from one to nine; 94 percent received either seven, eight, or nine different grades, and no essay received less than five different grades" (p. 6). One discovery from the experiment, which makes the radical grading differences more understandable, was that judges disagreed on the relative priorities of five separate evaluation factors, including quality, clarity, and development of ideas, number of technical and grammatical errors, control of organization and analysis, propriety of wording and phrasing, and stylistic originality and flavor (pp. 6-8). The largest number of judges put quality of ideas first, the next largest emphasized technical correctness, and so on through the list. But even the fluctuating priorities did not explain all the differences in judgment. As Diederich notes, other factors which his researchers could not infer from the judges' comments on papers might have had an impact. And more interestingly, two other causes might also have complicated the measurements: "unique ideas about grading that are not shared by any other reader, and random variations in judgment" (p. 10), both subjective elements difficult to eradicate even with the most careful preparation of readers or the greatest sincerity of effort. We might add still further complications which Diederich did not consider: that the judges' definitions of the five factors need not have agreed even when different judges professed the same values, nor need any one judge's definition or application of criteria have remained constant.

Elsewhere in his book, Diederich also documents numerous reader biases in testing situations, either for or against particular students, based on the readers' own compositional preferences (say, plain versus ornamented style, or brevity versus length), their political commitments (liberal or conservative), their impressions of students apart from writing samples (energetic versus lazy, bright versus slow, teamplayer versus troublemaker), or their intolerance for particular errors (split infinitive or beginning a sentence with "but"), which could automatically lower grades. In one intriguing experiment, two groups of teachers, each from a different school, were given selected bits of information about the students whose essays they were to evaluate (boy or girl, ninth grade versus tenth). What the teachers did not know, however, was that the information was not always true: half of it was intentionally falsified. The one bit of information that seemed to influence teachers' judgments of writing (again, partly falsified) was the designation of regular or honors student — and its influence was precisely opposite to what teachers expected. They had originally requested the information believing that honors students should be judged by "higher standards" than regular students. But in practice, as Diederich writes, "the papers that were stamped 'honors' averaged almost one grade-point *higher* than the other copies of the very same papers that were stamped 'regular' " (p. 12). Diederich's conclusion is important: "grading is such a suggestible process that we find what we expect to find. If we think a paper came from an honors class, we expect it to be pretty good, and that is what we find. If we think it came from a regular class, we expect it to be only so-so, and that is what we find" (p. 12). If such biases, then, are added to the differences of grading criteria among even professional writers and experienced readers, and then personal idiosyncracies of grading philosophy or shifts of grading practice from essay to essay are thrown in as well, how strong a case can be made for the reliability and the interpretive validity of an individual teacher's efforts in the isolated classroom at measuring student performance in order to depict subtle degrees of improvement?

Diederich goes on to show that it is, in fact, possible to enhance reliability by controlling these variables of evaluation performance, but only by means of an elaborate and extensive procedure involving multiple writing samples, multiple readings of the samples, a training period for readers to enhance their collective reliability (that is, the likelihood that one reader will agree with another), and some method of concealing students' identities. If teachers don't know the students they are evaluating, many biases can obviously be eliminated. But this means that the teacher who has worked with students during a semester is not the sole teacher who judges their competence, and may not be involved in the judgment at all, a discomfiting fact for teachers who believe, perhaps with some justification, that they can be in some ways "fairer" to students when they know more about them than the raw quality of samples of their work. Meanwhile, idiosyncratic judgments of quality can be reduced somewhat if teachers are willing to come together to practice evaluating essays, talking over different criteria and agreeing on their relative importance, until they can reach fairly consistent conclusions. Then, if teachers are prepared to test students on at least two different occasions, in order to get a more representative sample of their work, and if at least two teachers are willing to read each text, with a possible third reading to resolve disputes, the result can be a *single* evaluation of each student's ability with restricted reference to the criteria agreed upon (obviously, other unprepared readers would still reach different conclusions), and with a statistical reliability which Diederich locates at about .7 (which he confesses is much lower than the .9 he would prefer).

This single measure enables a certain rudimentary contrastive analysis, allowing examiners to say, not with certainty but with some articulatable justification, that one essay is "better" than another. It does not, of course, allow the judgment that one student "writes better" than another: only that a given text appears to be superior to some other given text on one occasion. Presumably, the greater the differences between two essays with reference to stated criteria, the more reliable the judgment that one is better, as in the case of these two samples, both of which attempt to argue a position:

Essay I
Fith National Bank, Adams and Alexito's are public places that entertain in the most elegant and fashionable style. The sofisicated atmosphere pronounce for enduce a unwimeing split of the soul, searching, in the mis of poetic ventilation; smoking should not be banned in public places.

Essay II
There are not many people in politics today who strike me as real leaders. Not Reagan, not Kennedy and certainly not Carter. No one seems to have a vision of a better society, a dream I can share. There are too many phonies and hucksters — those who might have the words or the looks of a leader, but none of the passion which can inspire people from every corner of the

culture. Politicians today are boring, they lack that spirit which moves people to act.

A real leader is someone who knows what is wrong, has a plan to fix it and convince us his plan can work. We all share a common fate no matter what our differences. If Arabia cuts off our oil we will all suffer. The real leader hears all points of view and accepts their validity. But when a decision has to be made, one side must win and one side must lose. Principle is a good way to summarize what it takes to be a leader.

We will hazard the guess that most readers, evaluating on the basis of standard school criteria for acceptable writing, will find the second essay superior to the first. It contains more writing, with fewer surface errors, greater syntactic complexity, subtler meanings, more powerful intellectual connections, and a maturer communicative sensitivity than does Essay I. But now consider this sample, which also argues a position:

Essay III
As in most laws, there is no clear-cut answer to the age when people should be allowed to drink. However, my feeling is that by raising the drinking age to nineteen, we are not getting to the heart of the problem. There are two main reasons for the change: to reduce the number of alcohol-related car accidents and to keep alcohol out of high schools. The first reason is valid and I can understand the reason behind it. I do not agree that the raise will keep alcohol out of the high school. Students have been drinking for years, and a one-year age hike is not going to stop them.

I suggest that instead of raising the drinking age we should make alcohol harder to maintain. If every bar, grocery store, and liquor store asked each customer for proof of identity, alcohol would be extremely difficult for minors to obtain.

It is also unfair that at the age of eighteen a citizen has the right to vote in elections, fight and die for his country in war, and get married but not have the right to drink. If we are allowed all these other responsibilities, we should be able to drink if we so desire.

Readers may consistently judge III to be better than I, but our experiments with over 200 teachers suggest that they will not consistently judge III better than II, or II better than III, or the two essays equal in quality, regardless of how carefully they are prepared for the reading. Indeed, judgments on a five-point scale will regularly vary as much as two points in favor of each essay. The conclusion is evident enough: the gross testing instruments available to us can yield no more than gross measures of qualitative difference. At the extremes of comparison (I and II or I and III) reliability is fairly high; but as essays reflect subtler varieties of difference (II and III), reliability will drop, whatever the preparation of readers, the number of test samples, the number of readings, and so forth.

Remember, now, all this effort that Diederich describes yields a single evaluation at a particular moment in time. If something like "improvement" is to be measured, at least one more evaluation at a later moment would be required. That would entail all of the same steps as before, but with some additional difficulties. Naturally, students would have to be set to exactly the same type of writing task they attempted the first time, which introduces the problem of insuring that four assignments — two on the first occasion and two on the second — are sufficiently similar to produce the same kinds of rhetorical responses from writers. Some interesting questions here: How shall it be determined that a particular task is best representative of writing ability? Is instruction throughout the semester to be focused on that one type of writing task? To what extent is instruction in other tasks likely to add to or detract from students' ability to manage the one stipulated for the exam? Then, consider the time, numbers, and administrative labor involved. All the readings would take place at the conclusion of the second exam, the essays from the first test coded and mixed with those of the second, which would eliminate the possibility of rating bias from knowing that one writing sample was elicited earlier than another. Suppose 200 students take the tests: that means 800 essays, four from each writer, and at least 1600 readings, minimally two for each student's work, a large but manageable operation. However, suppose 2000 students take the tests every semester: 8000 essays and at least 16,000 readings. The staff commitment and expense would be substantial! And then, a final difficulty, consider the gains from all this labor. Although the results of the second set of readings would undoubtedly be different from the first to some extent, there is no way to tell for sure what the differences mean, especially if the tests occur a mere four or five months apart. It is hard enough just to show that the writing in any one set of two essays is objectively better than the writing in another; but it is harder still to show that the difference in quality is more than random, that it represents a writer's "improvement."

Our experience in large writing program evaluation (2000 + students) has been that, although many students who scored 3 on a five-point scale at the start of a semester received 4 on that scale at the end, many other students reverse those numbers. The reasoning that would enable the first group of students to be regarded as "improved" also requires the second group to be regarded as "degenerating." Surely, it is better reasoning, given the complexities of verbal maturation, to argue that the first and second testing occasions really comprise a single measurement period with differences in score accounted for simply by the degree of unreliability in the test. To believe otherwise is to accept three dubious assumptions: that real growth (or degeneration) can occur in a very short space of time, that differences between two writing samples necessarily represent this growth (or deterioration), and that testing instruments are subtle enough to measure the differences successfully and stipulate the degree of change. It seems by now impossible to ignore an uncomfortable implication: if comparisons of measurements cannot guarantee a portrait of improvement, then what is the relevance of the concept for classroom purposes — that is, as something that ought to be happening during the span of a writing course? Certainly, writers improve — at least over extended periods of time. And surely evaluators could apply some set of criteria to a writer's efforts at age 10 and the same set to the same writer's efforts at age 25, distinguishing differences quite reliably and characterizing them as a demonstration of improved performance. But "improvement" here means intellectual, imaginative, and emotional maturation — the difference between a child's orientation to the world and an adult's orientation. It is not impossible during the short duration of a writing course, say four or five months, that the ongoing process of maturation might be further stimulated. But it is surely unlikely that such growth occurs invariably as the direct result of writing instruction, or that its occurrence will be signalled reliably in changes of quality in a handful of writing samples, or that five months' worth of subtle mental development will be susceptible to measurement according to such gross indicators as "quality of ideas" or "sophistication of style."

The insights of reader-response theory further complicate notions of the objective quality of writing and the nature of improvement. Given the complex character of responses to discourse, as Rosenblatt and others have described it, the conclusion appears inescapable that even the most careful preparation of readers will fail to homogenize their perceptions to the degree necessary for complete agreement about the excellences and limitations of even a single text, let alone the two texts minimally required for a statement about improvement. It does not matter, for example, that readers could readily decide to stipulate certain criteria by which to determine quality, because the superficial common agreement on labels — "quality of idea," "organizational effectiveness," "rhetorical awareness," "stylistic sophistication" — only covers over a deeper uncertainty about what they really signify and how, or the degree to which, individual texts manifest the characteristics they denote. For instance, the teachers who responded to drafts of the smoking essay introduced in Chapter 6 plainly thought they were looking at the same general determiners of excellence, yet they came to different conclusions about each draft because their reading responses were much richer, much more individualized, than their theoretical agreement. Hence, concerning organizational effectiveness on the second essay, different readers viewed the concept differently and came to diverse judgments of quality: "it is controlled and focused" — C + ; "it has problems, particularly as far as sequencing goes, but the framework is legitimate" — B-; "it flows nicely and the theme develops consistently" — A; "it is better organized around one argument" — B + ; "it flows freely and takes the reader through a logical and carefully presented position" — A-; "it shows an honest development of the writer's ideas" — B. For one reader or another, "organizational effectiveness" meant a focused topic, a framework for the argument, a restricted argument, a sequence of ideas, a consistency of development, a logical position, an appearance of flow, an appearance of care, and an appearance of honesty. To be sure, many of these ideas could be concretized so that "organizational effectiveness" takes on a sharper meaning for evaluators; but the more concreteness is achieved, the more potentially reductive or overrestrictive the criteria for "good writing" are apt to become. Hence, as reliability increased, validity might tend to diminish. In the face of such difficulties, it seems the developmental question whether or not "improvement" might possibly occur in the space of a five-month writing course is ultimately moot, because the inability to agree on precise meanings for the criteria that would serve to define it, or on the adequacy of the criteria, or on their applications to individual texts, renders the concept of improvement at best arbitrary and perhaps wholly fictional from a measurement standpoint.

Another relevant insight from reader-response theory, equally damaging to the concepts of evaluation and improvement, concerns the extent to which readers' awareness either of the authority of a writer or of their own authority to be judges affects their perceptions of texts. If, for example, readers know that a particular writer has a good reputation, so that they are disposed to grant his or her authority as composer, they will tend to view the writer's texts in terms of that reputation, regarding any challenges of their customary expectations — whether intellectual, formal, stylistic, or technical — as subtle excellences, requiring greater reader effort to appreciate and not a condemnation of the writer. Hence, having read Dylan Thomas' *Fern Hill* with pleasure, readers are prepared to work that much harder at reading *Altarwise by Owl-Light*.[10] The reverse is equally true: in the absence of confidence in the authority of a writer, or just given the opportunity to claim authority to judge (as is typically the case when teachers read student writing), readers will tend without hesitation to cite any idiosyncrasy of form or technique, idea or style, any authorial choice that challenges their personal preferences, as an "error." In short, readers simply do not view choices as deficiencies in circumstances where they accept a writer's authority and therefore do not take an evaluative stance toward the writing. But they will evaluate whenever they have leave to do so, in which case distinctiveness often becomes unacceptable performance. Joseph Williams has pointed out this intriguing reader behavior in an article on the number of "errors" that could be cited in Strunk and White's *Elements of Style*, errors which Strunk and White themselves identify in the book and exhort student writers to avoid.[11] Few readers are inclined to hold Strunk and White to their own prescriptions: indeed, our point is that it would not occur to most readers to view the text from an evaluative perspective. Once presented with the fact of rule violations, teachers would probably respond with the rationale that Strunk and White know the rules and are therefore free to violate them with impunity. But their reasoning would be quite different had the errors occurred in students' work.

We have asked several groups of teachers to read the following three essays, commenting on them as they would normally do in the classroom and estimating the writers' degrees of competence:

Essay I
Sometime I wonder what do "life" mean to some people. I once wanted to if people had to take their life by killing theirself and other people as well. I've

been hearing alot people killing new born babys that's something you should be put in jail for life you know what I mean. Because "life is beauty, so live and let live.

Essay II

A hunt. The last great hunt.

For what?

For Moby Dick, the huge white sperm whale: who is old, hoary, monstrous, and swims alone; who is unspeakably terrible in his wrath, having so often been attacked; and snow-white.

Of course he is a symbol.

Of what?

I doubt if even Melville knew exactly. That's the best of it.

He is warm-blooded, he is lovable. He is lonely Leviathan, not a Hobbes sort. Or is he?

But he is warm-blooded, and lovable. The South Sea Islanders, and Polynesians, and Malays, who worship shark, or crocodile, or weave endless frigate-bird distortions, why did they never worship the whale? So big!

Because the whale is not wicked. He doesn't bite. And their gods had to bite.

He's not a dragon. He is Leviathan. He never coils like the Chinese dragon of the sun. He's not a serpent of the waters. He is warm-blooded, a mammal. And hunted, hunted down.

It is a great book.

At first you are put off by the style. It reads like journalism. It seems spurious. You feel Melville is trying to put something over you. It won't do.

And Melville really is a bit sententious: aware of himself, self-conscious, putting something over even himself. But then it's not easy to get into the swing of a piece of deep mysticism when you just set out with a story.

Essay III

What is funny? Here I am almost finished a lot of material on humor, and I still don't know the definition of humor. I don't know what humor is but I continue to laugh my head off at certain things. I mean I really *sweated* it out with trying to figure out what humor is and what its sources are. But my wrestling continues.

Let's see. What's funny? I thought "Animal House" was funny. I thought "Airplane" was funny. I especially think the new issue of *The Plague* is very funny. Here's an item which I thought was hilarious. I mean, hilarious, as in I was laughing so hard, I was crying. Ok, let's analyze as we go along. (I haven't thought this out!) First off, look at the writing of "Godawful Falafel." When I first saw this writing, I thought it was Arabic. I mean it looks Arabic. But then I saw what it said and I laughed out loud. Why? Because it was funny. Is that a good reason? Isn't that why we usually laugh? Ok, we've established something. We laugh because something is funny. What's funny about it? Whenever I ask myself what humor is, I always come to this realization: It's funny because it's true. Well, this doesn't make sense. I mean, is it funny when I say $E = MC^2$? No. . . . When I spoke of laughter, I defined it as a kind of release, like crying. I said that laughter was a relief of built up anxiety and tension. (For example, in the cartoon depicting John Anderson's fantasy about being president, we laugh at our high expectation of ourselves when we have failed. We are emphathizing, I guess.) Shoot! All I've done here is come back to my original ideas. Darn it. Well, at least I fully understand why I laugh at this funny cartoon of John Anderson. I once wanted to be President too, you know.

The majority of the teachers we have polled are inclined to find the first of these essays the most problematic, citing its brevity and its grammatical and technical errors as indications that the writer probably belongs in a "basic writing" course. The majority also tend to find the third essay a good deal more promising, intellectually naive in some ways, of course, and a bit tongue-tied, but focused on some complex issues and earnestly concerned to make headway with them. More organized later drafts, teachers suppose, will solve some of the problems in this early version, the choppiness and slang, the muddled reasoning, and will yield a thoughtful, if not exceptional, essay. The middle text, meanwhile, is generally regarded as closer in quality to III than it is to I, though teachers differ on whether it is better or worse than III. Essay II has some evident virtues, especially in its occasionally sophisticated word-choices, but it is also repetitive and it lacks argumentative tightness as well as development of ideas. The word choices, many teachers say, may be flashy but they are also frequently incorrect, or at least not fully in the writer's control (as though he or she were trying to imitate a more learned style than present ability allows). Sentence fragments abound, and the phrasing seems unnatural at times, leading some teachers to conclude that the writer may be an advanced ESL student. The authors of both II and III, our teachers generally agreed, belong in a regular writing course.

At the close of discussion, teachers are nearly always surprised to learn that they have been tricked in this experiment, rather unfairly perhaps: for while the first and third essays are indeed student productions, the middle one is a published piece of criticism written by D.H. Lawrence. What the trick reveals, we believe, is not that teachers are unable to spot professional writing when they see it, but that tacit permission to assume a certain reading posture entices people to regard some textual features as "errors" which would probably not be so regarded were a nonevaluative posture assumed. We do not mean that readers would notice the errors and dismiss them: rather, the choices *would not be regarded as erroneous*. It appears to follow, then, that a reader's finding of errors and rendering of adverse judgments does not always depend on the text's conspicuous calling out for such a reading but sometimes results merely from the reader's sense of authorization to serve as judge, and therefore to deny the writer's authority any time a textual feature fails to validate preconceptions about what writing should look like. To be sure, where communication is expected and then truly thwarted by deficient choices, the disruption can prompt an evaluative response (hence, while readers might pay little or no attention to Lawrence's idiosyncracies in a nonevaluative context, they would certainly notice deficiencies in Essay I because the lapses cause an anticipation of learning about the writer's subject to go unsatisfied). But where subtler challenges to expectation arise, the evaluative response is more troubling. Many perceptions of quality or deficiency are little more than consequences of a disposition to regard texts in a certain way, to assert a privileged reader's right of judgment. This final realization about the subjectivity of evaluation should speak to teachers more emphatically than any of the technical measurement difficulties we have described; for teachers *are* especially privileged readers, enjoying the right to intervene in student writing any time they wish. Given the extent of their authority, they should be particularly cognizant of the dangers of self-satisfaction regarding their understanding of how well students are writing on particular occasions or developing as writers in the course of a semester.

But where does all of this leave us? If individual responses to texts are so persistently and legitimately divergent, then how strong a case can be made for the authenticity of evaluation, particularly in the isolated classroom where a single reader undertakes the measuring? And if evaluation enjoys only a limited objective validity, then how can anyone argue for "improvement" — the two-fold conclusion (a) that later writing is better than earlier, and (b) that the difference is due to the writer's maturation — as the immediate consequence of writing instruction or as a criterion for assessing the worth of that instruction? And finally, if such a poor case is to be made for the definition and perception of short-term improvement, then how will it be possible to determine the value of writing courses either to students or to a results-oriented society? A perplexing chain of reasoning, to be sure, but let's point out, first, that evaluation is not really a villain here. Teachers can cheerfully concede the subjectivity of grading, the imperfect reliability of measurement, without giving up on their own rough but nonetheless experienced and perfectly useful estimates of the intellectual and communicative strengths of their students' writing. Provided evaluation is not credited with more clarity or power than it deserves, a lack of precise, objective validity need not imply gross unfairness or inconsistency in an individual teacher's or a program's use of grades. After all, people judge writing all the time: editors evaluate the quality of submissions; business executives evaluate the persuasiveness or clarity of reports, proposals, and memos; law courts pronounce on the effectiveness of argumentative briefs; potential customers are moved or unmoved by advertising campaigns. Judgment of effort is a fact of life: fairness and reliability are important aspects of judgment but their imperfect realization will never serve to discredit the activity.

Students generally know, and in any case ought to learn, that they will be judged both in school and out, and that a desirable consequence of anticipated evaluation is often increased effort, even if a less desirable consequence is increased pressure to perform adequately. A teacher who is both skilled as a reader and sensitive to the needs, anxieties, and motivations of students can use grades effectively to lend an impression of completeness to the cycle of writing, reading, and rewriting in a workshop. He or she can reassure students through grading that they are, in fact, making progress — as defined by their willingness to take intellectual and formal risks, listen to readers, make revisions, and offer advice to other writers. Teachers err in their use of grades only when they allow the fiction of "improvement" to distort their judgments. The sequence of grades a student receives through a semester represents nothing more than a locus of points suggestive of his or her competence at a certain stage of personal development. If grades get higher during the semester, that fact no more indicates actual growth than the fact of progressively lower grades indicates degeneration. In each case, the fluctuations typically result from the crudeness of evaluation, the degrees of student effort on different occasions, the differences of writing task, good or bad luck, and unconscious or intentional shifts in the grader's standards or perceptions of different students. Naturally, grades can be manipulated to rise or fall consistently, and from the standpoint of incentive, perhaps they should be allowed to rise somewhat over a grading period. But real danger, the possibility of real unfairness or other misconduct, lurks in the myth of measurable improvement. There lies the villain, both in the practices of teachers and the attitudes of those who monitor writing programs.

The most debilitating illusion associated with writing instruction is the belief that teachers can, or at least ought to be able to, control writers' maturation, causing it to occur as the explicit consequence of something they do or ought to do. The myth of improvement is a villain because of what it leads people to think and the ways it leads them to behave where composition programs are concerned. It is this myth of improvement, for example, which has led teachers and others to regard writing courses, indeed even the liberal arts curricula of which they are a part, in minimal functionalist terms. It is this myth which has prompted some administrators to define teaching and curricular success with reference to trivial but readily demonstrable short-term "skill" acquisitions. It is also the myth of improvement that allows certain narrowly conceived competency tests, which exaggerate copy-editing procedures and the ability to memorize artificial performance recipes, to dictate the character of classroom activity, sometimes making parodies of the teaching and learning processes out of an obsession with test survival. It is this myth which leads some teachers to imagine it is fair to "grade on improvement," mistaking a willingness to follow orders for real development, even occasionally to the point of rewarding students who can most skillfully anticipate the teacher's prejudices while penalizing those who can't or won't. It is this myth which encourages faculty in other disciplines to regard the writing course as though it were the academic equivalent of a bandaid dispensary or an auto body shop — a place where people can get something "fixed" so that they can proceed about more important business. It is this myth which seems to justify those who blame English teachers when students entering composition courses with poorly developed verbal skills leave them in substantially the same condition, as though a writing instructor's responsibility were to create instantaneous literacy, or as though literacy were the English teacher's "area" in the same sense that accounting belongs to the business school and eighteenth-century France to the history department. The myth of improvement creates misunderstanding, anxiety, and frustration on all sides, among students, teachers, administrators, and the public alike, each of whom legitimately expects tangible benefits to come from educational effort. There certainly *are* benefits to writing courses, we insist. But instantaneous improvement cannot be one of them.

How paradoxical, critics might now say, that we should imply some value to writing instruction while also insisting that the one thing society reasonably expects it to accomplish is something it cannot do, at least not by itself. And how convenient, they might well add, that we should construct an argument supporting that instruction which also protects it from public scrutiny by denying the possibility of determining the character of its success. Our intent, however, is neither to deny a role for composition teaching in the development of verbal abilities (quite the contrary!) nor to deny the legitimacy of institutional demands for the evaluation of writing programs. It is rather to preserve the intellectual validity of that teaching by freeing it from a degrading scramble among instructors as well as administrators to guarantee visible results by appeal to artificial definitions of growth. A functionalist view of writing classes, emphasizing such low-level technical accomplishments as the manufacture of a business letter, is seductive because it assures a measure of teaching "success," yielding public evidence of productive effort. But its effect, often, is to encourage a rudimentary behaviorism in the classroom, not unlike the training of pigeons to push levers, where students are drilled to affect the *appearance* of literacy without striving to acquire the humane values or the intellectual competences that literacy really entails. To emphasize skill acquisition is finally, ironically, to distract from the nurturing of literacy by asserting a false, mechanistic priority at once meaningless to students and irrelevant to growth. We want to enhance, not diminish, the role of writing courses in stimulating that growth by enriching their content while also locating them in an environment of realistic expectations about what they can accomplish. And we want to urge their public evaluation, too, but not on the basis of trivial gains in superficial skills having little bearing on real development. The judgment of instructional worth should be a function of the perceived relationship between teaching and its desired end, which means focusing on the known long-term benefits of classroom activities whatever the difficulties of assessing their short-term results.

It is, for instance, a common enough experience that students who have been encouraged to read extensively through childhood and adolescence tend to be better readers than others who have not, even though the most exhaustive monitoring of their progress would undoubtedly fail to reveal the single parental act, or classroom strategy, or book, or personal experience, or technical aid, which accounted for the development of competence. Presumably, the value of a reading program would lie mainly in its effectiveness at creating new incentives and offering additional support for readers, so that school reading reinforces and intensifies the literary experiences students are also accumulating elsewhere. The special advantage of school reading is the opportunity for sharing books and insights with others, and especially for receiving feedback from the more experienced teacher-reader whose maturer conclusions about texts can excite student readers to additional effort and deeper perception. This, surely, would be considered the main value of a literature course, not the number of books in its syllabus or the number of critical, biographical, or historical "facts" articulated in lectures. Where reading program evaluation is concerned, then, it would surely be the encouragement to read, the environment in which reading takes place, the favorable change in student attitudes about reading, the energetic pursuit of important ideas, the developing awareness of what reading involves as an intellectual process, that would be monitored — the *kind* of instruction, in other words, not its local results — from a realization that these appropriate activities cause desired, long-term results. Literature teachers seldom defend their enterprise (and are seldom asked to defend it) on the basis of their measurable success at producing "better" literary critics, or even better readers. The experience of literature, teachers would surely argue, is valued in itself because it leads students to seek literacy and aspire to civility, though they receive neither from the literature course itself. Writing courses, we suggest, have a similar value, finding their justification in the activities they make available, the attitudes and awarenesses they foster, not the facts they convey, or their immediate performance gains. And we would readily hold those courses to the same standards applicable to courses in literature or indeed any other of the liberal arts — standards of serious involvement and application.

Writing — writing about things that matter, writing to make sense out of experience, writing to discover new knowledge, writing to reach ethical judgments, writing to examine the problems and complexities of the world, writing in response to meaningful reading — is an activity both truly liberal and truly artful. As such, it deserves equal status with other courses in a liberal arts curriculum. It is not "contentless," as some critics charge, nor is its content the random bits of information from logic, rhetoric, and grammar haphazardly assembled in textbooks. Its content is the ranges of experience that matter enough to teachers and students to be worth examining through discourse. What a writing course shares with other liberal arts courses is a powerful but also an inconveniently subtle value for the enrichment of mind and spirit, not altogether susceptible to measurement. Teachers in other humane disciplines would do well to consider whether they might be implicating themselves in a posture fundamentally antagonistic to their own academic tradition when they seek to hold writing courses to standards of empirical validation they would certainly not choose to have applied to them. We assume that an English department or a history department would not ordinarily regard true/false or multiple choice tests of the "content" of their fields as fitting measure of what they intend their students to learn — which suggests to us that they value the "improvement" of historical understanding and the ability to study history, or the "improvement" of literary understanding and the art of literary appreciation, more than the memorization of details or the sterile imitation of an instructor's views. But how shall program administrators or the society that schools serve make judgments about the progress of historical understanding, or literary appreciation, or the thinking abilities important to these disciplines? The answer, again, and it is an ancient one for the liberal arts, is that evaluation emphasizes, not short-term outputs, which are always inconclusive, but the character and appropriateness of activities going on in such courses, and the impact of those activities on students' dispositions to learn. Are students being exposed to substantial literary works and given an opportunity to discuss them with a mature teacher-reader? Are students being made aware of how historians conceive the past, how they define and locate historical evidence, how they interpret the significance of deeds and events? Are students active in class, free to think and explore on their own, free to talk to each other? Are they challenged to go beyond lectures and textbook summaries in their engagement with the richness of literature or history? Are students more aware of the value of literary or historical writings at the conclusion of a course? Are they willing to continue the disciplined work that will eventually make them literate about Russian history or English poetry or the American novel?

Writing courses certainly ought to be evaluated, but with reference to the same sorts of questions applicable to literature or history courses. Meaningful evaluative questions include the following: Are students receiving many and varied opportunities to write? Is the environment of the writing workshop supportive of their efforts by offering diverse and provocative responses from readers? Are they free to explore ideas in their own ways, just as other writers do? Are they given time to rethink their conclusions, time to revise, time to push beyond the trivial and into the fresh, unpredictable, and problematic? Do students leave the workshop aware that they have a new sense of themselves as writers, sensing a new authority to assert their own intelligence, believing in their capacities to make worthy statements, unwilling to settle for less than a best effort at explaining themselves? Or on the negative side: Is a teacher occupying center-stage, controlling expression so restrictively that students are only passive observers or timid mimics of the teacher's views and rhetorical preferences? Is lecturing more important than writing in the course? Are students just writing to formula, on subjects that don't seem to matter to them or within formats that make writing a mechanical exercise? Are students passive, bored, frustrated, or rebellious, reluctant to attend regularly, eager to escape the course, and hopeful of avoiding writing from that time on? The only outcomes measured by such questions are attitudinal adjustments, not changes in performance. A course should strive to create desirable attitudes about the personal and public value of writing, recognizing that a willingness to improve, to be serious about composing, will enhance the likelihood of improvement, just as a literature course creates a receptiveness to reading poems or short stories in order to promote sophistication of reading ability and aesthetic response. Indeed, a liberal arts course should be judged a failure to the extent that it fosters attitudes detrimental to the intellectual development it seeks to stimulate. At the same time, a writing course should also create in students a sense of its own integrity by requiring that its "contract" be honored, that students work responsibly, not perfunctorily, at their tasks, that they come to class, respond willingly to each other's writing, and make earnest efforts to revise on the basis of serious consideration of reader responses.

In short, any writing classroom features definable teacher obligations, definable student obligations, definable ends to be achieved, and an environment definable as productive or otherwise for the pursuit of those ends.[12] Society has every right to hold its schools to their responsibility of stimulating the growth of mind, the maturation of intellect, imagination, and ethical awareness, in writing courses as well as the rest of the curriculum. Schools have every right to hold teachers to sensible pedagogy, consistent with the best available research on how people learn to write and how their learning can be assisted. Teachers are entitled to hold students to their responsibility for developing their own abilities through application and enterprise. And students should expect to receive the assistance from teachers and others that they need in the process of educating themselves. But no one of these interdependent groups should imagine that any other can magically satisfy its demands without extended, reciprocal effort. It should not be supposed that teachers can produce instantaneous literacy in students, or that students can instantaneously translate instruction into improved verbal performance, or that writing programs can accomplish their goals autonomously, without an active commitment from teachers outside the English department, indeed from the world outside of schools, to encourage verbal literacy as energetically themselves as they wish writing teachers to encourage it. Each group, in other words, should look to the quality of its own effort as it evaluates the quality of others'.

This final point is crucial for understanding the usefulness of writing courses in liberal arts curricula. The concentrated composing, the thoughtful responding and revising, the wide-ranging exercise of abilities, the concern for productive attitudes about writing, all serve to stimulate writers' development and together constitute the central value of the workshop. Symptoms of growth — the willingness to take risks, to profit from advice, to revise, to make recommendations to others — may appear quickly, even if improved *performance* takes longer. For that reason, a course in composition deserves inclusion in any program devoted to humanistic education. But at the same time, if this concentrated stimulation occurs in a vacuum, if teachers of other courses implicitly deny the relevance of composing by failing to take advantage of writing-to-learn in their own classes, if school administrators are content to assume that one semester of writing instruction officially achieves the goal of verbal literacy rather than full immersion in a richly verbal school (not to mention social) environment, then the workshop is a rather expensive waste of energy, whatever its own quality and whatever the procedures for "proving" its local success by means of trumped up measurement schemes. How many American students can speak or even read French or Spanish despite having devoted anywhere from one to eight years learning it in isolated language classrooms, receiving one "A" grade after another along the way? People develop the competences that matter to them, when they have motive and opportunity to practice intensively, when those competences are conspicuously associated with the lives they lead or aspire to lead, and when other people whom they admire can be seen making use of the same abilities and encouraging their efforts to do likewise. This fact does not belittle the importance of expert assistance in developing some capability; it simply underscores the roles, the obligations, of nonexperts involved equally in the process. If educators in the liberal arts wish to assert that writing matters to the growth of mature human beings, they must accept an implication for their own teaching, their own encouragement of writers, regardless of the subjects they profess. When they also invite students to write, long after those students have completed composition courses, then they will begin to see the improvement they have looked for in the past. Perhaps, therefore, an added responsibility for philosophically aware writing teachers, beyond creating productive writing workshops, is to share their philosophical insights with colleagues in other fields, with school administrators, and with the public at large, who have a significant opportunity to make their own contributions to an educational goal that everyone values.

Notes

[1] Balanced and useful appraisals of the problematic state of present ability to measure growth in writing appear in the same issue of *College English*, 42 (September 1980): Lee Odell and Charles R. Cooper, "Procedures for Evaluating Writing: Assumptions and Needed Research," 35-43 and Anne Ruggles Gere, "Written Composition: Toward a Theory of Evaluation," 44-58. Both essays offer more optimism than we are inclined to do, but both also suggest that current instruments are not up to the expectations schools wish to have for them. See also the Preface to *The Nature and Measurement of Competency in English*, ed., Charles R. Cooper (Urbana, IL: NCTE, 1981). Most overviews of measuring growth in English are upbeat, of course, given the social and political pressures currently sustaining evaluation. But one need only look closely at the qualifiers in these studies — the difficulty of defining competence, the difficulties of creating reliable tests, the difficulties of interpreting the results — to notice the plain fact that evaluation hasn't as yet been proven effective.

[2] A particularly interesting work is William Perry, *Forms of Intellectual and Ethical Development in the College Years* (New York: Holt, Rinehart and Winston, 1970), which suggests the complexity and unpredictable progression of intellectual growth, especially over a short space of time. See also Jerome Bruner, who notes that "mental growth is not a gradual accretion" but "more a matter of spurts and rests" which "are not very clearly linked to age," *Toward a Theory of Instruction* (New York: Norton, 1968), p. 27. See also, though mainly in connection with the

education of younger children, Jean Piaget, *Science of Education and the Psychology of the Child* (New York: Viking, 1970), especially Part 2, Chapter 2.

3 This was initially Mina Shaughnessy's realization in *Errors and Expectations* (New York: Oxford University Press, 1977). See, for instance, p. 105. See also Sarah D'Eloia, "The Uses — and Limits — of Grammar," in *The Writing Teacher's Sourcebook*, eds., Gary Tate and Edward P.J. Corbett (New York: Oxford University Press, 1981), pp. 225-43. Loren Barritt and Barry Kroll have written, "The cognitive-developmentalist views the learner not as a passive slave to habits but as an active agent constructing a coherent view of the world. Errors are clues to the system of organized rules and intelligent strategies that a student draws on to perform a composing task," in "Some Implications of Cognitive-Developmental Psychology for Research in Composing," in *Research on Composing: Points of Departure*, eds., Charles R. Cooper and Lee Odell (Urbana, IL: NCTE, 1978), p. 54.

4 Aviva Freedman and Ian Pringle, "Writing in the College Years: Some Indices of Growth," *College Composition and Communication*, 31 (October 1980), 311-324.

5 For elaboration of this point, see Charles R. Cooper, "Competency Testing: Issues and Overview," in *The Nature and Measurement of Competency in English*, pp. 1-17.

6 See Kellogg W. Hunt, "Early Blooming and Late Blooming Syntactic Structures," in *Evaluating Writing: Describing, Measuring, Judging*, eds., Charles R. Cooper and Lee Odell (Urbana, IL: NCTE, 1977), pp. 91-106.

7 Joseph Williams notes the difficulty, for instance, of relating the concept of stylistic "complexity" to the concept of stylistic "maturity" in "Defining Complexity," *College English*, 40 (February 1979), 595-609.

8 This point is made in John C. Mellon's well-known study, *Transformational Sentence-Combining* (NCTE Committee on Research Report Number 10, 1969), and also in James Moffett, *Teaching the Universe of Discourse* (Boston: Houghton Mifflin, 1968), p. 170.

9 Urbana, IL: NCTE, 1974. Arguments elaborating Diederich's as well as other methodologies of evaluation can be found in several of the essays in Cooper and Odell, eds., *Evaluating Writing*.

10 This corresponds to I.A. Richards' general observation about the impact on readers of a writer's authority in *Practical Criticism* (New York: Harcourt, Brace, 1929), p. 297.

11 Joseph Williams, "The Phenomenology of Error," *College Composition and Communication*, 32 (May 1981), 152-68.

12 A responsible set of recommendations for evaluating the quality of writing instruction has come out of the Conference on College Composition and Communication Committee on Teaching and Its Evaluation in Composition. See "Evaluating Instruction in Writing: Approaches and Instruments," *College Composition and Communication*, 33 (May 1982), 213-29.